I0019262

Ju
Alexandar Ignjatovic
Sri Parameswaran

Power Analysis Side Channel Attacks

Jude Ambrose
Alexandar Ignjatovic
Sri Parameswaran

Power Analysis Side Channel Attacks

The Processor Design-level Context

VDM Verlag Dr. Müller

Impressum/Imprint (nur für Deutschland/ only for Germany)

Bibliografische Information der Deutschen Nationalbibliothek: Die Deutsche Nationalbibliothek verzeichnet diese Publikation in der Deutschen Nationalbibliografie; detaillierte bibliografische Daten sind im Internet über http://dnb.d-nb.de abrufbar.

Alle in diesem Buch genannten Marken und Produktnamen unterliegen warenzeichen-, marken- oder patentrechtlichem Schutz bzw. sind Warenzeichen oder eingetragene Warenzeichen der jeweiligen Inhaber. Die Wiedergabe von Marken, Produktnamen, Gebrauchsnamen, Handelsnamen, Warenbezeichnungen u.s.w. in diesem Werk berechtigt auch ohne besondere Kennzeichnung nicht zu der Annahme, dass solche Namen im Sinne der Warenzeichen- und Markenschutzgesetzgebung als frei zu betrachten wären und daher von jedermann benutzt werden dürften.

Coverbild: www.purestockx.com

Verlag: VDM Verlag Dr. Müller Aktiengesellschaft & Co. KG
Dudweiler Landstr. 99, 66123 Saarbrücken, Deutschland
Telefon +49 681 9100-698, Telefax +49 681 9100-988, Email: info@vdm-verlag.de
Zugl.: Sydney, University of New South Wales, 2009

Herstellung in Deutschland:
Schaltungsdienst Lange o.H.G., Berlin
Books on Demand GmbH, Norderstedt
Reha GmbH, Saarbrücken
Amazon Distribution GmbH, Leipzig
ISBN: 978-3-8364-8508-1

Imprint (only for USA, GB)

Bibliographic information published by the Deutsche Nationalbibliothek: The Deutsche Nationalbibliothek lists this publication in the Deutsche Nationalbibliografie; detailed bibliographic data are available in the Internet at http://dnb.d-nb.de .

Any brand names and product names mentioned in this book are subject to trademark, brand or patent protection and are trademarks or registered trademarks of their respective holders. The use of brand names, product names, common names, trade names, product descriptions etc. even without a particular marking in this works is in no way to be construed to mean that such names may be regarded as unrestricted in respect of trademark and brand protection legislation and could thus be used by anyone.

Cover image: www.purestockx.com

Publisher:
VDM Verlag Dr. Müller Aktiengesellschaft & Co. KG
Dudweiler Landstr. 99, 66123 Saarbrücken, Germany
Phone +49 681 9100-698, Fax +49 681 9100-988, Email: info@vdm-publishing.com

Copyright © 2010 by the author and VDM Verlag Dr. Müller Aktiengesellschaft & Co. KG and licensors
All rights reserved. Saarbrücken 2010

Printed in the U.S.A.
Printed in the U.K. by (see last page)
ISBN: 978-3-8364-8508-1

Abstract

The rapid increase in the use of embedded systems for performing secure transactions, has proportionally increased the security threats which are faced by such devices. Side channel attack, a sophisticated security threat to embedded devices like smartcards, mobile phones and PDAs, exploits the external manifestations like processing time, power consumption and electromagnetic emission to identify the internal computations. Power analysis attack, introduced by Kocher in 1998, is used by adversaries to eavesdrop on confidential data while the device is executing a secure transaction. The adversary observes the power trace dissipated/consumed by the chip during the encryption/decryption of the AES cryptographic program and predicts the secret key used for encryption by extracting necessary information from the power trace.

Countermeasures proposed to overcome power analysis are data masking, table masking, current flattening, circuitry level solutions, dummy instruction insertions, balancing bit-flips, etc. All these techniques are either susceptible to multi-order side channel attacks, not sufficiently generic to cover all encryption algorithms, or burden the system with high area cost, run-time or energy consumption.

The initial solution presented in this book is a HW/SW based randomised instruction injection technique, which infuses random instructions at random places during the execution of an application. Such randomisation obfuscates the secure information from the power profile, not allowing the adversary to extract the critical power segments for analysis. Further, the author devised a systematic method to measure the security level of a power sequence and used it to measure the number of random instructions needed, to suitably confuse the adversary. The proposed processor model costs 1.9% in additional area for a simplescalar processor, and costs on average 29.8% in runtime and 27.1% in additional energy consumption for six

i

industry standard cryptographic algorithms. This design is extended to a processor architecture which automatically detects the execution of the most common encryption algorithms, starts to scramble the power waveform by adding randomly placed instructions with random register accesses, and stops injecting instructions when it is safe to do so. This approach has less overheads compared to previous solutions and avoids software instrumentation, allowing programmers with no special knowledge to use the system. The extended processor model costs an additional area of 1.2%, and an average of 25% in runtime and 28.5% in energy overheads for industry standard cryptographic algorithms.

Due to the possibility of removing random injections using large number of samples (due to the random nature, a large number of samples will eliminate noise), the author proposes a multiprocessor *algorithmic* balancing technique. This technique uses a dual processor architecture where two processors execute the same program in parallel, but with complementary intermediate data, thus balancing the bitflips. The second processor works in conjunction with the first processor for balancing only when encryption is performed, and both processors carry out independent tasks when no encryption is being performed. Both DES and AES cryptographic programs are investigated for balancing and the author shows that this technique is economical, while completely preventing power analysis attacks. The signature detection unit to capture encryption is also utilised, which is used in the instruction injection approach. This multiprocessor balancing approach reduces performance by 0.42% and 0.94% for AES and DES respectively. The hardware increase is 2X only when balancing is performed. Further, several future extensions for the balancing approach are proposed, by introducing random swapping of encryption iterations between cores.

Acknowledgement

First of all, I wish to thank my supervisor, Prof. Sri Parameswaran, for all his support and advice, without which I would not have achieved my PhD. I would also like to thank my co-supervisor Dr. Aleksandar Ignjatovic for his valuable advice and support. My sincere thanks goes to Swarnalatha, Roshan and Thiruvaran for guiding me and helping me in every aspect of my PhD life. I wish to thank all my colleagues and friends at CSE, UNSW, present and past, for providing a wonderful working environment and a huge moral support.

I also take this opportunity to thank my Uncle, Mano Phillip, and his family for their support and faith. Because of them, I am in this good position in my life. I will not forget Paheetharan and my school friend Hammondson for their help and support, even when they were having a hard time. Thanks to all my friends who have thought about me and helped me in every stage of my life.

I know that thanking is not enough to express how much I owe my life to my family: dad (Ambrose), mum (Pavalavathy), brother (Jeyanthan) and sister (Jothini). All their sacrifices and hardship is what developed me and motivated me as a person. I wish I could turn around things and provide them a much better days than they have had.

I wish to add my friend Roshan G. Ragel as another co-author to this book and due to the limitations from the publisher I could not do so. However, I am gratefully declaring him as one of the co-authors to this book.

Finally, I dedicate this book to each and everyone of you who made my life a happy place to be.

Contents

List of Tables

List of Figures

Chapter 1

Introduction

Ever since the first fully programmable mechanical computer was invented by Charles Babbage in 1837, computing has significantly contributed to society in many different forms. Such computing entities are present in systems ranging from tiny devices (such as watches, hearing aids, etc.) to supercomputers. Embedded systems, formally introduced around the 1960s, paved the way for computing to be used ubiquitously in society . Large and expensive analog components were replaced by microprocessors or microcontrollers, creating a genre of small, energy efficient systems. A plethora of embedded devices emerged for applications in avionics, automobile industry, military, communications, electronic and consumer markets [3].

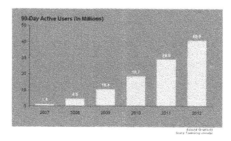

Figure 1.1: US Mobile Banking Forecast; taken from [1]

Recent surveys (such as banking industry) reveal an increasing number of people using embedded devices for small financial transactions rather than cash (i.e., the usage of "cashless wallet" is increasing). Smart Cards [37], PDAs [90] and Mobile Phones [242] are key examples of popular embedded devices used for secure transactions. Figure 1.1 depicts a forecast on the usage of mobile banking in US. The forecast illustrates that the mobile banking in US will hit an astounding 40 million users by 2012.

The survey of Smart Card usage (i.e., credit cards and debit cards) in Australia, as presented in Figure 1.2, reveals that the average number of payments made by a person using a Smart Card has doubled since mid 1990s, every five years.

Figure 1.2: Growth of Smart Card Usage in Australia: taken from [11]

Such an increase in the usage of embedded systems in secure transactions has proportionally increased the attacks imposed on such devices. Popular attacks include physical attacks [129], electrical attacks [211], Application Specific Integrated Circuit (ASIC) reverse engineering [28], fault injection [201], code injection attacks [194] and side channel attacks [249].

Side channel attacks are known for the ease with which they can be implemented, and the effectiveness with which it is possible to steal secret information without leaving a trace on the device [249]. Adversaries observe side channels such as power usage [143], processing time [49] and electro magnetic(EM) emissions [192], when the chip processes secure transactions as shown in Figure 1.3(a). The adversary feeds different input values into the system, while recording the side channels during the execution of a cryptographic algorithm (e.g., encryption using a secret key). These recorded external manifestations are then correlated with the internal computations. Figure 1.3(b) depicts some of the external manifestations during a typical communication session between Alice and Bob, where Alice encrypts the input M using a secret key K_a and sends the ciphertext to Bob. The ciphertext is deciphered using a secret key K_b by Bob and the real message M is revealed. Despite the fact that this standard secure communication (shown in Figure 1.3(b)) prevents the person in the middle from reading the real data, side channel attacks can still be performed successfully at both ends (i.e., sender and receiver) to identify the secret keys used for encryption/decryption.

As shown in Figure 1.3, external manifestations are used to obtain critical information,

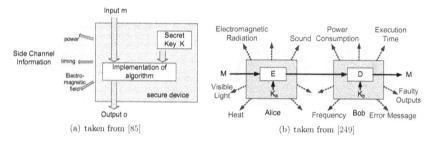

(a) taken from [85]   (b) taken from [249]

Figure 1.3: Manifestations used for Side Channel Attack

such as the secret key of a secure application. Analysing the power consumption/dissipation (i.e., power analysis) has been one of the most effective techniques to extract secret keys during the execution of cryptographic algorithms using Side Channel Attacks (SCAs) [143, 156, 177]. There are two main types of power analysis attacks: (1), Simple Power Analysis (SPA); and (2), Differential Power Analysis (DPA) [127].

SPA involves the identification of computations and instructions used in a system by analysing the power wave observed. Typically, the adversary observes the power dissipated, and tries to identify specific power wave segments of corresponding rounds in the encryption of data within cryptographic programs [127]. Typical examples of such cryptographic programs are Data Encryption Standard (DES), Advanced Encryption Standard (AES), RSA and ECC. Figure 1.4 depicts an example for Simple Power Analysis (SPA), where the adversary tries to identify the instructions executed by observing certain patterns in the power profile. As shown in Figure 1.4 the highest periodic peaks are identified as XOR instructions and the lower peaks are identified as AND instructions. The accuracy of instruction identification depends on the expertise of the adversary and the training sets simulated before the real attack. After the instruction identification, the Hamming weights (denotes the number of bits set to 1 during an instruction execution [46] — higher the Hamming weight, the higher the power consumption) are decided for each magnitude as shown in Figure 1.4. If the adversary identifies the data processed at the last XOR peak as 11111, the previous peak (which is less in magnitude) could have one less zero, and could well be 11011. A detailed explanation of the SPA is provided in Chapter 2.2.

Differential Power Analysis (DPA) is a more powerful technique than Simple Power Analysis (SPA), and is based on the hypothesis that there is a significant difference in the power

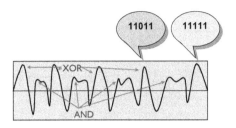

Figure 1.4: An example Simple Power Analysis

consumption in processing 1's and 0's [127]. Figure 1.5 depicts a brief overview of a DPA, where the adversary feeds several inputs to the chip and records the power traces. The analysis is then taken offline and several key guesses are made. Each guessed key is simulated with the data values used for power measurement to find an intermediate value in the algorithm (i.e., value of Bit as shown in Figure 1.5). For each of the key guesses the output power traces (of several separate inputs) are separated into two, depending upon whether the Bit value is a "1" or a "0". The difference between the averages of these sets is known as the DPA signal (also known as DPA bias signal). A peak in this DPA signal trace, which is plotted against possible key guesses, will reveal the correct key. A detailed explanation for DPA is provided in Chapter 2.3. A complete DPA attack on AES algorithm is demonstrated in Appendix A.

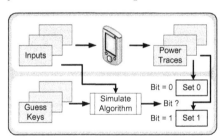

Figure 1.5: An overview of DPA

Extended versions of DPA and several other power analysis techniques exist, which are discussed in the literature review (i.e., Chapter 2). Pivotal vulnerable parts in an encryption for power analysis are key scheduling [16] (where subkeys are generated from the key), SBOX accesses [86] (where tables are looked up) in symmetric block ciphers (such as AES, DES, etc.) and conditional branching in public cryptosystems [88] (such as RSA and ECC). Researchers have proposed countermeasures for power analysis ranging from masking to bal-

4

ancing. Chapter 3 elaborates such countermeasures and their pros and cons. Most of the software countermeasures had a significant performance penalty, whereas the hardware countermeasures had substantial area overheads. In addition to that, most of the countermeasures for SPA failed to prevent DPA and vice-versa [152, 178, 180].

Hence, in this book, the author proposes effective countermeasures at system level to prevent power analysis based side channel attacks, with considerably reduced area and performance overheads. The author's first countermeasure (named *RIJID*) is a hardware software randomised instruction injection method which injects random instructions, random number of times, at random places during the encryption. Such randomisation scrambles the power wave so that the adversary is unable to identify specific segments such as encryption rounds within the entire power wave. A random generator is attached to the processor to chose a random number of instructions from an instruction pool containing instructions which do not change the state of the processor. The system identifies the encryption by having two special instructions around the encryption routine (at the start and at the end).

The special instructions have to be manually inserted in the assembly code of the program to implement *RIJID*. Such a software instrumentation would be an extra workload for the designer when dealing with more than one encryption programs. To overcome this additional instrumentation, signatures are obtained for the encryption routines inside any program. These signatures, which attempt to capture only the encryption routine, would allow the processor to detect the encryption at runtime. Concomitance [112] can be used to find signatures in a program based on instruction executions. A concomitance analysis is performed on instruction traces and the signatures are identified (e.g., XOR instructions executed within a certain window of instructions, suggests a type of encryption algorithm). A circuit was attached to the *RIJID* processor to perform such signature detection by listening to the instructions which are fetched by the processor. Hence, the modified processor (called *A-RIJID*) would detect the encryption at runtime and starts injecting random instructions, random number of times. The processor would stop the obfuscation when the signature expires.

One of the initial tasks for the adversary is to analyse the entire power profile and extract the required segments (e.g., the place where SBOX is looked up). This is done by analysing certain patterns in the power profile. Note that, similar instruction sequences will produce similar power patterns. If the adversary cannot extract these patterns from the power profile, it is almost impossible to achieve a successful attack. Hence, showing that the power patterns could not be extracted from the entire power profile would be sufficient to prove that the attack is not possible. The author used a rapid analysis (called *RIJID* index), based on cross-correlation, to realise the obfuscation provided by the random injection techniques (i.e., *RIJID* and *A-RIJID*). Key reason for this was to avoid the large amount of time taken for power simulations to perform the power analysis attacks.

The random injections in the power profile using *RIJID* and *A-RIJID* could still be removed using a millions of samples. For example, recording a million samples and averaging them might help to reconstruct the original power profile, by simply averaging out the randomness inserted. This has not been investigated in this book, but is a concern raised by several security experts. Thus, while *RIJID* can slow down an adversary, it is likely a persistent adversary could well find the secret key after a long time. Due to such a concern in the level of security provided by the random injections, a multiprocessor balancing architecture is introduced (called *MUTE*) to prevent power analysis based side channel attacks. Key motivations are that balancing is considered the better way to prevent power analysis, and the increasing deployment of multiprocessors in the embedded systems. *MUTE* contains at least two identical processors/cores which generally execute independent tasks. When one processor starts to execute the encryption algorithm, the second processor automatically starts the complementary version of the encryption program and executes in parallel (i.e., instruction-wise). Such an algorithmic balancing obfuscates the useful information from the power profile. *MUTE-DES* is designed to protect DES algorithm and a similar design (named *MUTE-AES*) is proposed for AES. DPA attacks are performed on *MUTE-DES* and *MUTE-AES* to show that both techniques prevent power analysis. In addition to that, a Fast Fourier Transform (FFT) analysis is performed to show that there is a reduced level of information in the power profile when data or key is changed.

Book Organisation

This book is broken down into seven major chapters,

- **Chapter 2** presents the literature review on the power analysis attacks proposed in the past. This Chapter is divided into several sections based on the type of attacks proposed. Critical encryption programs (such as DES, AES, RSA and ECC) targeted for the attacks are detailed at the start of the chapter, articulating the attack points and concepts. The other main sections are dedicated to Simple Power Analysis (SPA) and Differential Power Analysis (DPA), which are the key power analysis attacks. All the other power analysis attacks, except SPA and DPA, are bundled into Section 2.4. SPA attacks are classified into attacks using Hamming weights and attacks using conditional branching. DPA attacks are categorised into attacks targeted on block ciphers (such as DES and AES), attacks on public cryptosystems (such as RSA and ECC) and finally, the DPA extensions. Other attacks discussed here, apart from SPA and DPA, are Correlation Power Analysis (CPA), Big Mac attack, template attack, Davies-Murphy power attack and power analysis on FPGA. The attacks are compared against each other, identifying their limitations and severity.

- **Chapter 3** is a literature review of the countermeasures proposed to combat power analysis based side channel attacks. Most investigated countermeasures are masking, algorithm modification and hardware balancing, which are further expanded into subsections. Masking techniques are classified into data masking, table masking and window method. The rest of the countermeasures discussed in this chapter are dummy instruction insertion, signal suppression, current flattening, non-deterministic processors, handling clock and special instructions. Each countermeasure is explained in detail, presenting its advantages and drawbacks.

- **Chapter 4** describes the *RIJID* processor design.

- **Chapter 5** presents the secure *A-RIJID* processor.

- **Chapter 6** introduces the *MUTE-DES* architecture which prevents power analysis for DES algorithm.

- **Chapter 7** elaborates the *MUTE-AES* multiprocessor design for AES execution.

- **Chapter 8** presents an initial work on the future extensions of the multiprocessor balancing architecture. Three different extensions are proposed: (1), *MUTE-C*, a slightly corrupted balancing; (2), *MUTE-SWAP*, swapping consecutive rounds between processors while balancing; and (3), *MUTE-RSWAP*, randomly swap rounds between processors.

All the other technical efforts attempted during the research are given in the Appendices. Appendix A details the differential power analysis on AES. The development of RINDEX tool in matlab to calculate *RIJID* index (to realise the degree of obfuscation) is briefed in Appendix B. Appendix C explains the implementation of *MUTE* in the XUPV2P development board using the Embedded Development Kit (EDK) 8.2i. The SimpleScalar processor implementation for FPGA, using Xilinx8.2i, is summarised in Appendix D.

Chapter 2

Power Analysis

Kocher et al. [127] introduced power analysis in 1999, where secret keys used in an encryption program were successfully predicted by observing the power dissipation from a chip. Since then, power dissipation/consumption of a chip is one of the most exploited properties to predict secret keys using side channel attacks based on power analysis [132, 249]. Devices like Smart Cards [37, 58], PDAs [90] and Mobile Phones [242] have microprocessor chips built inside to perform secure transactions using internally stored secret keys. Smart Cards are increasingly used in secure applications by the customers of banks, credit card companies, cellular telephone operators, pay-TV broadcasters and ID token manufacturers, among others [37]. Since such devices have to perform secure transactions from remote locations, an adversary is able to exploit the chip (which is not necessarily physically secured) using power analysis. Kocher et al. [126] explain the power consumption of the Integrated Chips (IC), which are built out of individual transistors. As shown in Figure 2.1, current flows across the transistor when a charge is applied to (or removed from) the gate, where such current delivers a charge to the gates of other transistors, interconnect wires and circuit loads. This motion of electric charge consumes power which is externally detectable. Microprocessor logic units perform regular transistor switching, where individual transistors produce externally observable electrical behaviour, which reveals the microprocessor's activities in the power profile [126].

The adversary observes the Vcc pin of the chip to measure the power profile, while feeding inputs to the chip to perform secure transactions (such as encryption). A general technique to measure a circuit's power consumption is to connect a resistor in series with the power or ground input. The voltage difference across the resistor divided by the resistance reveals the

9

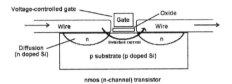

Figure 2.1: Power Consumption of a Transistor in an IC [126]

current, which is used to compute the power dissipation [127].

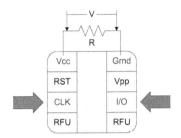

Figure 2.2: Power Measurement on a Smart Card

Smart Card is a 32-bit microprocessor [38, 85] which has clearly visible segmented parts outside the chip, revealing control pins like Vcc, Ground ($Grnd$), Input/Output (I/O), Clock CLK, etc. as shown in Figure 2.2. A resistor can be attached across Vcc and $Grnd$ as shown in Figure 2.2, to measure the voltage drop, which can be used to compute the power dissipation in Vcc. The adversary feeds in CLK and inputs through I/O pin to the chip for the execution of the encryption program stored inside. While the program is running for different inputs, the voltage across Vcc and $Grnd$ is recorded.

Messerges et al. [154] explained a much more detailed model of power measurement in a smart card as shown in Figure 2.3. Resistor (R1), which is connected between the true ground and V_{ss} pin on the card, is used to monitor the power dissipation. When there is a voltage change in V_{gate} the transistors $Q1$ and $Q2$ conduct the current, which discharges the C_{load} capacitance, causing the current to flow through the V_{ss} pin [154]. As per Messerges et al. [154], useful information is leaked when the circuit is clocked, changing the state of C_{load}, which will result in drawing current from all related gates. This is a general property of CMOS circuits and the changes can be observed at V_{scope} [154].

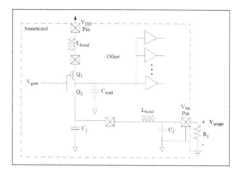

Figure 2.3: Power Model in a Smart Card [154]

A Complementary metal oxide semiconductor (CMOS) is widely used in microprocessors, microcontrollers, static RAM and other digital circuits... – Wiki

A simple power model of a Smart Card is defined in [53] as quoted in Equation 2.1 and Equation 2.2. The power consumption of a Smart Card at a state s in time t is $P(s,t)$ as shown in Equation 2.1. Let $f(e,t)$ denote the power consumption of event e at time t. The function $occurs(e,s)$ is a binary function which is 1 if e occurs when the relevant state is s and 0 otherwise. The $delay(e,s)$ is the time delay of the occurrence of event e in state s from the clock edge [53]. Hence, the total power consumption $P(s,t)$ at time t is the *sum* of power consumptions of all the events which took place.

$$P(s,t) = \sum_{e \in \mathcal{E}} f(e, t - delay(e, s)) * occurs(e, s); \quad [53] \tag{2.1}$$

In practice, the actual power component will include a noise component as shown in Equation 2.2. $\mathcal{N}(e,t)$ is a Gaussian noise component of event e, where $\mathcal{N}_d(e,s)$ is the noise component affecting the delay and $\mathcal{N}_c$ is the external noise function.

$$P(s,t) = \mathcal{N}_c(t) + \sum_{e \in \mathcal{E}} (f(e, t - delay(e, s) + \mathcal{N}_d(e, s)) + \mathcal{N}_d(e, t)) * occurs(e, s); \quad [53] \tag{2.2}$$

11

Gaussian noise is noise that has a probability density function of the

normal distribution... – Wiki

Such a power model [53] as shown in Equation 2.1 and Equation 2.2 can be used to predict power consumption using different events and filter the noise from the actual power measurements. A detailed study of power models and their weaknesses are presented in [66]. Similar power consumption models are referred to in [22]. The noise models are further discussed in [156].

A block diagram of a power measurement setup for power analysis of a chip is shown in Figure 2.4. Several devices are needed to record power samples such as: a computer (PC) to control the measurement, a high-sample-rate oscilloscope to measure and store the samples, a current probe (inductive probe) and a *Multi ICE* device to feed several inputs to the chip. A trigger signal is used to synchronize measurements, and an inductive probe is connected at the chip's power supply [86].

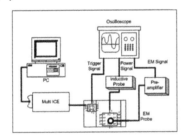

Figure 2.4: Power Measurement Setup on a chip [86]

High-sample-rate oscilloscope, TDS7254 Tek: US $40,000 and

Current Probe, TCP202: US $ 1,500... – Ebay

As shown in Figure 2.4 the chip is fed different inputs to execute the encryption program and the power samples are recorded for analysis. A real life practical setup is shown in

Figure 2.5, where a prototype IC is used for power anaysis with an HP54542C oscilloscope and a CT1 current probe from Tektronix [222].

Figure 2.5: Power Measurement Setup [222]

After the adversary has recorded the power values for different inputs, where a fixed secret key is used for encryption as shown in Figure 2.6, the power profiles are analysed with the known input values to predict the unknown secret key.

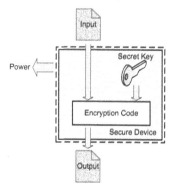

Figure 2.6: Power Dissipation as Side Channel

This chapter is divided into several sections based on the type of attacks proposed. Critical encryptions programs (such as DES, AES, RSA and ECC) targeted for the attacks are detailed in the first section, articulating the attack points and concepts. The second and third sections are dedicated to Simple Power Analysis (SPA) and Differential Power Analysis (DPA), which are the key power analysis attacks. All the other power analysis attacks, except SPA and DPA, are presented in the fourth section. SPA attacks are classified into attacks using Hamming weights and attacks using conditional branching. DPA attacks are categorised into attacks targeted towards block ciphers (such as DES and AES), attacks on public cryptosystems (such as RSA and ECC) and finally, the DPA extensions. Other attacks discussed here, apart from SPA and DPA, are Correlation Power Analysis (CPA), Big Mac attack, template attack, Davies-Murphy power attack and power analysis on FPGA. The attacks are compared against each other, identifying their limitations and severity.

2.1 Encryption Programs

An encryption program receives a plaintext and converts the plaintext into a ciphertext using a secret key by means of a fairly complex algorithm, so that the useful data becomes unreadable to the adversary. Encryption programs like DES, AES, RSA and ECC are currently attacked by the use of power analysis. A brief explanation of these encryption programs is provided detailing only the necessary parts related to power analysis attacks.

2.1.1 Data Encryption Standard (DES)

The Data Encryption Standard (DES), the basis for most popular embedded system encryption algorithms, is a symmetric-key block cipher encryption algorithm [63]. The author provides only the basic description for DES, which is sufficient for the adversary to predict the secret key using power analysis. Interested readers are referred to [63] for a detailed explanation of DES. Figure 2.7 depicts the DES algorithm, where the key is divided into subkeys before the start of the encrypion using a key permutation algorithm.

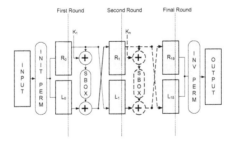

Figure 2.7: Data Encryption Standard Algorithm

Data Encryption Standard is a deprecated cryptographic block cipher ... – Wiki

In Figure 2.7, the input is passed through an initial permutation and then split into two parts, L0 and R0. XOR is first applied to the fragment of data present in R0 and the sub key K1. The output, which is the XOR of R0 and K1, is used for SBOX look-up. XOR is now applied to the output from the SBOX, and data in L0, thus resulting in output being placed in R1. R0 is passed to L1. This way of swapping the halves of input data and then XORing with the subkey for SBOX lookup will continue for 16 rounds. After the final round, the data values R15 and L15, as shown in Figure 2.7, are given to an inverse permutation and the output is the ciphertext.

2.1.2 Advanced Encryption Standard (AES)

Like DES, Advanced Encryption Standard (AES) is a symmetric-key block cipher encryption algorithm [167]. AES, the successor of DES, is used in a wide range of embedded applications [143]. Figure 2.8 depicts the AES algorithm (128 bits), where the secret key is used to generate round keys (subkeys) using a Key Scheduler. AES with 192 bits and 256 bits are also currently under practice.

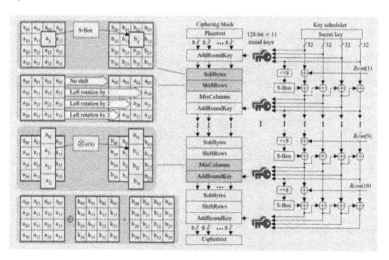

Figure 2.8: 128-bit Advanced Encryption Standard Algorithm [210]

AES is fast in both software and hardware, is relatively easy to implement, and requires little
memory and currently being deployed on a large scale ... – Wiki

As shown in Figure 2.8, the plaintext is XORed (*AddRoundKey*) with the first round key
(which is also the original secret key [143]) and the output is fed into a round. Each round
includes four actions, which are SubBytes, ShiftRows, MixColumns and AddRoundKey. The
SBOX lookup happens in SubBytes, where the rows and columns are swapped in ShiftRows
and ShiftColumns respectively. A different subkey is XORed after each round in AddRound-
Key. There will be ten rounds in 128 bits AES [167]. The last round, which is slightly different
from the previous rounds, includes only SubBytes, ShiftRows and AddRoundKey operations.
The ciphertext is produced after all the rounds are executed as shown in Figure 2.8.

2.1.3 RSA

RSA, a public-key encryption, is widely used in many applications like E-commerce, E-money
and smart cards [17, 105]. Figure 2.9 denotes the important steps in encryption and decryption
using RSA. A detailed explanation of RSA can be found in [206]. Initially, two prime numbers
are chosen (p and q). Values n (called public modulus [17]) and $\phi(n)$ are computed using p
and q as shown in Figure 2.9. A public key e is chosen and a private key d (which is the secret
key) is computed. The public key e and the value n are made visible for encryption.

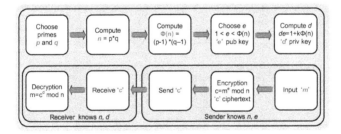

Figure 2.9: RSA Algorithm

No one can duplicate the confidence that RSA offers after 20 years of
cryptanalytic review... – Bruce Schneier

The sender, who knows the public key e and n of the receiver, encrypts the message (input) m as shown in Figure 2.9. The encrypted ciphertext c is sent to the receiver, who has the private key d and n for decryption. The decryption, which involves the operation with secret key d, is performed using exponentiation as shown in Figure 2.9 ($m=c^d \bmod n$, where d is the secret private key). The classical *Square-and-Multiply Algorithm*, as shown in Figure 2.10, is the simplest way to perform such binary exponentiation [17].

```
s=m
for i from 1 to b − 1 do
    s = s * s (mod n)
    if dᵢ = 1 then
        s = s * m (mod n)
return s
```

Figure 2.10: Square-and-Multiply Exponentiation Algorithm [17]

As shown in Figure 2.10, m is the input data, d is the secret key, which is a b-bit number, and n is the public modulus (explained above). For each bit of the secret key d_i squaring happens first ($s*s$) and the multiplication ($s*m$) takes place only when the bit is set. The result s is returned after the whole operation.

2.1.4 Elliptic Curve Cryptography (ECC)

Claimed to be better than RSA, Elliptic Curve Cryptography (ECC) is a public-key cryptographic algorithm, using a smaller key size with faster computation to suit small devices [99]. Figure 2.11 shows the elliptic curve, which is defined in Equation 2.3. The sender chooses a private key d in the interval between 1 to $n-1$ where n is a prime number. A public key P_d is created, such that $P_d = dG$, where G is a known point in the elliptic curve shown in Figure 2.11.

$$E : y^2 = x^3 + ax + b \tag{2.3}$$

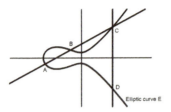

Figure 2.11: The Elliptic Curve [228]

Elliptic Curve Cryptography is emerging as an attractive public-key cryptosystem for

mobile/wireless environments... – Sun

The ECC is combined with different encryption schemes like Diffie-Hellman, Digital Signature Algorithm and MQV (Menezes-Qu-Vanstone) [228]. Detailed explanation of ECC and the encryption schemes can be found in [65, 157, 228]

The operation of computing the public key ($P_d = dG$) involves an addition of point G to itself d times. This operation is called *scalar multiplication* [65], where the binary version of *double-and-add approach* is used, as shown in Figure 2.12. The binary version of double-and-add algorithm [30] (shown in Figure 2.12) takes in the point G and the private key d as inputs. The output will be the public key P_d. For each bit of d, where the length of d is l, the Q is doubled at the start of each iteration. When the bit value d_i is one, G is added after doubling.

```
Input G, d
Output P_d = d.G
    Q ← G
    for i from l-2 to 0 do
        Q ← 2.Q
        if d_i = 1 then
            Q ← Q + G
        end if
    end for
    P_d ← Q
return P_d
```

Figure 2.12: Double-and-Add Algorithm [30]

There are two main power analysis methods: (1), Simple Power Analysis (SPA); (2),

Differential Power Analysis (DPA).

2.2   Simple Power Analysis (SPA)

In Simple Power Analysis (SPA), the power profile resulting from an encryption is analysed directly for different characteristics and patterns to predict the confidential data processed. Kocher et al. [127] state that the SPA reveals the device's operation as well as the secret key. Each instruction operates a set of gates, which results in a unique signature of that instruction in the power profile [71, 193]. Akkar et al. [22] claim that every type of instruction (arithmetic, Boolean, load and store) and every type of addressing mode has a distinctive consumption profile, resulting in the adversary classifying every assembly instruction by its power consumption. Thus the main property in SPA exploited by the adversary is that similar instruction executions (such as iterations) will generate similar patterns in the power profile, easily distinguishable by the naked eye. The adversary tries to predict the encryption segments in the power profile and then tries to identify certain instruction executions (like jump, xor, mov, etc.) to predict the data values processed.

Figure 2.13 shows that the adversary observes 16 clearly visible patterns relating to the 16 rounds in the DES encryption (explained in Section 2.1.1). Since these patterns are different from the other patterns as shown in Figure 2.13, it is obvious that the 16 power segments correspond to the encryption part of DES.

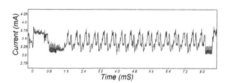

Figure 2.13: DES Rounds [127]

Similarly, Oswald et al. [180] showed that the power profile taken from AES clearly reveals the 16 iterations as shown in Figure 2.14 during the AddRoundKey and SubByte routines as explained in Section 2.1.2. Each iteration is applied for a byte in a 128-bit encryption, thus resulting in 16 iterations. Since the instruction sequence executed in each iteration of the loop is the same, similar patterns appeared.

RSA performs squaring and multiplication for exponentiation, as explained in Section 2.1.3.

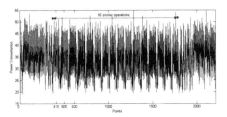

Figure 2.14: AES Rounds in AddRoundKey and SubByte [180]

Since the instructions executed are distinctively unique for squaring and multiplication, distinguishable patterns will be visible in the power profile of RSA for each of such operations, as shown in Figure 2.15. As Figure 2.15 shows, squaring (*Square*) produces similar patterns, where multiplication (*Multiply*) produces significantly different patterns.

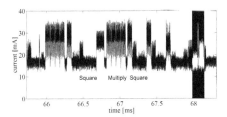

Figure 2.15: Square and Multiply patterns in RSA [172]

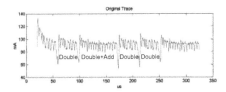

Figure 2.16: Double and Add patterns in ECC [87]

The double-and-add execution in ECC as explained in Section 2.1.4, also shows similar patterns for a similar sequence of instruction executions, as shown in Figure 2.16. Clearly visible patterns appear for double and add operations.

After finding the encryption block in the power profile, the task for the adversary is to figure out certain instruction executions within the encryption part. Kocher et al. [127] further showed that *jump* instruction executions inside the DES encryption (shown in Figure 2.13)

20

are visible for the adversary, where higher power is dissipated when a *jump* is executed as shown in Figure 2.17.

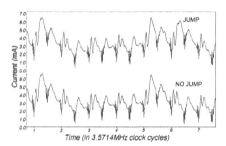

Figure 2.17: Power Variation due to Jump [127]

Figure 2.17 clearly shows that at clock cycle six, higher power consumption is observed (upper figure) when a *jump* instruction is executed and a comparatively lower power consumption is observed (bottom trace) when a *jump* is not performed. Similarly, *mov* instruction [147], *xor* instruction [185] and *load* (LDA) instruction [154] are some of the key instructions the adversary examines in the power profile to predict the data values used for secure computations using Simple Power Analysis (SPA). After the adversary has identified specific instruction executions in the power profile, the data processed at that instruction execution can be predicted by observing the power magnitude or height. The adversary analyses an instruction execution for its power magnitude with its Hamming weights (*which denotes the number of bits set to 1 after an instruction execution* [46]). The magnitude from real measurements is mapped into such pre-computation to predict the Hamming weight of the data.

2.2.1 Prediction of data using Hamming Weights

Hamming weight is defined as the number of 1's in the result after an instruction execution [154]. Messerges et al. [154] state that knowing the Hamming weight of a secret key reduces the brute-force key search space. The adversary needs to try only the secret key guesses with certain Hamming weights. For example, if the Hamming weight predicted of a secret key with 8 bits is 3, 0b01001001 (in binary) is one of the suitable candidates where 0b00100111 (in binary) is not, which has a Hamming weight of 4. The Hamming weight is proportional to the power height produced at the clock cycle of an instruction execution. This is true in

21

cases where a precharged bus is used and the number of 0's driven into the bus determines the amount of discharged current [156].

The adversary analyses the power dissipation of an instruction (such as *xor*) for different Hamming weights. Based on this analysis, the power values are categorised into different magnitude levels for different Hamming weights. For example, if an input is eight bits there will only be nine levels of magnitude possible based on nine possible Hamming weights (there are only nine Hamming weight possibilities, from zero to eight, since there are only eight bits). When a power value is observed during the attack for the already analysed instruction, the power height is simply mapped to the analysis to predict the Hamming weight [156]. Aigner and Oswald [21] show that *mov* instructions produce a significant power variation when executing 0x00 and 0xFF. Figure 2.18 shows the practical measurements in a current profile dissipated by *mov* instruction, where execution with 0xFF (the upper figure, with hamming weight 8) consumes more current than the execution with 0x00 (the middle figure, with hamming weight 0). The power difference between *mov*ing 0xFF and 0x00 is significantly visible, as shown in the bottom figure of Figure 2.18, where the adversary can predict the possible values processed inside the *mov* instruction based on the power magnitude. Sommer [147] also performed similar analysis on the *movwf* instruction to find the Hamming weight correlation with the power peaks.

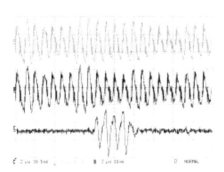

Figure 2.18: Hamming weight analysis on *mov* instruction [21]

Park et al. [185] analysed the *xor* instruction for its power dissipation for different Hamming weights as shown in Figure 2.19. An eight bit *xor* instruction is tested after its execution, where the power values for each Hamming weight (from 0x10 to 0xFF) of the result are subtracted from the power dissipated for 0x00, which has a Hamming weight of zero, to deduce the exact power dissipation. The y axis of Figure 2.19 denotes the voltage in mV, where the x axis specifies the Hamming weights produced in the result after the xor instruction execution. If an adversary extracts the power magnitude for an xor instruction execution in a real attack, the value of result (i.e., Hamming weight) can be easily predicted by mapping the power height in the analysis shown in Figure 2.19. For example, if the extracted power magnitude from real measurements is $0.02mV$, the Hamming weight after the xor execution is predicted by the adversary as 0x70 (which is 3).

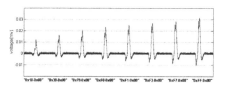

Figure 2.19: Hamming weight analysis on xor instruction [185]

A similar demonstration, predicting the Hamming weight using the power magnitude is presented by Messerges et al. [156], and is shown in Figure 2.20. The authors state that the attacker is assumed to know the locations of the pulses which contain the Hamming weight information. As Figure 2.20 depicts, the power magnitude is assigned certain levels based on different Hamming weights, which are specified in the y axis next to their magnitude. Knowing the Hamming weight of the data processed will lead to the secret key.

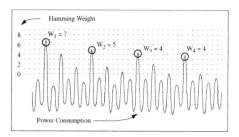

Figure 2.20: Hamming weight analysis [156]

Messerges et al. [154] came up with a formula as specified in Equation 2.4 to calculate the secret key in DES, if the Hamming weights are known during the key scheduling process. As the Hamming weight model shown in Equation 2.4, $\vec{w}$ denotes a vector of Hamming weights

23

w_i, $\vec{k}$ denotes the secret key to be computed and A is a 0-1 matrix such that A_{ij} is 1 if and only if weight w_i includes key bit k_j [154]. In DES encryption, the registers are shifted each time to create a subkey, which will be used for each round, as explained in Section 2.1.1. If the adversary knows each byte for eight shifts, then there is enough information to solve the Equation 2.4 to find the secret key k.

$$A\vec{k} = \vec{w}; \quad [154] \tag{2.4}$$

Messerges et al. [156] further state that another occurrence of information leakage, revealing secret information, is the transition count leakage (Hamming distance: the number of bitflips happening in an instruction execution [16]). Hamming distance can leak information when the dominant source of current is due to the switching in gates. The changes in gates dissipate current, where the greater the number of bits that change state, the greater the power that is consumed [156]. The experiment conducted in [156] to identify the power magnitudes for different numbers of bit transitions, uses a smart card which contains an 8-bit HC05-based microprocessor. The instruction tested is load (LDA), where an eight bit input is transferred into a register from memory. Figure 2.21 shows the Hamming distance analysis, which is similar to the Hamming weight analysis shown in Figure 2.20. The voltage levels are defined for possible bit transitions (i.e., the number of bits changed in the register after the LDA instruction execution), where the difference between transitions i and $i+1$ is observed to be $6.5mV$. Similar to the Hamming weight prediction, the adversary knowing the power magnitude of an LDA instruction execution will be able to realise the number of bit transitions by simply mapping the power profile on to the graph shown in Figure 2.21.

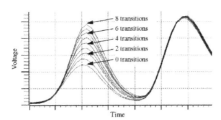

Figure 2.21: Hamming distance analysis [156]

The analysis in [156] showed that both Hamming weight and Hamming distance (bit transitions) can cause leakage in secure information. Messerges et al. [156] concluded that the type of information the adversary can use to reveal secret keys depends on the circuit design of the microprocessor, the type of operation the card is executing or the memory access. Knowing the system properly will reduce the attack time and complexity.

Brier et al. [45] defined a Hamming distance consumption model, based on a Hamming weight model. The Hamming weight model considered in [45] for an m-bit microprocessor, to a binary data D $(D = \sum_{j=0}^{m-1} d_j 2^j)$ is $H(D) = \sum_{j=0}^{m-1} d_j$. Equation 2.5 depicts the Hamming distance model, where the number of flipping bits from R to D is described by $H(D \oplus R)$, W is the consumed power and a, b are scalars. This model assumes that switching from 0 to 1 and 1 to 0 requires the same amount of power and there is a linear relationship between current consumption and Hamming distance [45].

$$W = aH(D \oplus R) + b; \quad [45] \tag{2.5}$$

Kunz-Jacques et al. [136] observed that predicting Hamming weights during simultaneous instruction executions would be much harder, since the execution has to be correlated with the sum of possible Hamming weights. For example, in DES two SBOX lookups are done simultaneously, where the observed power consumption would be from the execution of an SBOX pair [136]. The authors, however, managed to find a linear combination between the Hamming weights and simultaneous instruction executions. Figure 2.22 denotes the power variation based on Hamming weights, where the lower Hamming weight corresponds to lower power consumption and the higher Hamming weight corresponds to higher power consumption.

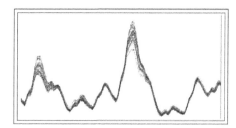

Figure 2.22: Hamming weight plots for simultaneous SBOX accesses in DES [136]

However, the experiments of Akkar et al. [22] show that Hamming weight correlation with power magnitude does not always work. Figure 2.23 shows the power consumption for storing a value in RAM ordered by Hamming weight in two different smart cards. Despite the general Hamming weight hypothesis, where an increasing curve is expected with the increase in Hamming weight, Figure 2.23 does not show a linear increase with increasing Hamming weight. This made Akkar et al. [22] conclude that the Hamming weight model is sometimes inadequate, as Hamming weight might not produce equal difference in power consumption in certain smart card designs.

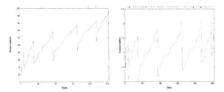

Figure 2.23: Hamming weight analysis on two different smard cards [22]

Biham and Shamir [37] describe the steps of attacking the Key Scheduling part of the DES algorithm (explained in Section 2.1.1) using Simple Power Analysis (SPA). The attack is based on Hamming weights to predict the subkeys. In smart cards the subkeys are stored in RAM in chunks of eight bits and the amount of power dissipation is proportional to the number of 1's in the eight written bits [37]. As per Biham and Shamir [37], the adversary first extracts the power consumption graph related to the key scheduling part from the whole power profile. The next step is to extract the power consumption graphs of separate subkey schedulings (16 subkeys) to analyse the Hamming weights. The measurement may contain many errors, but can be smoothed by averaging the power consumption by a large number of executions with a common key [37]. The authors also stress the necessity of the linear equation, which is explained in Equation 2.4, where there are 56 secret key bits to be predicted using the 96 (six subkey bytes for 16 rounds) Hamming weight of subkeys written into RAM. This proves that there are a sufficient number of equations to compute the secret key. Biham and Shamir [37] propose the following two ways to eliminate the effects caused by the imperfect knowledge of Hamming weights in the attack:

1. standard techniques from error correcting codes can be used, since there are 96 equations to be solved for only 56 variables;

2. since the DES algorithm divides the key into two halves and the subkeys contain bits

26

from one of these halves, the analysis of these segments separately will minimise the effect of measurement errors.

Similarly, the key scheduling segment (Key Expansion [143]) in AES encryption, where the roundkeys are generated from the secret key (explained in Section 2.1.2), has been attacked using Simple Power Analysis (SPA) exploiting Hamming weights, by Mangard [143]. In AES, the 128-bit secret key is expanded to eleven round keys as explained in Section 2.1.2. Mangard [143] identifies four main requirements to conduct the simple power analysis attack on AES key expansion:

1. the attacker needs to measure the power consumption of the device while it is performing at least one full AES key expansion. More samples can be used to find the average power trace to reduce the effect of noise;

2. the attacker should be able to extract the power traces relating to the occurrence of each intermediate result during AES key expansion, from the whole power trace;

3. the attacker needs to be able to obtain enough information from the extracted power trace, mainly caused by processing the intermediate result, to perform a brute-force search;

4. the attacker should know one ciphertext and certain properties of the corresponding plaintext to perform a brute-force search of possible keys.

If the AES key expansion is examined in greater detail, one byte of a roundkey calculation does not need all the bytes from the previous or the next roundkey. Figure 2.24 shows the equations for creating $RoundKey_1$ in AES key expansion, where $W_{i,j}$ represents the jth byte of the ith key, $S\text{-}Box$ represents the table lookup and $Rcon$ contains fixed values. This clearly shows that given an arbitrary $RoundKey_i$ all other round keys, including the secret key, can be calculated [143]. Hence, Mangard [143] claims that knowing a round key and its round number is equivalent to knowing the secret key.

As shown in Figure 2.24, four 32-bit roundkey segments are created from the previous roundkey. This observation of four overlapping parts in the AES key expansion is used for the SPA attack by Mangard [143], where the four segments of a round key are attacked independently. For example, Figure 2.25(a) indicates the four overlapping parts for $RoundKey_3$.

27

$$W_{4,j} = S\text{-}Box(W_{3,j+1}) \oplus Rcon_{1,j} \oplus W_{0,j}$$
$$W_{5,j} = W_{4,j} \oplus W_{1,j}$$
$$W_{6,j} = W_{5,j} \oplus W_{2,j}$$
$$W_{7,j} = W_{6,j} \oplus W_{3,j}$$

Figure 2.24: Computation of $RoundKey_1$ in AES key expansion [143]

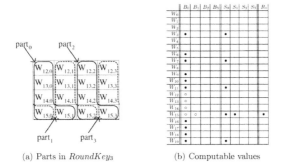

(a) Parts in $RoundKey_3$ (b) Computable values

Figure 2.25: Partitions and Computations using $RoundKey_3$ [143]

Based on $part_0$ in $RoundKey_3$, as shown in Figure 2.25(a), the other computable values such as the round keys and the intermediate results are analysed. Figure 2.25(b) indicates possible computable values, if $part_0$ of $RoundKey_3$ is known. The notations used in Figure 2.25(b) are $B_{0...3}$ referring to the bytes of the key word W_i, S_x is the output of the SBOX(B_x) and $R_0 = xor(S_1, Rcon)$. A $\circ$ is inserted into the cells for the known $part_0$ of $RoundKey_3$ ($part_0$ includes $W_{12,0}$, $W_{13,0}$, $W_{14,0}$, $W_{15,0}$ and $W_{15,1}$ as shown in Figure 2.25(a)). A $\bullet$ is inserted for the cells where the values can be computed from the known values of $part_0$ of $RoundKey_3$. Based on this partition and the possible computation of values, Mangard [143] proposes the simple power analysis attack on the AES key expansion. Figure 2.26 details a summary of the attack proposed by Mangard [143].

As shown in Figure 2.26, the preparatory steps before the attack involve the adversary deciding which round key to attack and to determining the Hamming weights based on the power magnitudes at necessary places like computation of W, SBOX(W) and $xor(SBOX, Rcon)$. The adversary should also find one ciphertext and information about the corresponding plaintext. The execution (attack) starts off with determining the list of possible computable values for each $part$ from 0 to 3 (as explained in Figure 2.25) for the SubKey part of all 5-byte values (since the Hamming weights are known, all the values which contain that Hamming weight

28

Preparation:

1. Decide which round key to attack. The round keys starting with the words W_t where $t \in \{12, 16, 20, 24, 28, 32\}$ are possible.
2. By power analysis determine the Hamming weights of the bytes $W_{t+x,0...3}$ $\forall x \in \{-9, -6, -5, -3, -2, -1, 0, +1, +2, +3, +4, +5, +6, +7\}$. Additionally, determine in the same manner the Hamming weights of the bytes $S\text{-}Box(W_{t+y,0...3})$ and $xor(S\text{-}Box(W_{t+y,1}), Rcon_{\frac{t+1+y}{4},0})$
   $\forall y \in \{-9, -5, -1, +3, +7\}$
3. Find one ciphertext and sufficient information about the corresponding plaintext.

Execution:

1. For $part = 0 \ldots 3$ do
   - Determine the list, $Subkey_{part}$, of all 5-byte values whose Hamming weights are equal to the measured Hamming weights of $W_{t,part}$, $W_{t+1,part}$, $W_{t+2,part}$, $W_{t+3,part}$ and $W_{t+3,(part+1) \bmod 4}$.
   - Run through all elements of $Subkey_{part}$ and for each 5-byte value of this list calculate the bytes
     $W_{t+x,part}$ $\forall x \in \{-9, -6, -5, -3, -2, -1, 0, +1, +2, +3, +4, +5, +6, +7\}$
     Additionally, calculate the bytes $S\text{-}Box(W_{t+y,0...3})$ and
     $xor(S\text{-}Box(W_{t+y,1}), Rcon_{\frac{t+1+y}{4},0})$ with $y \in \{-9, -5, -1, +3, +7\}$.
     Delete all 5-byte combinations from the list $Subkey_{part}$ that do not lead to the Hamming weights determined by power analysis.
   end for
2. Based on the four lists, $Subkey_{0...3}$, determine a list of 128-bit values that are possible for the attacked round key.
3. Perform a brute-force search of this list to identify the correct key.

Figure 2.26: Summary of the attack on AES key expansion [143]

have to be tried) as shown in Figure 2.26. All 5-byte combinations from the list that do not match the Hamming weights determined by power analysis are then deleted. Based on these lists, which are computed for each part of the RoundKey of concern, a list of 128-bit values for possible round key candidates is determined. And finally, a brute-force search of this list to identify the correct key is performed [143]. Mangard [143] claims that this attack (summarised in Figure 2.26) is a very reasonable compromise between the freedom to use the Hamming weight information and the computational effort.

Similar to the SPA attack of Mangard [143] on AES key expansion, Xiao and Heys [244] presented an attack on the key schedule of Camellia [26], a 128-bit block cipher implemented in an 8-bit smart card. Xiao and Heys [244] state that this attack runs faster than the attack of Mangard [143] in AES and does not require any pairs of plaintext and ciphertext. Figure 2.27 briefs the key scheduling and the subkey generation of the Camellia block cipher.

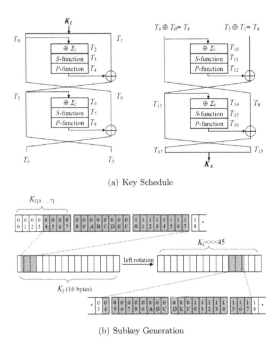

(a) Key Schedule

(b) Subkey Generation

Figure 2.27: Camellia Block Cipher [244]

nightly Firefox 3 builds now contain the Camellia cipher... – Bob Lord, Mozilla

As shown in Figure 2.27(a), the original key K_L is used to derive another key K_A, where $\sum_i$ is unique for each round i, *S-function* performs bit-wise substitution and *P-function* performs a linear transformation. Each subkey is obtained as one half of K_L or K_A after they are left rotated a specific number of bits, as shown in Figure 2.27(b). Xiao and Heys [244] claim that this attack exploits the redundancy in the key schedule of Camellia to determine the complete key without any knowledge of plaintext and ciphertext. There are three prerequisites identified for this attack:

1. the attacker has access to the power consumption information,

2. the attacker has the ability to identify clock cycles for the steps in the key schedule and

3. there exists a monotonic relationship between power and Hamming weight.

The first step of the attack of Xiao and Heys [244] identifies the Hamming weight at each left shift to generate subkeys as shown in Figure 2.27(b). Since there is going to be an overlap in the subkey computation, because of shifting, possible candidates related to the measured Hamming weights are tested for the key. The second step of the attack is to exploit the Hamming weight during the derivation of K_A from K_L, which is shown in Figure 2.27(a). The Hamming weights at T_2 and T_3 are predicted from the power magnitude at those clock cycles, and are compared with the Hamming weights computed from the chosen key candidates of K_L in step one. Similar Hamming weight checks are deployed at each round of Camellia key schedule as defined in Figure 2.27(a) to predict the 128-bit key.

The Simple Power Analysis (SPA) attacks discussed above exploited the relationship between the power magnitude and the Hamming weight to predict the secret key. Conditional branching in algorithms, like RSA and ECC, can also be used to predict the secret key using SPA, which is discussed in the next section.

2.2.2   Prediction of data using Conditional Branching

Public key cryptosystems like RSA [206] and ECC [157] use conditional branching based on key bits as explained in Section 2.1.3 and Section 2.1.4. The conditional branches of the square-and-multiply algorithm can be identified in the power trace because additional register loads are required for multiplication, which typically increase the width of the leading spike [105]. Since the number of instructions executed in the square-and-multiply operation is higher than the number of instructions executed in the square operation, the power profile will have significantly different patterns to distinguish between these two operations (i.e., more lengthy patterns denote the square-and-multiply operation and short different patterns denote the square operation). In fact, Kocher et al. [127] in 1998, predicted that the conditional branches will reveal useful information from the power profile. Figure 2.28 shows the power profile used for attacking RSA implemented on a *Hitachi H8/300* processor by Hollestelle et al. [104], where the Square-and-Multiply (SM) segments are distinguishable from the pure Square (S) operations.

As the square-and-multiply algorithm explained in Section 2.1.3, the square happens for all the bits in the key where multiplication is executed only when the key bit is 1. Hence, based

Figure 2.28: Square-and-Multiply power patterns in RSA [104]

on whether a square S or square-and-multiply SM is executed the key bits can be revealed. The key is predicted in [104] as shown in Figure 2.28, where SM patterns reveal the bit value as 1 and the S patterns reveal the bit value as 0. A similar way of exploiting the conditional branches in the square-and-multiply algorithm to predict the key in RSA is stated and also subjected to experiments by several other researchers in [18, 78, 93, 155, 172, 238].

Similar exploitation of conditional branching to predict the secret key is applied to Elliptic Curve Cryptography (ECC) where the double-and-add algorithm (explained in Section 2.1.4) performs branches based on key bits. Figure 2.29 depicts the power profile of double-and-add algorithm executed on the $SC140$ DSP processor. As Figure 2.29 shows, the double (D) operations and double-and-add (S) operations are clearly distinguishable in the power profile because the number of instruction executions for S is higher than D, where the adversary can predict the value of key bits used just by looking at the patterns. In this example, shown in Figure 2.29, the key processed is 0b001001.

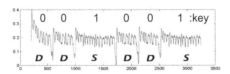

Figure 2.29: Double-and-Add power patterns in ECC [88]

The Simple Power Analysis (SPA) based on conditional branching in ECC (as shown in Figure 2.29) is further researched and proved by several other researchers [30, 47, 65, 178]. Even though the conditional branching reveals information about secret keys as discussed above, some real measurements, such as the one from Novak [172], did not provide enough variations in the power profile to distinguish between square and square-and-multiply in RSA. Novak [172] claimed that the patterns could not be distinguished from the measurements taken by power sampling equipments. Similar failure to find distinguishable patterns in RSA is reported by Messerges et al. [155], where the authors tried a simple cross-correlation [48] experiment to determine specific patterns (i.e., separate patterns related to square and multiply) from the indistinguishable power profile. Figure 2.30 shows the attempt of Messerges et al. [155] to extract the multiplication and square separately, where the multiplication power signal (middle trace) is cross-correlated with the whole exponentiation power signal (top trace). The resulting wave after cross-correlation is shown in the bottom trace in Figure 2.30, where peaks appear at the locations of the individual squares and multiplies.

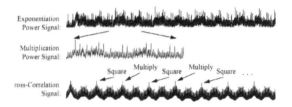

Figure 2.30: Cross-correlation on power profile to extract patterns [155]

Since the exponent wave is known to the authors, the square and multiply operations are labelled at the peaks in the bottom trace of Figure 2.30. However the height of the peaks are uncorrelated with the type of operation [155]. Based on these observations, Messerges et al. [155] claim that cross-correlation is not useful in differentiating between squares and multiplies.

Brier and Joye [47] presented a unified classical formulae for point doubling and addition, in the double-and-add algorithm in ECC (presented in Section 2.1.4) to perform a constant number of multiplications inside both operations to mask from SPA as explained above (i.e., different patterns for addition and doubling). The authors used Montgomery Modular Multiplication (MMM) [161]. However, Walter [239] performed an SPA successfully on the solution of Brier and Joye [47] where the conditional subtraction in the MMM [240] was exploited. Figure 2.31 briefly shows the attack of Walter [239] on the Montgomery Modular Multiplication (MMM) with the Brier and Joye [47] formulae for point addition. As shown in Figure 2.31, the Key bits (first row) with their respective double (D) or addition (A) operations are specified (key bit 1 executes DA, where 0 executes only D as explained in Section 2.1.4). The conditional subtractions used for operations u_1, u_2, s_1 and s_2 in MMM (the operations are explained in [239]) are denoted. The key point of the attack is whether there is a difference in subtractions between operations or not (specified as Y if a difference exist in Figure 2.31).

If there is a difference in subtraction (Y), that is detected as an add operation (A) by Walter [239]. As per the double-and-add algorithm, a double operation (D) will be executed on either side of an add (A) operation. Based on this observation, the last row in Figure 2.31 is filled with Y when the predicted operation (which is related to the key bit) is correct and the unknown operations are indicated with an asterick $(*)$.

Key	1 1 1 1 1 1 1 100 100 100 100 1 1 100 1 1 1 1 10 1 10 1 1 1 1 1 1
Pt Op^n	DADADADADADADADDDADDDADDDDADDDADADADDDADADADADADDDADADDADADADADADA
u_1 sub^n	0101100000010101000011001100010101010001010000001000101000001100
u_2 sub^n	0100100101000001010011001000000100010000000000000000111000011101
s_1 sub^n	0000101111000010001110010100001111000001000110001000010000100000
s_2 sub^n	0100101011010110001110010100011010000101100111001100110001000110
Diff^{nce}	Y Y Y Y Y Y Y Y Y Y Y Y Y Y Y Y Y Y Y Y
Known	YYYYY*YYYYYYYYY*YYY****YYY*YYYYYYY*YYYYYYYYY**YYYYYYYY***YYY*YY

Figure 2.31: Exploiting conditional subtractions [239]

Montgomery Modular Multiplication is used in modular arithmetic as an efficient way of performing an exponentiation of two numbers modulo a large number... – Wiki

As shown in Figure 2.31, Walter [239] proved that most bits in the key can be predicted with the implementation of Brier and Joye [47] on the double-and-add algorithm using Montgomery Modular Multiplication (MMM), which was claimed as secure against SPA. The attack of Walter [239] is further experimented upon by Sakai and Sakurai [202], using NIST recommended primes [171]. The authors [202] state that even if the unified codes are used, the underlying field operations should also be implemented in constant time, where the unified approach, in itself, is still vulnerable to power analysis.

Yen [247] identified an SPA vulnerability in AES, where the operation *xtime* (to compute $a(x) \cdot x$ mod $m(x)$, used in MixColumn operation which is explained in Section 2.1.2) performs a conditional branching based on the carry bit as shown in Figure 2.32. The instruction "XOR PRI" is only executed when the carry bit is one, using the jump instruction "JR NC, NEXT", as shown in Figure 2.32. A timing attack on this conditional branching is proposed in [131], but the possibility of exploiting this for Simple Power Analysis (SPA) is not extensively investigated. However, Yen [247] claims that SPA in *xtime* is possible and the conditional branching will reveal useful information to the adversary.

```
xtime:
        SL   A
        JR   NC, NEXT
        XOR  PRI        % PRI=1Bh (in hexadecimal)
NEXT:
```

Figure 2.32: An *xtime* implementation [247]

As explained above, Simple Power Analysis (SPA) directly analyses the power profile measured from a single attempt by feeding an input to the processor. However, this has several limitations for the adversary to perform a successful attack. Differential Power Analysis (DPA), which is much more successful than SPA, uses more than one sample of the power profile for the analysis to predict the secret key.

2.3 Differential Power Analysis (DPA)

Kocher et al. [127] introduced Differential Power Analysis (DPA) and observed that the variations in the power dissipation related to the manipulated data tend to be smaller and overshadowed by measurement errors and noise. DPA [127], one of the most successful power analysis methods, uses statistical functions to exploit the target algorithm, and to predict the secret key from smaller power variations. The underlying theory behind DPA is that, for some instruction I, the average power consumption is correlated to the value of at least one input bit or a function of input bits [71]. In simple terms, when the actual processing is correlated with the predicted behaviour, a higher correlation has to be observed when the prediction matches the actual processing. DPA is demonstrated by several researchers in block ciphers like DES, AES and public cryptosystems like RSA, ECC.

2.3.1 Differential Power Analysis (DPA) on Block Ciphers

Block ciphers encrypt a group of characters (blocks) of plaintext message using a fixed transformation [149]. Examples for block cipher encryption programs are DES, 3DES, AES, IDEA and RC5. The nature of block ciphers (i.e., independent operations between blocks) is convenient for the adversaries, where a successful attack on a single block can be simply repeated on all the other blocks to reveal the whole secret key.

35

2.3.1.1 Differential Power Analysis on DES

The DPA by Kocher et al. [127] is demonstrated on the DES encryption program which is explained in Section 2.1.1. As shown in Figure 2.33, Kocher et al. [127] observed in DES that at the beginning of the 16th round, the intermediate result L is XORed with subkey K, where the result is fed into the $SBOX$ lookup to generate the ciphertext C. The DPA selection function $D(C,b,K_s)$ is defined to compute the bit b ($0 \leq b < 32$) of L, where the 6 key bits entering the $SBOX$ corresponding to bit b are represented by K_s ($0 \leq K_s < 2^6$) [127].

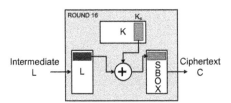

Figure 2.33: The First DPA definition on DES

As per Kocher et al. [127], to perform DPA on a processor chip the adversary observes m encryption operations and records the power traces $T_{1..m}[1..k]$ containing k samples each, including ciphertexts $C_{1..m}$ (note that no knowledge of plaintext is required). The main aim of the adversary is to determine the subkey K_s. If the adversary can guess a value of K_s, the DPA selection function to compute the value of bit b is computable (reverse computation of the DES algorithm) using the known values of ciphertext C. The attacker performs a k-sample differential trace $\Delta_D[1..k]$, finding the average of the traces for which $D(C,b,K_s)$ is one and the average of the traces for which $D(C,b,K_s)$ is zero. Hence, $\Delta_D[j]$ is the differential value at point j in the power profile. Equation 2.6 shows the derivation of the differential trace $\Delta_D[j]$ at point j. Kocher et al. [127] claim that if the chosen K_s is correct, the prediction correlates with what is being processed, thus producing a spike in the differential trace. Since the power consumption is correlated to the data bit values, the plot of differential trace Δ_D will be flat with spikes in regions where D matches with the values processed.

$$
\begin{aligned}
\Delta_D[j] &= \frac{\sum_{i=1}^{m} D(C_i, b, K_s) T_i[j]}{\sum_{i=1}^{m} D(C_i, b, K_s)} - \frac{\sum_{i=1}^{m} (1 - D(C_i, b, K_s)) T_i[j]}{\sum_{i=1}^{m} (1 - D(C_i, b, K_s))} \\
&\approx 2 \left(\frac{\sum_{i=1}^{m} D(C_i, b, K_s) T_i[j]}{\sum_{i=1}^{m} D(C_i, b, K_s)} - \frac{\sum_{i=1}^{m} T_i[j]}{m} \right); \quad [127]
\end{aligned}
\tag{2.6}
$$

36

Figure 2.34 depicts the differential traces generated from the experiments of Kocher et al. [127]. The experiments were performed on a smart card, executing DES and the traces in Figure 2.34 are produced using 1000 samples ($m = 10^3$). The top trace in Figure 2.34 refers to the average power trace of DES encryption, whereas the other three traces denote the differential traces. The second trace from the top reveals the correct guess of K_s (i.e., a significant spike in the trace) and, the third and fourth traces show incorrect guesses (i.e., no significant spikes).

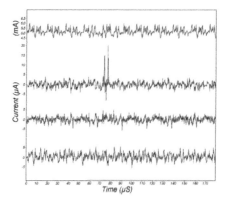

Figure 2.34: Traces on DPA of DES [127]

As shown in Figure 2.34, the correct subkey part K_s (which is 6 bits) can be successfully predicted, and the other parts can be predicted in a similar fashion to completely predict the 48 bits subkey. The presentation of Differential Power Analysis (DPA) on DES by Kocher et al. [127] is more abstract, lacking details, since it was the first paper on DPA. Messerges et al. [156] reviewed and investigated the DPA proposed by Kocher et al. [127] in detail on a smart card, executing DES encryption. As per Messerges et al. [156], DPA is much more powerful than Simple Power Analysis (SPA), where the attacker does not need to know as many details about the implementation of the algorithm.

The explanation of Messerges et al. [156] on Differential Power Analysis (DPA) goes as follows. The attack begins by executing the encryption program for N random values of plaintext inputs. A discrete power signal $S_i[j]$ is recorded for each of the N inputs, PTI_i and the ciphertext output CTO_i is also recorded. $S_i[j]$ is a portion of the power consumed during the attack part of the algorithm. The i index corresponds to the input PTI_i and the j index corresponds to the time of the sample. The partition function D, which is referred to as the selection function by Kocher et al. [127], is defined by Messerges et al. [156] in a much refined way as shown in Equation 2.7. The D function computes the value of one bit C_1 of CTO_i, which is XORed with the first bit (bit #1) of the SBOX1 (i.e., the first SBOX) output as shown in Equation 2.7. The metric C_6 represents the six bit intermediate result, which is XORed with the six bits of the last round's subkey K_{16} and the result is given as the index for the SBOX1 lookup.

$$D(C_1, C_6, K_{16}) = C_1 \oplus \text{SBOX1}(C_6 \oplus K_{16}); \quad [156] \qquad (2.7)$$

After recording the necessary power signals and other metrics, the adversary can guess a value for the subkey (i.e., values ranging from 0 to 2^6 for a 6-bit part of the subkey value) and perform the D function computation (shown in Equation 2.7). The power signals ($S_i[j]$) are placed into two sets using the computation from the partition function D, as shown in Equation 2.8. If function D generates a value of 0 for a subkey guess, the power signal $S_i[j]$ is given to set S_0. After placing the power signals in different sets of S_0 and S_1, the average power signal is computed for each set as shown in Equation 2.9, where $|S_0| + |S_1| = N$. Finally, the DPA bias signal is obtained by subtracting the two averages $A_0[j]$ and $A_1[j]$ as presented in Equation 2.10. Messerges et al. [156] claim that choosing an appropriate D function results in a DPA bias signal which exposes the value of the secret key. The main reason for choosing the specific D function, using the bits of $C_1.C_6$ and K_{16} as shown in Equation 2.7, is that when these bits are manipulated in the smart card, there will be a slight difference in power dissipation depending on whether the bit (computed using D function) is 0 or 1. Thus, if enough PTI samples are used, the DPA bias signal $T[j]$ will show power biases when the actual subkey is predicted and will converge to 0 at all other times [156]. But the experiments of Messerges et al. [156] show that the power biases for incorrect key guesses did not always converge to 0, but the largest biases are still observed for the correct key guess.

$$
\begin{aligned}
S_0 &= \{S_i[j] \mid D() = 0\}; \\
S_1 &= \{S_i[j] \mid D() = 1\}; \quad [156]
\end{aligned}
\qquad (2.8)
$$

$$A_0[j] = \frac{1}{|S_0|} \sum_{S_i[j] \epsilon S_0} S_i[j];$$

$$A_1[j] = \frac{1}{|S_1|} \sum_{S_i[j] \epsilon S_1} S_i[j]; \quad [156]$$

(2.9)

$$T[j] = A_0[j] - A_1[j]; \quad [156]$$
(2.10)

Figure 2.35 depicts the DPA experiment of Messerges et al. [156] on DES, which is executed in a smart card, using attack equipments such as a PC, a general-purpose interface bus (GPIB) card and a digital oscilloscope. The power consumption for the last three rounds (Round 14, Round 15 and Round 16) were collected and analysed as shown in Figure 2.35, with a total number of $N = 1300$ power signals.

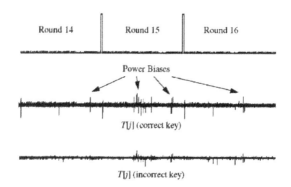

Figure 2.35: DPA bias signals in DES [156]

As shown in the DPA bias plot for the correct key (middle plot in Figure 2.35), the bias signals are twice as large compared to the DPA bias plot for the incorrect key (bottom plot in Figure 2.35). This shows that the correct key is easily recognised from the bias signal. The experiment of Messerges et al. [156] revealed the six bits of the secret key by exploiting the SBOX1 in round 16 of DES. Similarly, all 48 bits of the secret key can be revealed by attacking each SBOX access (there are eight SBOXes for each round in DES). The remaining eight bits of the secret key can be found by brute force or by successively applying this approach backwards to previous rounds [156].

Messerges et al. [156] state that more samples would be needed for a successful attack depending on the noise level in the signal. Hence the authors in [156] proposed noise level modelling and evaluated how to filter the noise from the actual signal to enhance DPA. The attack of Messerges et al. [156], as explained above, did not clearly explain how a prediction of the subkey will result in revealing the real secret key, since back tracking using the DES algorithm needs all previous subkeys. Koeune and Standaert [132] also investigated the Differential Power Analysis on DES encryption, which is similar to the attacks by Kocher et al. [127] and Messerges et al. [156] (explained above). According to Koeune and Standaert [132], the selection function is focused on an arbitrary output bit b of an arbitrary SBOX at the 16th round. Gebotys [86] also proved that the subkey in the 16th round for an SBOX lookup in DES is successfully revealed. Figure 2.36 shows the DPA performed on DES by Gebotys [86] where the store operation after the SBOX lookup is measured for power dissipation. The correct subkey (0x36) produces a significant peak in the DPA plot as shown in Figure 2.36.

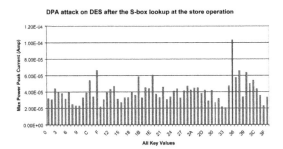

Figure 2.36: A successful DPA attack in DES [86]

Coron and Goubin [68] clearly define the steps to perform a DPA (a slightly different version than [156]) in DES, which are as follows:

1. measure the consumption on the first round, for n DES computations. Let the input values for those computations be $E_1,....,E_n$ and the electric consumption curves measured during the computations be $C_1,....,C_n$. The "mean curve" MC is also computed for the n consumption curves;

2. consider the attack, for instance on the first output bit (bit b) of the first SBOX during the first round. The bit b depends only on the six bits of the subkey. The attacker makes

40

a hypothesis on the 6 bits subkey, and the value of b is computed from those six bits and from input E_i. This allows the separation of the inputs $E_1,....,E_n$ into two categories: those that yield b=0; and, those that yield b=1;

3. the mean MC' of the curves C, corresponding to inputs of the first category (where b=0) is computed. If MC and MC' show an appreciable difference the chosen values of the six key bits are assumed to be correct. If MC and MC' does not show any significant difference, step 2 is repeated with another choice for the six key bits;

4. steps 2 and 3 are repeated with a target bit b in the second SBOX, then the third SBOX, till the eighth SBOX. This will help the adversary obtain the 48 bits of the secret key (subkey);

5. the remaining eight bits can be found exhaustively.

The steps of Coron and Goubin [68] for DPA in DES, with a greater level of explanation than the previous papers [127, 156], claim that the actual secret key is revealed by attacking the first round, and that the attacker does not require any knowledge of the individual electric consumption of each instruction, nor the position in time of each of these instructions. However, it seems the authors were trying to predict the subkey, but not the real secret key, since the secret key has gone through permutations, as explained in Section 2.1.1 to generate subkeys, which are then supplied as 6-bit chunks for encryption. Recent attacks on DES show [86] that the attacker needs power samples dissipated at specific instructions to perform a successful attack, where the mean of the whole power sample contains noise, masking the actual computation. Coron and Goubin [68] have presented a slightly different DPA bias calculation, where the mean of the original power samples are subtracted from the mean of the set which has $b = 0$. The other DPA attacks on DES [86, 127, 132, 156], as explained above, did not clearly state how the prediction of the subkey can be used to predict the exact secret key, and the method flow in attacking the DES encryption (such as permutation tables in DES, the places where the power should be measured, etc.) was not explained in detail. However, DES is becoming obsolete, since it is not sufficiently secure for embedded systems, due to its vulnerabilities for different type of attacks, especially fault attacks [29]. Hence, few DPA attacks for DES have been described in recent years.

2.3.1.2 Differential Power Analysis on AES

Advanced Encryption Standard (AES) [167], the successor of DES, is a popular target of attackers using DPA. Daemen and Rijmen [71], the inventors of the AES, explain the steps of DPA. The authors assume that the average power consumption P_I of an instruction I is correlated to bit op_1. However their analysis applies to any bit op_i as shown in Equation 2.11. Equation 2.11, $E_{op_2,...,op_n}$ denotes the average over all values of $op_2,...,op_n$. The correlation between P and op_1 implies that $P_I(0) \neq P_I(1)$ and difference D_I is computed, as shown in Equation 2.12.

$$
\begin{aligned}
P_I(0) &= E_{op_2,...,op_n}[P(I,0,op_2,...,op_n)]; \\
P_I(1) &= E_{op_2,...,op_n}[P(I,1,op_2,...,op_n)]; \quad [71]
\end{aligned}
\tag{2.11}
$$

$$
D_I = P_I(0) - P_I(1); \quad [71]
\tag{2.12}
$$

In Equation 2.12, the correlation between P_I and op_1 is more exploitable when D_I has a larger contribution from the actual operation than the noise [71]. Daemen and Rijmen [71] further state the steps for a DPA attack as follows:

1. identify a bit a in the intermediate encryption result, which will act as an input to an instruction I, that will produce larger D_I for bit a. It is assumed that bit a is computable from known bits D such as input, output and using a guessed unknown key bits K, by applying the encryption function; $a=f(K,D)$;

2. record the power profiles of n executions of the AES encryption, making sure that the bits of D vary over the sample;

3. guess a value for K and partition the power samples into two groups: those for which $a = 0$ and those for which $a = 1$, for a given K. Accumulate the power consumption in the groups and find the difference between the results as shown mathematically in Equation 2.13.

$$
T_1(K) = \sum_{f(K,D)=0} P(D) - \sum_{f(K,D)=1} P(D); \quad [71]
\tag{2.13}
$$

If the value of K is correct, then $T_I(K)$ will not be equal to 0, but if it is not correct, then the value of $T_I(K)$ is expected to be much closer to 0, since both side of the results will contain samples corresponding to $a = 0$ and $a = 1$. Hence, the predicted key value K that maximises $|T_I(K)|$ is likely to be the correct secret key [71]. However, Daemen and Rijmen [71] did not perform a DPA attack on AES, but just defined the steps for the attack. Golic and Tymen [94] state that the intermediate variables identified in the fundamental hypothesis for the DPA attack on AES are the output bytes of the SBOXes in the first round. Since each SBOX access is a function of an input byte which itself is a bitwise sum of a byte of plaintext and its corresponding expanded key byte, knowing the plaintext byte and guessing the key byte correctly will result in computing the correct SBOX output. The main objective in the DPA of AES is to recover the expanded key (it is the actual secret key in the first round as explained in Section 2.1.2) in a byte-by-byte divide-and-conquer manner [94]. Golic and Tymen [94] also identified the necessary steps to perform DPA in AES, specifically saying that the output bit of the SBOX output is used to divide power samples into two categories, where the steps, explained above from Daemen and Rijmen [71], are more general.

Ors et al. [177] performed Differential Power Analysis (DPA) on an ASIC (Application Specific Integrated Circuit) AES implementation. The target for this DPA in [177] were the eight most significant bits (MSBs) of the *Register* after the initial key addition, as shown in Figure 2.37. Since the key used for this operation is the original secret key (as explained in Section 2.1.2) and the *Shift Rows* operation does not change the eight MSBs of the result after the *Add RoundKey* operation, the storage of these eight MSBs in the *Register* is observed for power consumption [177]. This place of power measurement to predict the secret key is quite different from the other techniques explained above [71, 94], where such techniques observed the power consumption of almost the whole encryption. Ors et al. [177] measured the power consumption of the first clock cycle, where the initial key addition operation occurs and the second clock cycle where the result is written into the *Register*, to perform DPA. Tiri et al. [222] also demonstrated a DPA on an AES coprocessor and noted that the eight state bits can be predicted by guessing a key byte, requiring $16 * 2^8$ key guesses, while brute force requires 2^{128}. This shows that DPA takes significantly less attack time than a brute force attack. Gebotys [86] explains the attack point in Rijndael (AES) as shown in Figure 2.38. The store after the table lookup (which is fed by the result of the XOR of key and plaintext) is stated

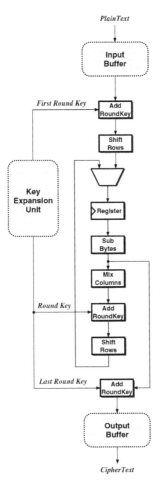

Figure 2.37: Block Diagram of the AES crypto-chip [177]

as the attack point, as shown in Figure 2.38(a), where the power magnitudes during the store after the table lookup are recorded for a DPA attack. The attacker guesses the key value (such as the eight bits of the key, which is shown as ? in Figure 2.38(b)), which is XORed with known plaintext and input to the SBOX table. The power traces are then partitioned into two groups according to the expected value of bit j (a zero, 0? or one, 1?), as shown in Figure 2.38(b), to perform DPA.

44

Rijndael (pronounced rain-dahl) is the algorithm that has been selected by the NIST as the candidate for the AES... – TechTarget

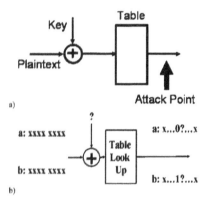

Figure 2.38: Attack point and Partitioning in Rijndael [86]

Boracchi and Breveglierli [44] explain the DPA on AES SBOX in detail as shown in the flowchart in Figure 2.39. The adversary collects the power traces by feeding possible inputs and guessing a key value and performing the DPA bias calculation (also explained in steps above from [71]). A similar procedure will be iterated for all possible key guesses of secret key KG as shown in Figure 2.39. The DPA bias will be plotted and the key guess KG, which generates the highest peak, will be predicted as the correct key. The reliability r of the attack can be measured, as clearly explained in [44].

In the Differential Power Analysis (DPA) experiments of Boracchi and Breveglierli [44], the decision function D_{SB} to partition the power traces for DPA is defined as $D_{SB}(PTI_i,kg)$ = $[SBOX(PTI_i \oplus kg)] \wedge 2^j$, $j = 0,...,7$, where PTI_i is the ith plaintext and kg is the guessed key. The output of the decision function is the SBOX output bits. The DPA traces, based on this selection function, are presented in Figure 2.40, where 256 DPA traces for possible key guesses are plotted, considering the power consumption samples of the initial part of an AES round. The trace having the highest peak is obtained when the decision function exploits the correct key guess kg, as shown in Figure 2.40.

45

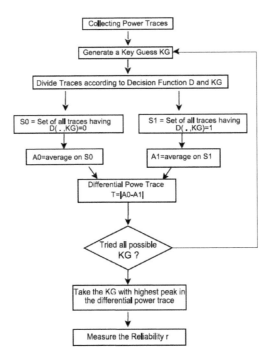

Figure 2.39: Operational Flowchart of DPA on AES [44]

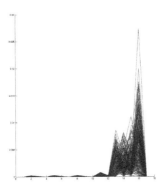

Figure 2.40: DPA traces to an AES SBOX [44]

Boracchi and Breveglierli [44] observed that the Decision Function was the key element in Differential Power Analaysis (DPA), where it had to be designed accurately depending on

46

the algorithm implemented in the device. Figure 2.41 depicts the AES pseudocode (AES encryption is explained in Section 2.1.2), where the attack points are denoted. The data at * can be taken as target bits when the attacker knows the plaintext, while the data at ** can be extracted for target bits when the attacker has the ciphertext output. The experiment of Boracchi and Breveglierli [44] was based on AES SBOX output, because the authors claim that the SBOX execution greatly influences the power consumption within the whole encryption. But the authors also say that one would attack at the AddRoundKey operation (lines are denoted as *** and **** in Figure 2.41), which is investigated by [177].

```
Cipher(byte in[4*Nb], byte out[4*Nb], word w[Nb*(Nr+1)])

begin
byte state[4,Nb]

state = in

AddRoundKey(state, w[0, Nb-1]) //***

for round = 1 step 1 to NrÛ1
    SubBytes(state)
    ShiftRows(state)                // at round =1, *
    MixColumns(state)
    AddRoundKey(state, w[round*Nb, (round+1)*Nb-1])
end for

SubBytes(state)    // **

ShiftRows(state)

AddRoundKey(state, w[Nr*Nb, (Nr+1)*Nb-1]) //****

out = state

end
```

Figure 2.41: AES pseudocode and Target bits [44]

DPA in AES is not clearly demonstrated or presented as DES, but realised and experimented on, so that the researchers are able to propose techniques to prevent DPA. In brief, to perform DPA in block ciphers, the adversary selects a key block to attack and perform the analysis to predict that block, which is independently executed from the other blocks in the algorithm. The same set of steps will be repeated until all key blocks are successfully predicted. However, the DPA on Public Cryptosystems would be quite different, as public key and private key are used, with large prime number multiplications.

2.3.2 Differential Power Analysis on Public Cryptosystems

Kocher et al. [127] forecasted the vulnerability of Public Cryptosystems, like RSA and ECC, against Differential Power Analysis (DPA) attacks, stating that public key algorithms can be analysed for DPA by correlating the intermediate computations with power consumptions.

The authors further predicted that the exponent bits in modular exponentiation operations can be guessed for correlation to realise the actual computations. However, few researchers successfully attempted to break the private key in public cryptosystems using DPA, compared to block ciphers.

2.3.2.1 DPA on RSA

The first power analysis on RSA was performed by Messerges et al. [155], which is slightly different from DPA and presented in Section 2.3.3.6. Following this, Boer et al. [42] experimented with DPA on an RSA implementation, exploiting the dependency of the power consumption on the value of intermediate data of the Square-and-Multiply algorithm (explained in Section 2.1.3). The attack model is based on the correlation between the power consumption and the Hamming weight of intermediate data (refer [120]). The attack of Boer et al. [42] further assumes that the adversary can vary the input data x and the simple power consumption measurements $P(x,t)$ are carried out using a digital oscilloscope and recorded in a PC. The selection function $d(x)$, used in the attack, is shown in Equation 2.14, where $W(x)$ refers the Hamming weight of the intermediate data and $E(n)$ refers to the expected Hamming weight value of the n-bit bus of the RSA coprocessor. However, Boer et al. [42] state that the easiest selection function would be the Hamming weight of the intermediate data or just a byte of transported data.

$$d(x) = W(x) - E(n); \quad [42] \tag{2.14}$$

The correlation formula for the DPA attack on RSA of Boer et al. [42] is presented in Equation 2.15, where the correlation is carried out between the result of the selection function $d(x, j)$ based on the key hypothesis j, the input data x and the power consumption $P(x,t)$ at time t for the input x. Note that the mean value of each element is denoted using a line at the top. The metric t can be narrowed down to a small interval if the simple power characteristics of the implementation are obvious. The metric i runs through all single measurements and the correlation coefficient $c(t, j)$ has to be computed for each key guess j. Significant correlation results will be generated for the correct key guess and the correlation will be near zero for all the other key guesses (i.e., wrong guesses) [42].

$$c(t,j) = \frac{\sum_i (d(x_i, j) - \overline{d(x_i, j)})(P(x_i, t) - \overline{P(x_i, t)})}{\sqrt{\sum_i (d(x_i, j) - \overline{d(x_i, j)})^2} \sqrt{\sum_i (P(x_i, t) - \overline{P(x_i, t)})^2}}; \quad [42] \qquad (2.15)$$

Boer et al. [42] performed a DPA attack on the implementation of RSA using the Chinese Remainder Theorem (CRT) (refer [64] for the definition and details of CRT). CRT is popularly known for the speedup it provides in the RSA signature and decryption, where the basic definition of CRT says that the congruence $x \equiv y \pmod{N}$ can be computed as simultaneous congruences $x \equiv y \pmod{n_i}$ for all $1 \leq i \leq k$, where $N = n_1.n_2.n_3...n_k$ [248].

The Chinese remainder theorem is said to have been used to count the size of the ancient Chinese armies... – PlanetMath.org

According to Boer et al. [42], the conventional modular exponentiation using the Square-and-Multiply algorithm (explained in Section 2.1.3) is computed using CRT as follows:

1. split the exponent: $d_p = d \bmod (p - 1)$, $d_q = d \bmod (q - 1)$, where $n = pq$;

2. perform the two exponentiations using the Square-and-Multiply algorithm: $v_1 = x^{d_p} \bmod p$, $v_2 = x^{d_q} \bmod q$;

3. using the precalculated multiplicative inverse $P_q = p^{-1} \bmod q$ from Garner's algorithm [149];

    u: (v2 - v1)*P_q mod q

    y: v1 + u*p

    return y.

The DPA attack of Boer et al. [42] (named as Modular Reduction on Equidistant Data (MRED)) on the above CRT implementation, assumes that the adversary can choose the input values and the inputs are categorised into a series with each series containing several elements. Step 1 is the attack place for DPA, where the key task is to find the prime number q by attacking the "*d mod q*" computation while changing the input d.

The attacker chooses a series of inputs (x_i) to be fed into the algorithm as shown in Equation 2.16. Starting value x_0 is chosen as a random number. There are k sets of inputs used, where k reaches the size of the prime number to be attacked. By selecting such inputs, the attacked computation can be interpreted, as shown in Equation 2.17, where r_0 is the remainder. The DPA involves predicting r_0, which will eventually be used to predict prime q.

$$x_i = x_0 - i.(256)^k; \quad [42] \tag{2.16}$$

$$(x_0 - i.(256)^k) \bmod q = r_0 - i.(256)^k; \quad [42] \tag{2.17}$$

A brief explanation of the MRED attack [42] is as follows: the adversary starts predicting each byte of r_0 starting from the least significant byte. Each byte of r_0 can hold 256 values, hence there will be 256 hypothesis H_j, to predict that byte. Hypothesis H_{ji} is defined as $\{r_i \bmod 256 = (j - i) \bmod 256\}$, where j refers a specific hypothesis and i refers a specific input for hypothesis j. For example, Table 2.1 shows the Hamming weights and hypothesis table populated for the attack, where the values for each input for all 256 hypothesis are computed (i.e., $H_{ji} = (j - i) \bmod 256$). Based on the Hamming weight of the values for each input in the set in Table 2.1, the decision function d_{ji} values are calculated, as shown in Table 2.2. These values are just the Hamming weights of each hypothesis values (i.e., value of 255 has a Hamming weight of 8). The correlation values $c(t, j)$ as shown in Equation 2.15 are evaluated from the values of d_{ji} computed and the power values $P(x_i, t)$ recorded for each input. Table 2.1 and Table 2.2 are examples showing how a byte value of remainder r_0 can be predicted. The correlation $c(t, j)$ which produces the highest peak (referred as f_0 in [42]) is predicted as the correct byte value for r_0.

H_{ji}	x_0	x_1	x_2	x_3	x_4	···	x_i
H_{0i}	0	255	254	253	252	···	$-i$ mod 256
H_{1i}	1	0	255	254	253	···	$(1 - i)$ mod 256
H_{2i}	2	1	0	255	254	···	$(2 - i)$ mod 256
.....	...	...	...	...	..		....
H_{255i}	255	254	253	252	251	···	$(255 - i)$ mod 256

Table 2.1: Hamming weights and hypothesis [42]

The correlation $c(t, j)$ plot for a byte of an r_0 prediction is shown in Figure 2.42, where the f_0 value, which has the highest peak is revealed as 66. Finding r_i successively in similar fashion

d_{ji}	x_0	x_1	x_2	x_3	x_4	$\cdots$	x_i
d_{0i}	0	8	7	7	6	$\cdots$	$W(H_{0i})$
d_{1i}	1	0	8	7	7	$\cdots$	$W(H_{1i})$
d_{2i}	1	1	0	8	7	$\cdots$	$W(H_{2i})$
....	..	..	..	..	..	..	....
d_{255i}	8	7	7	6	7	$\cdots$	$W(H_{255i})$

Table 2.2: Decision function and Hamming weights [42]

and, finding gcd of x_0 and the final f revealing the secret prime q. A detailed explanation of the MRED attack can be found in [42].

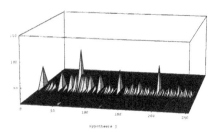

Figure 2.42: Correlation plot to find f_0 [42]

Aigner and Oswald [21] also stated that the RSA is vulnerable to DPA and the authors explained the mean method of Messerges et al. [155], which is elucidated in Section 2.3.3.6. There were very few attempts to attack RSA using DPA.

2.3.2.2 DPA on ECC

One of the first DPA attacks on Elliptic Curve Crytosystems (ECC) was performed by Coron [65], where the author modified the conventional Double-and-Add algorithm (explained in Section 2.1.4) which is proved to be vulnerable to Simple Power Analysis (refer Section 2.2.2). The modified version, as shown in Figure 2.43, precludes branching execution. Both double and addition are computed without any branch and the result is chosen based on the value of bit d_i. The main observation of Coron's DPA attack [65] is that at iteration j the processing point Q depends only on the first bits $(d_{l-1}.....d_j)$ of d and the attack assumes that the adversary knows how points are represented in memory during computation. When a point Q is processed, the power consumption will be correlated to some specific bits of d. Hence, such correlation can be used to successively recover the bits of d by guessing the points computed inside the card. For example, to predict the second most significant bit d_{l-2} of d, the power consumption should be correlated with any specific bits of the binary representation of $4P$. If $d_{l-2} = 0$, $4P$ is computed in the algorithm shown in Figure 2.43 and the power consumption will correlate with any specific bits of $4P$. If $d_{l-2} = 1$, there will not be any correlation between power consumption and bits in $4P$, because $4P$ is never computed. Bits of d can be recursively predicted in a similar fashion [65].

$$\texttt{input P}$$
$$Q[0] \leftarrow P$$
$$\texttt{for } i \texttt{ from } \ell - 2 \texttt{ to } 0 \texttt{ do}$$
$$\qquad Q[0] \leftarrow 2Q[0]$$
$$\qquad Q[1] \leftarrow Q[0] + P$$
$$\qquad Q[0] \leftarrow Q[d_i]$$
$$\texttt{output } Q[0]$$

Figure 2.43: SPA resistant Double-and-Add algorithm [65]

Briefly, the attack is to predict the secret key d in the computation $Q = dP$ by changing different data inputs for P. The DPA attack of Coron [65] goes as follows:

1. perform the double-and-add algorithm shown in Figure 2.43, k times with distinct $P_1, P_2, ..., P_k$ to compute $Q_1 = dP_1$, $Q_2 = dP_2, ..., Q_k = dP_k$;

2. record the power consumption $C_i(t)$ associated with the ith execution of the algorithm, where $1 \le i \le k$;

3. compute s_i which can be any bit of the binary representation of $4P_i$, where $1 \le i \le k$;

4. perform the correlation function $g(t)$ between s_i and $C_i(t)$ as shown in Equation 2.18, where the difference between the average power consumptions for those points for which $s_i=1$ and the average power consumption for those points for which $s_i=0$ is calculated;

5. a peak will be observed in the trace of $g(t)$ if $4P_i$ is processed (i.e., $d_{l-2} =0$) as shown in Figure 2.44 and no peaks will be seen when $4P_i$ is not processed (i.e., $d_{l-2} = 1$) as shown in Figure 2.45;

6. this process can be iterated recursively until all the bits of d are predicted. For example, the bits of $8P_i$ should be correlated with the power consumption to predict d_{l-3}.

$$g(t) = < C_i(t) >_{i=1,2,...,k|s_i=1} - < C_i(t) >_{i=1,2,...,k|s_i=0}; \quad [65] \qquad (2.18)$$

Figure 2.44: A peak, revealing $d_{l-2} = 0$ [65]

Figure 2.45: No peak, revealing $d_{l-2} = 1$ [65]

Coron [65] also extended the attack to any scalar multiplication algorithm. The attack of Coron [65] is explained clearly except the part at which the power consumption should be measured, since, the prediction of a portion of the total power consumption may be unsuccessful due to high noise effects. Hasan [102] also proposed a similar attack on ECC scalar multiplication, stating that the Simple Power Analysis (SPA) resistant implementation (shown in Figure 2.43) includes equal amount of computations irrespective of the data, which can be exploited for a Differential Power Analysis (DPA) attack. Similar to Coron's attack [65], Hasan [102] also begins the DPA by feeding inputs $P_0, P_1, ..., P_{t-1}$ to the system which computes kP_i and monitoring the power consumption at the place where two elliptic curve points are added for each iteration. According to Hasan [102], the power consumption signal at the jth iteration of the ith execution is defined as S_{ij}, where $0 \leq i \leq t$ - 1 and $0 \leq j \leq n$ - 1; key k is of size n. If a certain number of most significant bits of k, such as $k_{n-1}, k_{n-2}, ..., k_{j'+1}$, are known, the attack of Hasan [102] to predict the next most significant bit $k_{j'}$, proceeds as follows:

1. chose a partition function, such that the function depends on k, more specifically $j = j'$, it depends on $k_{n-1}, k_{n-2}, ..., k_{j'}$;

2. denote the actual value of the bit $k_{j'}$ used in the device as $\gamma_{i,j'} \in \{0,1\}$, $0 \leq i \leq t\text{-}1$. The adversary comes up with a guess value for $k_{j'}$ and computes $\gamma'_{i,j'}$, $0 \leq i \leq t - 1$, for the partition function;

3. split the power signals $S_{i,j'}$, for $0 \leq i \leq t - 1$, into two sets: $S_0 = \{S_{i,j'}|\gamma'_{i,j'} = 0\}$ and $S_1 = \{S_{i,j'}|\gamma'_{i,j'} = 1\}$;

4. compute the differential signal $\delta(j') = \dfrac{\displaystyle\sum_{S_{i,j'} \in S_0} S_{i,j'}}{\displaystyle\sum_{i=0}^{t-1} \gamma'_{i,j'}} - \dfrac{\displaystyle\sum_{S_{i,j'} \in S_1} S_{i,j'}}{\displaystyle\sum_{i=0}^{t-1} (1 - \gamma'_{i,j'})}$;

5. A non-zero value in differential signal $\delta(j')$ indicates a correct guess for $k_{j'}$.

The attack of Hasan [102], as explained above, fails to address the details of the partition function, but states that the power consumption should be measured at the point addition of each iteration. Okeya et al. [175] stated that even though the Montgomery scalar multiplication in ECC (refer to [161] for more about the Montgomery multiplication) is immune to timing attacks [173], the implementation of such multiplication does not always guarantee that it is immune to Differential Power Analysis (DPA). For example, the implementation of Montgomery in [162] performs one addition and one doubling on the elliptic curve independently, where the order of computation is flexible and decided on the bit value. Okeya et al. [175] claim that such an implementation is vulnerable to DPA, where the attacker can use DPA to identify the order of the computation. However, the authors did not perform a DPA attack to prove their claim. Oswald and Aigner [178] also state that ECC can be attacked using DPA, partitioning power measurements into two different sets based on some prediction, such as the guess of a secret key bit.

2.3.3 Extensions of Differential Power Analysis

DPA has been very successful in most used cryptosystems like DES, AES, RSA and ECC, as explained above. While some part of the research community is proposing various countermeasures to combat DPA, another part is still be able to crack the system by extending the standard DPA attack with slight tuning and variations. Various such extensions on DPA attacks are categorised and presented. This section is divided into subsections for each of the DPA extensions, which are multiple bit DPA, higher order DPA, hamming distance based

DPA, hamming weight based DPA, amplified DPA on xtime implementations, attacks on modular exponentiations using averaging and subtraction, and the sliding window DPA.

2.3.3.1 Multiple Bit Differential Power Analysis Attack

The traditional DPA technique (also called single-bit DPA [247]) proposed by Kocher et al. [127] used only one bit to partition the power signals (i.e., the value of one bit is decided from the partition function). Messerges et al. [156] observed that one way to improve the Signal-to-Noise Ratio (SNR) is to increase the signal magnitude, where the signal is dependent on the number of bits output by the partition function. Hence, Messerges et al. [156] implemented a Multiple bit (also called *d-bit*) DPA attack on DES, extending the single-bit DPA of Kocher et al. [127] to partition more than one bit (d bits). There are three sets used in partitioning as shown in Equation 2.19, where if the D function outputs d 0s or 1s, then the signal is placed into set S_0 and S_1 respectively, while other cases are placed into set S_2 and not used.

$$\begin{aligned} S_0 &= \{S_i[j] \mid D(\cdot) = 0^d\}; \\ S_1 &= \{S_i[j] \mid D(\cdot) = 1^d\}; \\ S_2 &= \{S_i[j] \mid S_i[j] \notin S_0, S_1\}; \quad [156] \end{aligned} \tag{2.19}$$

The Multiple bit attack on DES by Messerges et al. [156] uses 4-bit D function, as shown in Equation 2.20, based on the fours bits output from an SBOX. As Equation 2.20 depicts, C_6 represents the 6 bits that are XORed with the 6 bits of the last round subkey (K_{16}). SBOX14 returns all four bits after the lookup. A similar choice of D function on other SBOXes can be used to determine the rest of the key bits [156].

$$D(C_6, K_{16}) = \text{SBOX}14(C_6 \oplus K_{16}); \quad [156] \tag{2.20}$$

Messerges et al. [156] experimented with their Multiple bit DPA attacks on a smart card with $N = 1000$ random inputs as shown in Figure 2.46, where the single-bit (1-bit) DPA plot is drawn at the top and a 4-bit DPA plot is shown in the middle and the bottom plot refers to an 8-bit DPA trace. The correct subkey guess is predicted at the places where significant peaks appear within the DPA traces, as shown in Figure 2.46, where the DPA plots (magnitude

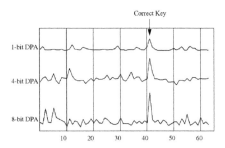

Figure 2.46: DPA bias traces [156]

of the significant peaks) clearly reveal that the Multiple bit DPA attacks are superior to the conventional single-bit DPA attacks.

Coron and Goubin [68] also explained the steps of a 4-bit Multiple bit DPA attack on DES. However, the author's method uses 16 categories, which slightly varies from the attack of Messerges et al. [156] (which utilising only two categories). The attack (in [68]) uses a partition function which outputs 4 bits (the output bits from the SBOXes) and the inputs and power samples are separated into 16 categories based on these partition values: those giving 0000, those giving 0001, ..., those giving 1111. According to Coron and Goubin [68], the next step for the adversary is to compute the mean MC' of the power curves of the last category (i.e., the set placed for 1111), instead of finding the mean based on a single bit. The mean of the whole power sample MC is subtracted with MC' to compute the DPA bias signal. However, the real attack was not implemented in [68], where the authors predict that more input samples might be needed, compared with the single bit DPA, to realise an appreciable difference between MC and MC'. Koeune and Standaert [132] also emphasised the Multiple bit DPA attack of Messerges et al. [156], stating that the signal to noise ratio is improved by separating the measurements into two sets based on b bits: one set corresponding to *all zeroes* and other to *all ones*. Boracchi and Breveglieri [44] proposed a Multiple bit DPA on AES. The authors state an example, where the decision function uses two bits of the target byte (2-bit DPA). In such a case, the possible values are $\{00, 01, 10, 11\}$ and the traces have to be divided into four sets, corresponding with each possible decision value. Boracchi and Breveglieri [44] observed that the power consumed depends significantly on the target bit values, especially a clearer peak in the difference between selection bits $\{11\}$ and $\{00\}$. Hence, the authors claim that such a decision function between {11} and {00} is equivalent to considering only Hamming weights of the input value. The attack based on Hamming weight is presented later in this section.

2.3.3.2   Higher Order Differential Power Analysis Attack

Kocher et al. [127] defined higher order DPA, stating that more sophisticated selection functions can be used to combine multiple samples (one or more) within a trace. The second-order DPA attack of Messerges [152] on a smart card is one of the earliest work on higher order DPA attacks. Most encryption algorithms, especially the block ciphers, start the execution by combining the input data (PTI) with a secret key. Messerges [152] refers such an initial process as a *whitening process* which uses the XOR operation with the input data, which, the author states, it is done in Twofish encryption (refer to [207] for an explanation of Twofish).

Twofish was one of the five AES finalists... – Bruce Schneier

A simple example is used by Messerges [152] to explain the second-order DPA attack, as shown in Figure 2.47. The algorithm W_1, to the left of Figure 2.47, immediately performs the XOR operation in line **A**. Such a straight operation can leak information about the secret key. Hence, the algorithm W_1 is vulnerable to a first-order DPA attack (i.e., the conventional DPA, explained in Section 2.3). The W_2 algorithm at the right side of Figure 2.47, attempts to overcome the DPA vulnerability by performing an indirect whitening approach, where a random mask is generated at line **B** followed by the XOR operation of the data *PTI* and the random mask, to produce an intermediate result *mPTI*. The XOR of *mPTI* and the secret key is computed in line **C**. The random mask is generated internally and not observable by the adversary. Messerges [152] realises that the results at lines **B** and **C** leak only random information making the DPA fail. However, the author claims that combining the information at lines **B** and **C** together for analysis will still lead to a successful DPA attack.

The second-order DPA of Messerges [152] exploits the relationship between the instantaneous power consumption and the Hamming weight of the data being processed. Figure 2.48

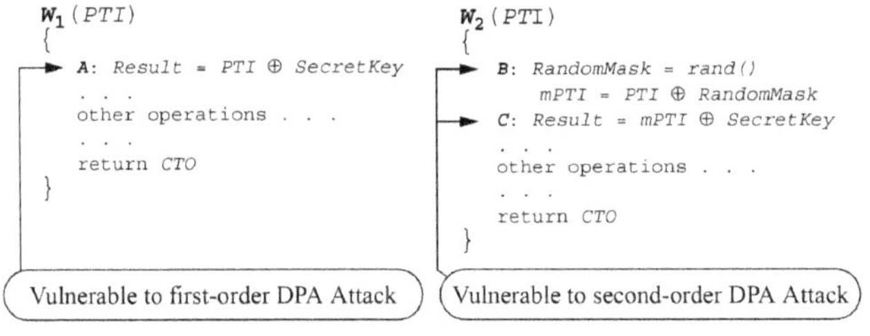

```
W₁(PTI)                              W₂(PTI)
{                                    {
   ► A: Result = PTI ⊕ SecretKey        ► B: RandomMask = rand()
      . . .                                    mPTI = PTI ⊕ RandomMask
      other operations . . .           ► C: Result = mPTI ⊕ SecretKey
      . . .                                 . . .
      return CTO                            other operations . . .
}                                           . . .
                                            return CTO
                                     }
```

(Vulnerable to first-order DPA Attack)   (Vulnerable to second-order DPA Attack)

Figure 2.47: A simple example for second-order DPA [152]

depicts the second-order DPA attack algorithm, where an N-bit processor is attacked using the power samples P_B and P_C at lines **B** and **C** respectively. The main aim of the adversary is to predict the secret key (which is of size N bits) at the whitening process using the power samples P_B and P_C. As the algorithm explains in Figure 2.48, to predict bit i of the key from 0 to N-1, the ith bit of the input PTI is set to 0 and the other bits are set to random values, and an average statistic $\bar{S}_0$ is computed using the instantaneous power signals P_B and P_C at lines **B** and **C**. The ith bit of the input PTI is then set to 1 and the steps are repeated to find the average statistic $\bar{S}_1$. The DPA bias statistic T is computed from the average statistics $\bar{S}_0$ and $\bar{S}_1$ as shown in Figure 2.48. If T is greater than 0, the ith bit of the key is predicted as one, otherwise zero. The same procedure is iterated till all the bits of the key are analysed.

1. *Repeat for i equal to 0 through $N-1$ {*
2. *Repeat for b = 0 to 1 {*
3. *Calculate average statistic $\bar{S}_b = |P_B - P_C|$ by repeating the following: {*
4. *Set the ith bit of the PTI input to b.*
5. *Set the remaining PTI bits to random values.*
6. *Collect the algorithm's instantaneous power consumption as lines B and C. Call these values P_B and P_C, respectively. } }*
7. *Calculate the DPA bias statistic $T = \bar{S}_0 - \bar{S}_1$.*
8. *If $T > 0$ then the ith key bit is a one, otherwise it is a zero.*

Figure 2.48: Second-order DPA algorithm [152]

The second-order DPA result of Messerges [152] is presented in Figure 2.49, where the experiment is implemented on the ST16 smartcard executing algorithm W_2, which is shown in Figure 2.47. The plots in Figure 2.49 show an 8 bit key prediction using the attack algorithm in Figure 2.48; the x axis showing the number of power signals used and the y axis referring to the DPA threshold signal T, where the actual key being attacked is 0x6B. In most cases T

58

converged to the correct bit using fewer than 50 power signals, except bit # 5 which required more than 2,500 power signals to get the correct bit.

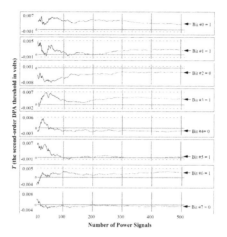

Figure 2.49: Second-order DPA plots [152]

As shown in Figure 2.48, the key is successfully attacked by combining the power measurements taken at different operations. Messerges [152] states that Chari et al. [54] suggested an alternative statistical method based on multiplying P_B and P_C, rather than taking the difference for a second-order DPA attack. Daemen et al. [70] define an N-th order DPA, which makes use of N different intermediate values calculated at N different times during the execution of the algorithm. The authors claim that second-order DPA is more difficult to implement than first-order DPA for three main reasons: (1), identifying which places should be combined together and computing the distance between operations is a complex process; (2), since the random delays make the identification of required power values in the trace harder, the samples needed to perform a successful attack increase to n^2, demanding more data storage and processing; and (3), the number of power samples needed to generate statistically significant results increases to about $2z^2$, because the increase in the number of partitions reduces the number of samples placed inside each partition [70].

Waddle and Wagner [235] state that higher-order DPA attacks come into play when some intermediate value that depends only on the plaintext and some small part of the key, but not correlated directly with power consumption at any particular time, contributes to the joint distribution of the power consumption executed at different times in the computation. Waddle and Wagner [235] presented two second-order DPA attacks: (1), *Zero-Offset 2DPA*, which is applied in a situation where the power correlation times for the two bits are coincident; and (2), *FFT 2DPA*, which applies to more general situations where the adversary does not know the time of correlation. The attacks in [235] assume that the adversary has guessed part of the key and has predicted an intermediate bit value b for each of the power traces and grouped them into a $b = 0$ (T^0) and a $b = 1$ (T^1) group, where there are n traces in each of these groups and each trace contains samples at m evenly spaced times. The power sample i at time t from group b is denoted as $T_i^b(t)$. The authors use a generic DPA subroutine, as shown in Figure 2.50, which takes in two groups of traces T^0, T^1 and a threshold value τ, which determines whether the groups' totalled traces differ by more than τ at any sample time. If the difference of the totalled traces is greater than τ at any point, DPA returns 1, indicating that T^0 and T^1 have different distributions. Otherwise, the DPA returns 0, indicating that T^0 and T^1 are identically distributed.

$$\text{DPA}(T^0, T^1, \tau)$$

1 :   for each $t \in \{0, \dots, m - 1\}$:
2 : $s \leftarrow 0$
3 :   for each $i \in \{0, \dots, n - 1\}$:
4 : $s \leftarrow s + T_i^0(t) - T_i^1(t)$
5 :   if $|s| > \tau$ return 1
6 :   return 0

Figure 2.50: Generic DPA subroutine [235]

The *Zero-Offset 2DPA* attack [235] is a slight variation of first-order DPA, where the system that performs masking (i.e., where a random number is generated and XORed with the actual key, as explained in algorithm W_2 of Figure 2.47) should have a power consumption at a time which contains both the effects of generating the random number and XORing with the secret key (shown in line **B** and line **C** of Figure 2.47 respectively). Waddle and Wagner [235] realise that such a coincident effect of the two masked values seems too specialised, but the authors cite the work of Messerges [153] which shows that some registers contain the multi-bit intermediate value. Another example given by Waddle and Wagner [235] is a paired circuit which computes both random and mask inputs in parallel. The *Zero-Offset 2DPA* attack from [235] is presented in Figure 2.51, where it is a simple squaring of the samples in the power

60

traces before running straight DPA. As shown in Figure 2.51, the algorithm uses a threshold of $2nd^2$, where n is the number of traces in each group and d is a parameter in units of the standard deviation of the noise. The authors further extend the Zero-Offset 2DPA attack by stating that if the difference is not known, a similar attack can be mounted by calculating the lagged product instead of calculating the squares of the samples.

$$\text{Zero-Offset-2DPA}(T^0, T^1)$$
1 : for each $b \in \{0, 1\}$, $i \in \{0, \dots, n\}$, $t \in \{0, \dots, m\}$:
2 : $\quad T_i^b(t) \leftarrow (T_i^b(t))^2$
3 : return DPA$(T^0, T^1, 2nd^2)$

Figure 2.51: Zero-Offset 2DPA algorithm [235]

The other second-order DPA proposed by Waddle and Wagner [235] is called the Fast Fourier Transform (FFT) 2DPA, where there is no requirement that the times of correlation be coincident. An *autocorrelation* is used in an *FFT 2DPA* attack where the correlation of the curve with itself is computed (refer to [79] for more information on autocorrelation). Figure 2.52 depicts the autocorrelation subroutine used for the attack, where the trace is FFTed and then Inverse Fast Fourier Transformed (Inv-FFTed) at the end, which results in autocorrelation.

$$\textbf{Autocorrelate}(T)$$
1 : $\quad F \leftarrow \textbf{FFT}(T)$
2 : $\quad$ for each $t \in \{0, \dots, m-1\}$:
3 : $\quad\quad F(t) \leftarrow |F(t)|^2$
4 : $\quad$ return $\textbf{Inv-FFT}(F)$

Figure 2.52: Autocorrelation subroutine [235]

Using the autocorrelation subroutine shown in Figure 2.52, the *FFT 2DPA* attack is created, as presented in Figure 2.53. As per the *FFT 2DPA* attack shown in Figure 2.53, the traces (from 0 to n - 1) are autocorrelated and then added together for each clock (t) and the summed traces Z^0 and Z^1 are fed to the DPA subroutine (shown in Figure 2.50) with a threshold nd^2.

The *FFT 2DPA*, as shown in Figure 2.53, does not require any knowledge of where the masking operations are executed in the trace to measure power magnitudes, since the auto-correlation identifies the required places. Both the *Zero-Offset 2DPA* attack and the *FFT 2DPA* attack of Waddle and Wagner [235] are mathematically proved as sound second-order

FFT-2DPA(T^0, T^1, τ)
1 :   for each $b \in \{0,1\}$, $t \in \{0, \ldots, m-1\}$:
2 : $Z^b(t) \leftarrow 0$
3 :   for each $b \in \{0,1\}$, $i \in \{0, \ldots, n-1\}$:
4 : $A^b \leftarrow$ Autocorrelate(T^b_i)
5 :   for each $t \in \{0, \ldots, m-1\}$:
6 : $Z^b(t) \leftarrow Z^b(t) + A^b(t)$
7 :   return DPA$(Z^0,\ Z^1,\ nd^2)$

Figure 2.53: FFT 2DPA attack [235]

attacks, but not implemented in a practical experiment. The authors also realise that the higher-order DPA attackers require the exact knowledge of the time at which the intermediate values and the power consumptions are correlated. Joye et al. [115] evaluated and analysed the second-order DPA attack of Messerges [152] on the *whitening* process in detail. The RC6 block cipher [199] is experimented on for the second-order DPA in [115], where Figure 2.54 shows the RC6 algorithm used for the attack. Let us concentrate only on the *whitening* process of the algorithm (For example, in line 2(b) in Figure 2.54 the value of the key bit S_{2i} is masked). To predict the key bit S_{2j}, which is used in round j, the adversary has to observe the power consumption when the random number is used (i.e., $(A \oplus t)$) and the place where the secret key S_{2j} is added to the intermediate result.

---

1. $B = B + S_0$ and $D = D + S_1$
2. for $i = 1$ to r do
   (a) $t = (B \times (2B + 1)) \lll \log_2 n$ and $u = (D \times (2D + 1)) \lll \log_2 n$
   (b) $A = ((A \oplus t) \lll u) + S_{2i}$ and $C = ((C \oplus u) \lll t) + S_{2i+1}$
   (c) $(A, B, C, D) = (B, C, D, A)$
3. $A = A + S_{2r+2}$ and $C = C + S_{2r+3}$

Figure 2.54: RC6 encryption algorithm [115]

RC6 is a parametrised algorithm where the block size, the key size, and
the number of rounds are variables... – Webopedia

Even though the second-order DPA of Joye et al. [115] claims that it is similar to the attack of Messerges [152] using Hamming weights in DPA, the methodology and the decision function are quite different from the latter. The second-order DPA bias computation is defined in Equation 2.21, where $\chi(t)$ refers to the power consumption at time t and τ_1, τ_2 are the time slots when the two power measurements are taken in the random operation, and the masking operation with the key respectively. The difference in power consumption of τ_1 and τ_2 for each sample is placed into one of two sections: a section which belongs to σ_1 and a section which belongs to σ_0 based on a decision function. The decision function proposed by Joye et al. [115] is based on Hamming weights, where in an Ω bit processor the word which has an average Hamming weight of $(\Omega - 1)/2$ is defined for set σ_0 and the word with an average Hamming weight of $(\Omega + 1)/2$ is defined for set σ_1. The value $\hat{s}$ for which $\Delta_2(\hat{s})$ is maximal is likely to be the correct key. This second-order DPA [115] is similar to the conventional DPA (single-order) as explained earlier in this section, except that the power consumption difference between two places are considered for the attack instead of at a single place.

$$\Delta_2(\hat{s}) = < |\chi(\tau_2) - \chi(\tau_1)| >_{x \in \sigma_1(\hat{s})} - < |\chi(\tau_2) - \chi(\tau_1)| >_{x \in \sigma_0(\hat{s})}; \quad [115] \qquad (2.21)$$

Figure 2.55 shows the second-order DPA trace on RC6 (algorithm presented in Figure 2.54) performed by Joye et al. [115] on the *whitening* process used by Messerges [152]. The traces at the left of Figure 2.55 show the wrong key guesses and the traces to the right reveal correct key guesses S_{2i} and S_{2i+1}, where significant peaks appear in round 5 and round 6 respectively (pointed in the trace). Around 3000 power traces are used for the word size of 8 (the top row) to realise the correct key and around 20000 power traces are used for the word size of 16 (the bottom row) to successfully predict the key. The authors also observed, from their experiments, that for words greater than 32, a much larger number of power traces are necessary to mount a practical attack.

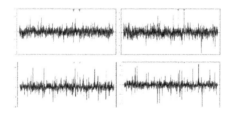

Figure 2.55: Second-order DPA trace [115]

Peeters et al. [188] presented a higher-order DPA on an FPGA (Field Programmable Gate Arrays) implementation of the SBOX masking as shown in Figure 2.56. A key k is XORed with the input b, while a random value r is generated and XORed with the intermediate value before the original SBOX (S) lookup. The masking SBOX (S') is precomputed, as shown in Figure 2.56, where the setup masks the actual computation. The higher-order DPA [188] on such an implementation works on the hypothesis that when the intermediate value x switches to another intermediate value x' at time t, the power consumption of the device at this time is proportional to the Hamming weight $W_H(x \oplus x')$.

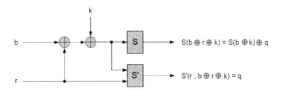

Figure 2.56: Masking of SBOX lookup [188]

According to the second-order DPA of Peeters et al. [188], the adversary feeds inputs $b_0, b_1, ..., b_n$ to the system and observes the power consumptions $o_1, o_2, ..., o_n$ at the SBOX lookups, where the power consumption is contributed by both S and S' lookups containing the sum of both Hamming weights. There are 2^{N_b} number of key candidates for an N_b bit key $k_i \in [0, 2^{N_b} - 1]$. For a fixed value of secret key state $\Sigma = \sigma_i$, the adversary can determine all the possible observations, for all different possible random states $R = r_j$. From this analysis it is possible to derive the probability density functions $P[O = o_i | \Sigma = \sigma_i]$, for all the possible secret states [188]. Since the adversary can only observe the power consumption o_i at the ith input, the probability density function for a key state is computed using the Hamming weight probability extracted from the power magnitude. The adversary computes the probabilities $P[O^* | \Sigma^*(k_j)]$ for each key candidate $k_j \in [0, 2^{N_b} - 1]$, as shown in Equation 2.22. The chain with the highest probability will reveal the correct key.

$$P[O^* | \Sigma^*(k_j)] = P[O = o_1 | \Sigma = \sigma_1(k_j)] \times P[O = o_2 | \Sigma = \sigma_2(k_j)] \times ...; \quad [115] \qquad (2.22)$$

The simulated results of the second-order DPA attack of Peeters et al. [188] are shown in

Figure 2.57 where the correct key is successfully predicted using around 4000 inputs. A real second-order attack in an FPGA is also presented in [188] where the authors found that it is harder and needs more computation than a simulation attack.

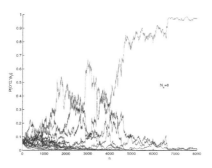

Figure 2.57: A simulated higher order attack [188]

Peeters et al. [188] state that higher-order DPA attacks require more traces than first-order DPA attacks, but the number of traces needed for a successful attack is no longer unrealistic. The authors also realise that the noise in the power measurements certainly affects the attack, and a better estimation of the statistical distributions would improve the success rate. Oswald et al. [180] performed a similar second-order DPA as Messerges [152] (explained earlier in this subsection where the key is predicted bit by bit, assuming that the instantaneous power is proportional to the Hamming weight), but extended and generalised the attack by predicting several bits of the secret key together. The attack of Oswald et al. [180] is explained as follows:

1. the adversary records the set of power traces $\mathcal{T}$ during the execution of a known algorithm using a set of known plaintexts P_i, a set of unknown masks M_i and an unknown key K;

2. an interval I of length l is fixed for all power traces $\mathrm{T} \in \mathcal{T}$, where the interval is guessed in a time frame which includes both the intermediate values of masking: $F_1(P_i) \oplus M_i$ and $F_2(P_i) \oplus M_i$ (explained in Figure 2.47) where $F_i(P_i)$ denotes an intermediate value that is computed with input P_i;

3. calculate a pre-processed trace that contains all values $|I_a - I_b| \ \forall \ I_a, I_b \in I \subseteq T$ for each trace T. There will be $l(l-1)/2$ points in the pre-processed trace, since $|I_a - I_b| = |I_b - I_a|$;

4. perform a standard first-order DPA attack, which is explained in Section 2.3, on the pre-processed power traces, by guessing the part of the key K to predict the value of $HW(F_1(P_i) \oplus F_2(P_i))$, where HW refers the Hamming weight;

5. the power magnitude difference $|C(F_1(P_i) \oplus M_i) - C(F_2(P_i) \oplus M_i)|$, which occurs in the pre-processed trace is due to the two attacked intermediate results $F_1(P_i) \oplus M_i$ and $F_2(P_i) \oplus M_i$. $C(a)$ refers the power consumption of the value a. Hence, the DPA plot on the pre-processed traces will produce a peak at such correlated positions, revealing the correct key.

Oswald et al. [180] implemented the above explained second-order DPA attack on a smart card, which is executing AES encryption. Two outputs of the masked SubBytes operation of the first round in AES (refer Section 2.1.2 for the information on AES) is attacked to predict the Hamming weight (i.e., $HW(S(P_1 \oplus K_1) \oplus S(P_2 \oplus K_2)))$, revealing the first two key bytes. During pre-processing the power magnitude, at a place in the selected interval, is subtracted by all the other power magnitudes in that interval. Hence, for each corresponding place there will be a set of subtracted values corresponding to other points. This set is called a segment [180]. For example, Oswald et al. [180] observed points from 410 to 620 as the attack interval in the whole AES power trace. The first step of the authors was to subtract points 411 to 620 from point 410, which will have 210 values and this set is named as segment 1. The next step is to subtract points 412 to 620 from 411, and this set (i.e., segment 2) will contain 209 values. A similar strategy will be followed till the end and there will be 210 segments in total. The power values in each segment are concatenated before applying DPA. Hence, there will be 210 segments in this case for AES. However, the concatenation of segments was not clearly demonstrated by the authors. Figure 2.58 depicts the DPA plot of the correct key guess in AES which uses 3000 measurements, showing significant peaks for several segments. The highest peak occurs at segment 61, as shown in Figure 2.58 which denotes the effective point to reveal the correct key.

Oswald et al. [180] further wanted to show that only the correct key produced the peak. The segment 61 (with 150 power samples), which caused the highest peak in Figure 2.58, is attacked on all 65536 key hypothesis. This fine tuned attack is shown in Figure 2.59 where the 65535 incorrect key guesses are plotted in gray and only the correct key guess is shown in

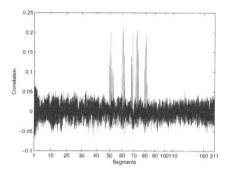

Figure 2.58: Second-order DPA using segments in AES [180]

black. As Figure 2.59 depicts, only the correct key leads to significant peaks.

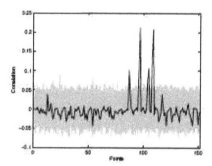

Figure 2.59: Second-order DPA on segment 61 [180]

As explained above, higher-order DPA attacks (specially the second-order) were very successful against masking techniques. The masking techniques, which are known as secure against power analysis, are explained in Chapter 3.

2.3.3.3 DPA based on Hamming distance

Messerges et al. [155] state that Hamming distance (number of bitflips that occur in an execution [16]) is also another property which leaks secure information. Joye et al. [115] claim that in most cases, it is necessary for the adversary to assume that the actual power consumption is linearly related to the Hamming distance of a hardware state that existed just prior to the moment when the data word is handled. The authors state that the energy required to transfer data over the bus will be related to the number of bits switched. Tiri et al. [222] exploited the correlation between the Hamming distance and the power measurements to attack the key in a coprocessor, executing AES encryption. Equation 2.23 presents the attack formula, which uses the Hamming distance (HamDist) of an intermediate result to correlate with the power measurement ($P_{measurement}$). Figure 2.60 depicts the component flow of round 11 and round 11+1 in the AES core (the attack place), where register RB in round 11 is observed for the Hamming distance by backtracking the value of D_{11} using the ciphertext C_{11} and guessed key K_{11}. The power is measured ($P_{measurement}$) at the RB in round 11+1 (the bottom component flow in Figure 2.60).

$$\max f_{cost}(K_{11}) = \text{corr}(P_{model}, P_{measurement});$$
$$\text{where} \quad P_{model} = \text{HamDist}(sub^{-1}(shiftrow^{-1}(K11 \oplus C_{11})), C_{11}) \qquad (2.23)$$
$$P_{measurement} = \max(I_{supply,11+1}); \quad [222]$$

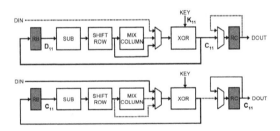

Figure 2.60: AES core: round 11(top), round 11+1(bottom) [222]

The DPA attack of Tiri et al. [222], using the formula in Equation 2.23, did not explain clearly how the correlation (*corr* function) is performed. However, their results show that the Hamming distance model successfully reveals the correct key by producing a significant peak in the correlation trace as shown in Figure 2.61. A key byte is predicted successfully using an average of 15,000 measurements.

Peeters et al. [188] performed a second-order DPA attack on an FPGA as explained earlier in this section. The authors realised that the Hamming distance power consumption model is generally true for any CMOS circuit and is especially applicable to FPGAs.

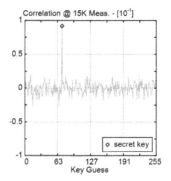

Figure 2.61: DPA trace using Hamming distance correlation [222]

2.3.3.4 DPA based on Hamming weight

Several researchers [115, 154, 188] have stated that Hamming weight models (number of 1's in the result) can be used to perform DPA attacks, where some type of electronic circuits like precharged logics show linear variations in power consumptions against the Hamming weights in the intermediate results. Messerges [152] proposed a DPA attack on the standard *whitening* process, which performs XOR operation with the input data (PTI) and the secret key. The attack of Messerges [152] is given as an algorithm in Figure 2.62. For an N-bit processor, the algorithm in Figure 2.62 is repeated to predict each key bit separately from bit 0 to $N - 1$. To predict a key bit i, the ith bit of PTI is set to 0 first and the remaining PTI bits to random values. Such PTI are fed into the operation and corresponding power signals are recorded. The average power signal $A_0[j]$ from these multiple power signals is calculated, where j refers the sampling time of the *whitening* operation. A similar step is repeated by having the ith bit of PTI to 1 and the other bits to random values to find $A_1[j]$. The DPA bias signal $T[j]$ is computed using the difference between $A_0[j]$ and $A_1[j]$ as shown in Figure 2.62. Observing a positive bias spike in $T[j]$ reveals the ith bit of secret key as one and a negative bias spike reveals its value as zero.

Figure 2.63 depicts the DPA bias plots based on the attack presented in Figure 2.62, which reveals the 8 bits secret key (value of 0b01101011 = 0x6B). All 8 bits converge to their correct values using fewer than 50 power samples. This attack of Messerges [152] is based on the hypothesis that processing data with higher Hamming weight will consume more power than processing data with lower Hamming weight.

1. *Repeat for i equal to 0 through N – 1 {*
2.   *Repeat for b = 0 to 1 {*
3.   *Calculate the average power signal $A_b[j]$ by repeating the following:{*
4.   *Set the ith bit of the PTI input to b.*
5.   *Set the remaining PTI bits to random values.*
6.   *Collect the algorithm's power signal. } }*
7.   *Create the DPA bias signal $T[j] = A_0[j] - A_1[j]$.*
8.   *$T[j]$ will have a positive bias spike when the ith secret key bit is a one, and will have a negative DPA bias spike when ith secret key bit is a zero. }*

Figure 2.62: DPA algorithm on whitening using Hamming weights [152]

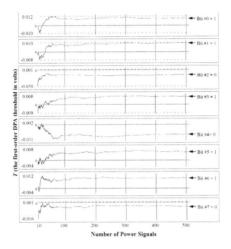

Figure 2.63: DPA bias plots on whitening revealing 8 bits secret key [152]

Boracchi and Breveglieri [44] claim that Multi-bit DPAs (explained earlier) can be performed as Hamming weight attacks, when they are used to divide the samples yielding all ones or all zeros based on some decision function. According to the authors, a decision function for DPA can be formulated based on Hamming weights and a threshold can be used for a decision considering the value of the Hamming weight of the result. Equation 2.24 depicts the decision function D_γ used in [44], where HW denotes the function that counts the Hamming weight and $SB_0(PTI_i, kg)$ are the target bits which are obtained as the output of an SBOX of the first AES round. A byte of the input data PTI_i and a byte of the subkey kg are XORed and fed into the SBOX. T_γ is the threshold operation which produces 1 when the argument is bigger than γ and 0 when it is not. The bytes having a Hamming weight which is equal to the threshold γ may or may not be considered.

70

$$D_\gamma(PTI_i, kg) = \text{T}_\gamma[HW(SB_0(PTI_i \oplus kg))]; \quad [44] \tag{2.24}$$

Boracchi and Breveglieri [44] observe that collecting power traces is the most time consuming part of a DPA attack. Hence, the authors proposed a technique to use several decision functions and fuse them together to predict the secret key with as few numbers of power samples as possible. Equation 2.25 presents the multiple set DPA function $\mathbf{D}(PTI_i, kg)$, which uses five DPA functions from $D_2(PTI_i, kg)$ to $D_6(PTI_i, kg)$. For example, $D_2(PTI_i, kg)$ function generates 1 when the Hamming weight is greater than 2 and it generates 0 when the Hamming weight is less than 2. These five different decision functions will produce five different differential power traces $T_{kg}^2[j],....,T_{kg}^6[j]$.

$$\mathbf{D}(PTI_i, kg) = \begin{bmatrix} D_2(PTI_i, kg) \\ \vdots \\ D_6(PTI_i, kg) \end{bmatrix}; \quad [44] \tag{2.25}$$

The differential power traces $T_{kg}^2[j],....,T_{kg}^6[j]$, corresponding to each decision function (defined in Equation 2.25), are fused together, as shown in Equation 2.26 to come up with a single powerful differential trace. The product of maximas of the individual traces excludes faulty peaks due to lack of power traces in a partition.

$$M(kg) = \prod_{i=2}^{6} \max(T_{kg}^i[j]); \quad [44] \tag{2.26}$$

Figure 2.64 reveals the DPA plots (first five plots) on AES, attacked at the SBOX output of the first round, based on different decision functions having different Hamming weight (HW) thresholds. For example, the first DPA plot has a threshold 2 (showing HW > 2), which denotes that the decision function produced 1 when the Hamming weight of the intermediate value is greater than 2, otherwise 0. The fused DPA plot based on the first five figures and using the function in Equation 2.26, is presented in the last plot in Figure 2.64. As observed in the fused DPA plot, the correct secret key (value of 60) is revealed by a significant peak, using just 2000 power traces.

One of the recent DPA attacks is by Park et al. [185], which correlates Hamming weight with the power consumption. The main hypothesis of this attack is that the higher the Ham-

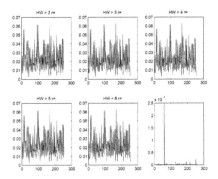

Figure 2.64: DPA plots for different thresholds (first five), M(kg) plot (last) [44]

ming weight, the higher the power consumption. Park et al. [185] implemented their attack in AES (refer Section 2.1.2) and ARIA (Academy, Research Institute, Agency [246]), which are block ciphers which operate based on an 8-bit input/output. ARIA is also a symmetrical key encryption algorithm which was proposed in 2004 [137]. Only the attack on AES is presented here, but interested readers can refer to the paper of Park et al. [185] for the attack on ARIA encryption, which is similar to AES.

ARIA is especially efficient in hardware implementations and 8-bit architectures and hence it is applicable to various environments like IC-cards, VPNs, etc... – NSRI, Korea

The DPA attack of Park et al. [185] on AES, which predicts each byte of the secret key iteratively, is illustrated as follows:

1. 256 possible values for the 8 bits of an input which is encrypted with an 8 bits secret key of interest (the first byte of the secret key - exact value of 0x2B), are created: denoted as $X_1,....,X_{256}$;

2. the power consumption signals are measured during the encryption when using the inputs $X_1,....,X_{256}$: power consumption signals are denoted as $P_1,....,P_{256}$. The power is

72

measured in the first round of AES encryption at the first SBOX storing point (around 1000 samples are measured);

3. each measured power consumption signal is differentiated from the other signals as follows; $P_1 - P_2$, $P_1 - P_{256}$,...., $P_2 - P_3$,...., $P_{255} - P_{256}$. Figure 2.65 shows several differentiated power consumption signals, where "0x56 - 0xD0" means the differentiation between the power consumption signals with input messages 0x56 and 0xD0;

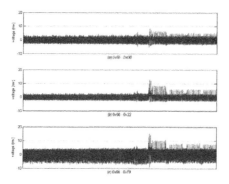

Figure 2.65: Differentiated power consumption signals [185]

4. the pair of the power consumption signals which has the highest difference is identified. In this case it is observed for the input message pair "0x56 and 0x79" (shown in Figure 2.65(c)), which is going to be used to predict the 8 most significant bits of the round one key of the AES algorithm;

5. based on the hypothesis that maximum power consumed is for 0xFF (i.e., Hamming weight of 8) within an 8 bit output, the output after the SBOX lookup for the highest difference pair (i.e., "0x56 and 0x79") is predicted as 0xFF. Because of the positive peak for the pair "0x56 and 0x79" in Figure 2.65(c), the output after the SubByte transformation (refer Section 2.1.2) for the input 0x56 is predicted as 0xFF;

6. the predicted output 0xFF after the SBOX can be backtracked in the particular SBOX to identify the index, as shown in Figure 2.66. As the SBOX shown in Figure 2.66 demonstrates, the value 0xFF is produced using the index 0x7D;

7. this shows that the input 0x56 became 0x7D after the AddRoundKey transformation,

73

	0	1	2	3	4	5	6	7	8	9	a	b	c	d	e	f
0	63	7c	77	7b	f2	6b	6f	c5	30	01	67	2b	fe	d7	ab	76
1	ca	82	c9	7d	fa	59	47	f0	ad	d4	a2	af	9c	a4	72	c0
2	b7	fd	93	26	36	3f	f7	cc	34	a5	e5	f1	71	d8	31	15
3	04	c7	23	c3	18	96	05	9a	07	12	80	e2	eb	27	b2	75
4	09	83	2c	1a	1b	6e	5a	a0	52	3b	d6	b3	29	e3	2f	84
5	53	d1	00	ed	20	fc	b1	5b	6a	cb	be	39	4a	4c	58	cf
6	d0	ef	aa	fb	43	4d	33	85	45	f9	02	7f	50	3c	9f	a8
7	51	a3	40	8f	92	9d	38	f5	bc	b6	da	21	10	ff	f3	d2
8	cd	0c	13	ec	5f	97	44	17	c4	a7	7e	3d	64	5d	19	73
9	60	81	4f	dc	22	2a	90	88	46	ee	b8	14	de	5e	0b	db
a	e0	32	3a	0a	49	06	24	5c	c2	d3	ac	62	91	95	e4	79
b	e7	c8	37	6d	8d	d5	4e	a9	6c	56	f4	ea	65	7a	ae	08
c	ba	78	25	2e	1c	a6	b4	c6	e8	dd	74	1f	4b	bd	8b	8a
d	70	3e	b5	66	48	03	f6	0e	61	35	57	b9	86	c1	1d	9e
e	e1	f8	98	11	69	d9	8e	94	9b	1e	87	e9	ce	55	28	df
f	8c	a1	89	0d	bf	e6	42	68	41	99	2d	0f	b0	54	bb	16

Figure 2.66: AES SBOX [185]

where the 8 bit key and an 8 bit input are XORed. Hence, the 8 most significant bits of the key is 0x2B, which is XORed with 0x56 and given as 0x7D as an index to the SBOX to get an output of 0xFF;

8. the same steps can be repeated to predict the rest of the key bytes.

Park et al. [185] claim that their attack (explained above) deduces the secret key directly using partial information of the target algorithm and intermediate values, instead of using a target algorithm simulator to predict some bits, as used in other DPA techniques (refer to Section 2.3). Han et al. [101] proposed a similar DPA attack on the AES of Park et al. [185], using Hamming weight at the SubBytes operation (i.e., SBOX access). The authors state that the single-bit DPA with simple partitioning criteria may fail on hardware implementations and the multi-bit DPA results in too many redundant power traces. Figure 2.67 depicts the attack power model of Han et al. [101] on AES, where $I_1 = SubBytes(K_s \oplus x_1)$, $I_2 = SubBytes(K_s \oplus x_2)$, K_s is the key byte to be attacked and x_1, x_2 are inputs. The authors set the values of $I_1 = 0x00$ and $I_2 = 0xFF$. If an adversary can guess values for key K_s the inputs x_1 and x_2 can be computed by backtracking the SBOX for values 0x00 and 0xFF respectively.

According to Han et al. [101], the DPA attacker keeps x_1 and x_2 inputs unchanged and feeds the other input plaintext bytes randomly, which will result in the elimination of the influence of the remained partial bits in the power measurements, if the number of samples are enough. For each subkey guess there are two plaintext sets prepared, as shown in Equation 2.27, where $PT_i[119:0]$ denotes the 120 random plaintext bits. Input values for x_1 and x_2 are precomputed for each subkey guess K_s, assuming the values at the SBOX output as 0x00 and 0xFF respectively. The encryption is performed for each subkey guess K_s and uses the

74

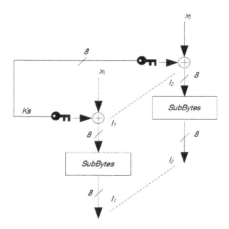

Figure 2.67: Attack power model [101]

plaintext sets, including the precomputed x_1 and x_2, as shown in Equation 2.27. Hence, there will be two power trace sets, $E(S_1(K_s),t)$ and $E(S_2(K_s),t)$. The difference between these power trace sets for the subkey guess K_s is illustrated in Equation 2.28.

$$S_1(K_s) = \{S_1[K_s,i] : (x_1, PT_i[119:0]) \mid 1 \leq i \leq m\}$$
$$S_2(K_s) = \{S_2[K_s,i] : (x_2, PT_i[119:0]) \mid 1 \leq i \leq m\}; \quad [101] \tag{2.27}$$

$$\Delta E(K_s,t) = \sum_{i=1}^{m} E(S_1[K_s,i],t) - \sum_{i=1}^{m} E(S_2[K_s,i],t); \quad [101] \tag{2.28}$$

The correct subkey guess will produce a significant peak in the differentiated power trace (shown in Equation 2.28), if the number of samples (m) is large enough [101]. This DPA attack of Han et al. [101] uses a hardware implementation of AES encryption. The critical power trace which includes the effects of the target intermediate results, is extracted with 100 data points from the whole power trace. Figure 2.68 depicts the DPA trace computed using Equation 2.28, which clearly shows a significant peak for the correct key guess. The authors observed that the peak occurred 4ns after starting the AES encryption, which proved that the maximum power difference was generated during the first AddRoundKey operation (refer to Section 2.1.2 for details on AddRoundKey).

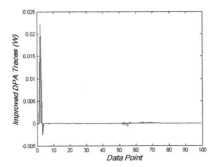

Figure 2.68: The DPA trace for 256 subkey guesses [101]

The attack of Han et al. [101] does not need the averaging of the power traces, since the number of power traces in the two input sets (shown in Equation 2.27) are equal. Hence, this improved DPA is claimed to be less time consuming in analysis, only performing sum and subtraction.

2.3.3.5 Amplified DPA on xtime implementations

The Rijndael (i.e., AES) uses a MixColumn operation where the columns of the intermediate values are swapped using $xtime$ operation (refer to Section 2.1.2 for more details) [247]. The MixColumn subroutine considered for the amplified DPA attack of Yen [247] is shown in Figure 2.69, which uses $xtime$ operations to mix columns. The $xtime$ operation used for the attack is specified in Figure 2.70. Yen [247] considers the Rijndael State as a four row and a four column grid, such that $c_{i,j}$ ($i,j \in 0,1,2,3$) is the value at each cell before the MixColumn is applied.

The amplified DPA attack on the xtime implementation of Yen [247] used on the MixColumn implementation (shown in Figure 2.69) of AES is explained as follows:

1. the adversary guesses the key bytes $k_{0,0}$ and $k_{1,1}$ randomly and computes corresponding values for $c_{0,0}$ and $c_{1,1}$ by simulating the AES algorithm for all the collected plaintexts M_i. Note that the adversary needs only these bytes since the others are not involved in the computation of the keys which are attacked here;

2. the adversary computes $Tm = c_{0,0} \oplus c_{1,1}$, as shown in the implementation in Figure 2.69, and obtains the most significant bit (MSB) of Tm. An MSB of "1" in Tm will result

```
Input:  first column of State before MixColumn {c_{0,0}, c_{1,1}, c_{2,2}, c_{3,3}}
Output: first column of State after MixColumn {d_{0,0}, d_{1,0}, d_{2,0}, d_{3,0}}
```

$$Com = c_{0,0} \oplus c_{1,1} \oplus c_{2,2} \oplus c_{3,3}$$
$$Tm = c_{0,0} \oplus c_{1,1}$$
$$Tm = \texttt{xtime}(Tm) \qquad \cdots \cdots \text{ first } \texttt{xtime}$$
$$d_{0,0} = c_{0,0} \oplus Com \oplus Tm$$
$$Tm = c_{1,1} \oplus c_{2,2}$$
$$Tm = \texttt{xtime}(Tm) \qquad \cdots \cdots \text{ second } \texttt{xtime}$$
$$d_{1,0} = c_{1,1} \oplus Com \oplus Tm$$
$$Tm = c_{2,2} \oplus c_{3,3}$$
$$Tm = \texttt{xtime}(Tm) \qquad \cdots \cdots \text{ third } \texttt{xtime}$$
$$d_{2,0} = c_{2,2} \oplus Com \oplus Tm$$
$$Tm = c_{3,3} \oplus c_{0,0}$$
$$Tm = \texttt{xtime}(Tm) \qquad \cdots \cdots \text{ fourth } \texttt{xtime}$$
$$d_{3,0} = c_{3,3} \oplus Com \oplus Tm$$

Figure 2.69: The attacked MixColumn Implementation [247]

```
xtime:
      SL   A
      LD   B, A
      SBC  A, A   % A ← A-(A+cf)
      AND  PRI
      XOR  B
```

Figure 2.70: The attacked xtime implementation [247]

in a value of 0xFF in the register A after the instruction execution "SBC A, A" in Figure 2.70. Otherwise, the value of register A becomes 0x00;

3. similarly to the ordinary DPA, for all M_i's which lead to an MSB = 1 in Tm, the related power traces are collected and averaged together and formed an average trace $Tr^{(1)}$. The average traces yielding MSB = 0 in Tm are collected and averaged into $Tr^{(0)}$. A differential trace $Tr^{(diff)}$ between $Tr^{(1)}$ and $Tr^{(0)}$ is computed and analysed;

4. if there is a significant peak in the differential trace $Tr^{(diff)}$ then the guessed key bytes for $k_{0,0}$ and $k_{1,1}$ are correct. Otherwise, the adversary has to repeat the attack again by guessing other possible values for $k_{0,0}$ and $k_{1,1}$;

5. once $k_{0,0}$ and $k_{1,1}$ are derived, the adversary can attack $k_{2,2}$ and $k_{3,3}$ using a similar approach by analysing and observing at the "third" xtime operation shown in Figure 2.69. This attack is repeated until all the key bytes are identified.

Yen [247] claims that the amplified DPA attack produced a much more significant peak (even when using a single bit) within the differential power trace without collecting exponentially more power traces, compared with the other DPA techniques. The author extended this attack further to another xtime implementation which can be referred to in the paper [247]. However, the amplified DPA attack is only defined and explained by the author but not implemented as a real attack.

2.3.3.6 Attacks on Modular Exponentiation using Averaging and Subtraction

Messerges et al. [155] performed three different Differential Power Analysis (DPA) attacks (which are a Single-Exponent Multiple Data (SEMD) attack, a Multiple-Exponent Single Data (MESD) attack and a Zero-Exponent Multiple Data (ZEMD) attack) on a smart card which is executing an authentication application using Modular Exponentiation for public cryptosystems. A brief explanation of the modular exponentiation in public cyptosystems is, input M is fed and the exponentiation $M^e \bmod N$ is performed using the secret key e and the public modulus N. In most implementations such exponentiation is performed using the Square-and-Multiply algorithm, which is explained in Section 2.1.3. Hence, the main aim of the attack is to successfully predict the private secret key e used in the exponentiation. The SEMD attack assumes that the smartcard is willing to exponentiate an arbitrary number of random values with two exponents: the secret exponent and a public exponent [155]. The adversary inputs L random values when the secret exponent is used and collects corresponding power signals, $S_i[j]$. Similarly, the L random values are used for exponentiation using the known exponent and the power signals $P_i[j]$ are recorded. The average of these power signals are computed and subtracted to form the DPA bias signal $D[j]$ as shown in Equation 2.29.

$$D[j] = \frac{1}{L} \sum_{i=1}^{L} S_i[j] - \frac{1}{L} \sum_{i=1}^{L} P_i[j] = \bar{S}[j] - \bar{P}[j]; \quad [155] \tag{2.29}$$

As shown in Equation 2.29, the differentiation between the power signals will average out to different values (based on whether it is Square or Multiply) if the portion of the power signals are dependent on the exponent bit. The portions which are dependent on the intermediate data will converge to a constant value. Thus, $D[j]$ can be used to determine the exact locations of the squares and multiplies in the secret exponentiation. The DPA bias trace of the SEMD attack performed on a smartcard by Messerges et al. [155] is presented in Figure 2.71, where about 16 exponentiation bits are attacked using $L = 10000$; thus 20000 trial exponentiations were needed to perform exponentiation with both secret and known exponents. As Figure 2.71

78

depicts, the energy in the DPA signal is greater when the two exponent operations are different (S denoting Square and M Multiply). The shaded horizontal bars show the output of a filter indicating the energy associated with each time interval.

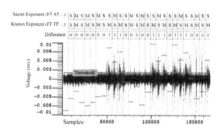

Figure 2.71: SEMD DPA on a smartcard [155]

As shown in Figure 2.71 the operations are easily distinguished from the DPA trace by averaging between the known and secret exponents. Messerges et al. [155] further propose another attack called the Multiple-Exponent Single Data (MESD) attack, which is claimed as more powerful than SEMD attack, especially in terms of improving the Signal-to-Noise Ratio (SNR). The assumption for the MESD attack is that the smart card will exponentiate a constant value using exponents chosen by the adversary. Figure 2.72 illustrates the attack flow of MESD. An arbitrary input M is chosen by the adversary and the exponentiation is performed with the secret exponent e. The average power signal $S_M[j]$ is observed. The next step, as shown in Figure 2.72, is to attack each exponent bit successively starting with the first bit used in the Square-and-Multiply algorithm and ending with the last bit. It is assumed that the adversary knows the first (i - 1) exponent bits. To attack the ith exponent bit the adversary guesses the ith bit as a 0 and then 1 and lets the card exponentiate using both guesses. If the ith bit is guessed correctly the intermediate results will also agree at the ith position. If the guess is wrong, then the results will differ [155]. Since the previous bits for a guessed bit are known, the correct bit guess produces a power signal that agrees with the secret exponent's power signal for the larger amount of time. Thus, whichever bias signal is zero for a longer time corresponds to the correct guess. Similarly, all the bits are predicted successively as shown in Figure 2.72. Figure 2.73 shows an MESD attack plot on a next bit guess, where the correct guess is clearly seen to be the signal that remains zero the longest. The authors used 1000 trial exponentiations for this attack shown in Figure 2.73.

```
M = arbitrary value and e_g = 0
Collect S_M[j]
for (i = n-1 to 0)
{  guess (ith bit of e_g is a 1) and collect S_1[j]
   guess (ith bit of e_g is a 0) and collect S_0[j]
   Calculate two DPA bias signal:
      D_1[j] = S_M[j] - S_1[j] and D_0[j] = S_M[j] - S_0[j]
   Decide which guess was correct using DPA result
   update e_g }
e_g is now equal to e (the secret exponent)
```

Figure 2.72: MESD Algorithm [155]

Figure 2.73: MESD key guess [155]

Messerges et al. [155] proposed another attack called Zero-Exponent Multiple Data (ZEMD) which is similar to MESD, but with a different set of assumptions. One assumption for ZEMD is that the smart card will exponentiate many random messages using the secret exponent. The adversary is not required to know any exponents, hence the attack is called zero-exponent. However, according to Messages et al. [155] the adversary needs to be able to predict the intermediate results of the Square-and-Multiply algorithm using an off-line simulation. The authors claim that since there are only few common approaches to implement modular exponentiation, it is not hard for the adversary to realise the algorithm used by the exponentiation hardware. Figure 2.74 depicts the ZEMD DPA attack algorithm, which starts with the adversary attacking the first bit of the secret exponent e and successively attacking all the other bits. At the ith iteration of the algorithm, it is assumed that the correct exponent e_g is correct up to the $(i - 1)^{th}$ bit. As the algorithm reveals, the adversary guesses the ith bit of the secret exponent as a 1 and performs the exponentiation with L inputs with a random value M in each run. The power signals $S[j]$ are collected during the exponentiation. Since all the bits up to the ith bit are known in the secret exponent e_g, the exponentiation can be simulated and the multiplication result in the ith step is observed and the Hamming weight is recorded. If the Hamming weight is high (i.e., a partition function can be used) the power signal $S[j]$ is added to the set S_{high}, or else to the set S_{low}. The DPA bias signal $D[j]$ is calculated by finding the averages of the two sets and subtracting each other as shown in Figure 2.74. The guess of the ith bit of e_g is declared correct (i.e., equals 1) if there are spikes in the DPA bias signal. No spikes in DPA bias signal represents the wrong guess, so the ith bit of the secret exponent e_g will be predicted as 0. Successive attacks on the remaining bits will finally reveal the whole secret exponent e.

```
e_g = 0
for (i = n-1 to 0)
{   guess (ith bit of e_g is a 1)
    for (k = 1 to L)
    {   choose a random value: M
        simulate to the ith set the calculation of  M^e_g mod N
        if (multiplication result has high Hamming weight)
            run smartcard and collect power signal: S[j]
            add S[j] to set S_high
        if (multiplication result has low Hamming weight)
            run smartcard and collect power signal: S[j]
            add S[j] to set S_low }
    Average the power signals and get DPA bias signal:
        D[j] = S_low[j] - S_high[j]
    if DPA bias signal has spikes
        the guess was correct: make ith bit of e_g equal to 1
    else
        the guess was wrong: make ith bit of e_g equal to 0 }
e_g is now equal to e (the secret exponent)
```

Figure 2.74: ZEMD Algorithm [155]

An example attack on the ZEMD implementation (illustrated in Figure 2.74), revealing the correct and incorrect guesses in the DPA bias signal, is presented in Figure 2.75. An 8-bit partitioning function is used in this example based on the Hamming weight of the multiplication result, where the power signals corresponding to results with Hamming weight eight are subtracted from the power signals with Hamming weight zero. The attack shown in Figure 2.75 clearly shows significant peaks for the correct key bit guess obtained using 500 power signals.

Figure 2.75: DPA bias plot using ZEMD [155]

Park et al. [185] claim that their Hamming weight DPA attack (explained earlier in this Section) is much similar to ZEMD, but does not involve any off-line simulation as has been performed in ZEMD. Aigner and Oswald [21, 178] also analysed and used the DPA attacks of Messerges et al. [155] (i.e., SEMD, MESD and ZEMD).

2.3.3.7 Sliding Window DPA

The adversary predicts the key using Differential Power Analysis (DPA) by observing the significant peak (explained in Section 2.3), assuming that all the power traces are synchronised. A popular countermeasure is to insert dummy instructions (also known as *Random Process Interrupts* (RPIs) [61]) during the normal execution of the CPU to produce time shifts so that the power samples' operation cycles do not match (the dummy instruction insertion countermeasure will be explained in Chapter 3 in detail). This desynchronisation effect, also known as *incoherent averaging* in digital signal processing [140], smears the peaks in the differential trace, failing the secret key guess. Clavier et al. [61] presented a *Sliding Window* Differential Power Analysis (SW-DPA) on such a failed DPA trace to reconstruct the peaks to successfully predict the secret key. An SW-DPA involves two steps: (1), a classic (Kocher-style [127]) differential curve should be obtained first, which will not produce peaks at the correct key guess because of the RPIs; and (2), adding points on k consecutive cycles from the differential trace obtained in (1) to integrate the RPI-protected differential trace. Figure 2.76 depicts the real-life SW-DPA differential curves on DES with an integration window size of 30. The top figure reveals the correct key guess, showing a peak, while the bottom figure reveals the wrong key guess.

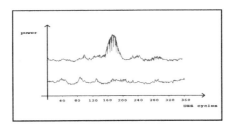

Figure 2.76: Differential trace using SW-DPA [61]

The attack in Figure 2.76 uses only one bit from the SBOX output in DES encryption to classify the power samples to generate a DPA trace. However, Clavier et al. [61] observed that some output bits leak more information than others by generating 4 different DPA traces based on 4 output bits from the SBOX. Figure 2.77 proves the statement by the authors, where the top figure (denoting the SW-DPA trace on the first output bit) shows more significant spikes than the bottom figure (denoting the SW-DPA trace on the fourth output bit).

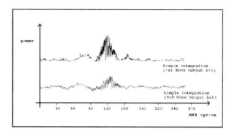

Figure 2.77: SW-DPA traces for different output bits [61]

The combination of multiple DPA traces to improve the spikes in the attack, based on the Hamming weight in the bus, is also explained by Clavier et al. [61]. The authors conclude that the main advantage of combining the multiple traces is the increase in Signal-to-Noise Ratio (SNR).

2.4 Other Power Analysis Attacks

The dominance of Differential Power Analysis (DPA) in the field of Power Analysis has not stopped the researchers from finding different attacks which are more or equally powerful than DPA. This section presents such attacks and discusses their benefits and drawbacks compared to DPA. The attacks presented here are Correlation Power Analysis, Big Mac attack, Template attack, Davies-Murphy attack and power analysis on FPGA.

2.4.1 Correlation Power Analysis (CPA)

Correlation Power Analysis (CPA) [46] is a technique equally popular to DPA, and recent power analysis attacks tend to prefer CPA over DPA. Brier et al. [46] proposed CPA stating that it is based on the Hamming distance model which can be seen as a generalisation of the Hamming weight model. The basic model for the attack is $W = aH(D \oplus R) + b$, where the $H(D \oplus R)$ yields the Hamming distance between D and R, W is the power consumption and a, b are scalars. N number of random words M_i are used for encryption and corresponding power curves W_i are extracted. A guessed key value along with the known data words M_i produce a set of N predicted Hamming distances $H_{i,R} = H(M_i \oplus R)$. R is a given state (i.e., previous state). An estimate $\hat{\rho}_{WH}$ of the correlation factor ρ_{WH} is presented in Equation 2.30. The authors claim that this model, in Equation 2.30, is the fitting model with the maximum likelihood, when R is exhausted, to maximise $\hat{\rho}_{WH}$. More description and analysis on this model can be referred to in [45].

$$\hat{\rho}_{WH}(R) = \frac{N \sum W_i H_{i,R} - \sum W_i \sum H_{i,R}}{\sqrt{N \sum W_i^2 - (\sum W_i)^2} \sqrt{N \sum H_{i,R}^2 - (\sum H_{i,R})^2}}; \quad [46] \qquad (2.30)$$

The CPA attack of Brier et al. [46] is experimented on DES during the SBOX access in first round with the original key values of 0x11 0x22 0x33 0x44 0x55 0x66 0x77 (hexadecimal format) and the first round subkey values of 24, 19, 8, 8, 5, 50, 43, 2 (decimal format). Figure 2.78 depicts the results of CPA using the Equation 2.30, which articulates the attack on the subkey in round one at each SBOX access. The first 6 subkey guesses (K) sorted by decreasing correlation rates (ρ_{max}) is tabulated for each SBOX. As shown in Figure 2.78, the correct subkey guesses (row 1) always stand out with good contrast and only 40 curves. Hence, the authors claim that a sound decision can be made without any ambiguity despite a rough estimation of ρ_{max}.

SBox$_1$		SBox$_2$		SBox$_3$		SBox$_4$		SBox$_5$		SBox$_6$		SBox$_7$		SBox$_8$	
K	ρ_{max}	K	ρ_{max}	K	ρ_{max}	K	ρ_{max}	K	ρ_{max}	K	ρ_{max}	K	ρ_{max}	K	ρ_{max}
24	92%	19	90%	8	87%	8	88%	5	91%	50	92%	43	89%	2	89%
48	74%	18	77%	18	69%	44	67%	32	71%	25	71%	42	76%	28	77%
01	74%	57	70%	05	68%	49	67%	25	70%	05	70%	52	70%	61	76%
33	74%	02	70%	22	66%	02	66%	34	69%	54	70%	38	69%	41	72%
15	74%	12	68%	58	66%	29	66%	61	67%	29	69%	0	69%	37	70%
06	74%	13	67%	43	65%	37	65%	37	67%	53	67%	30	68%	15	69%

Figure 2.78: CPA results on guessing subkeys in round one of DES [46]

Brier et al. [46] identified certain restrictions in implementing CPA in a practical scenario, such as complex architectures implementing separated buses for data and address which masks certain bit transitions, the pipeline may smear the correlation peaks, etc. The authors further investigate the practical problems in Differential Power Analysis (DPA), mainly stating that DPA produces peaks for wrong guesses (called *ghost peaks*) which prevent the adversary from making sound decisions from the DPA plots. According to the authors, this is because of the assumption in DPA that the target bit from a decision function for any wrong subkey guess does not depend on the value associated with the correct guess, which is not observed as always true. However, CPA is more demanding than DPA and difficult to implement, since it requires the characterisation of the leakage model parameters [46]. Koeune and Standaert [132] pointed out that the multiple bit attacks are suboptimal, since they consider only *all something* values, but not all possible texts. Hence, the authors found that Correlation Power Analysis (CPA) can solve this problem and identify the key steps in CPA for DES, which are as follows:

1. the adversary decides the place in the DES encryption for power measurement and the corresponding data to predict the Hamming weight. For 2^6 possible key guesses and N different input texts, the adversary simulates DES and computes the Hamming weight of the intermediate result of concern. The result of this prediction is stored in a **prediction matrix**. In most attacks the intermediate result of concern in DES is the output of the SBOX;

2. the adversary measures the power consumption at the place where the intermediate result of concern is computed in the device. The result of this measurement is stored in a **consumption vector**;

3. the adversary *compares* the Hamming weight predictions with the real power consumption measurements by computing the correlation coefficient using the Equation 2.30;

4. if the attack is successful, the correct key guess will be the only value producing a high correlation coefficient.

The correlation attack in DES for the 6 MSBs of the subkey from Koeune and Standaert [132] is presented in Figure 2.79. The correct guess is clearly identified as the component which is producing a higher correlation.

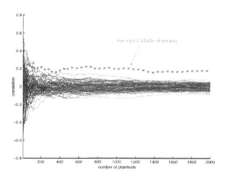

Figure 2.79: CPA attack in DES for 6 MSBs of the subkey [132]

Ors et al. [177] performed a Correlation Power Analysis attack on AES based on the value stored in a *Register* after the AddRoundKey operation (refer to Section 2.1.2 for more details on AES operations). The authors have used CPA, but in a slightly different way than Brier et al. [46]. Equation 2.31 shows the definition of CPA by Ors et al. [177], where the correlation is initially performed as a simulation before real power measurements to estimate the difficulty of the real attack. The correlation coefficient $C(T, P)$ identifies the degree of correlation between P, the predictions of the model, and T, the set of traces, as specified in Equation 2.31. $E(T)$ refers to the expectation (average) trace and $Var(T)$ denotes the variance of T.

$$C(T, P) = \frac{E(T \cdot P) - E(T) \cdot E(P)}{\sqrt{Var(T) \cdot Var(P)}}; \quad [177] \tag{2.31}$$

The CPA attack of Ors et al. [177] goes as follows:

1. the adversary chooses N random plaintexts and computes the total number of bit changes between previous and the current values of the *Register* during the execution of AES for each plaintext for a specific key. To attack the 8 Most Significant Bits (MSBs) of the secret key, all possible 2^8 key values are simulated with the N plaintexts to compute the bit changes in the *Register*. These values are stored into an $N \times 2^8$ matrix M_4;

2. the adversary measures the power consumption at the *Register* write, while the chip is executing AES with the N plaintexts. These power consumption traces with 1000 samples each are stored into an $N \times 1000$ matrix M_5;

3. power consumption matrix M_5 is preprocessed by averaging (refer to [177]) to compute the average of each power consumption trace. The averaged values are stored in an N matrix M_6;

4. for each key guess, compute $c_i = C(M_6, M_4(1 : N, i))$ using the Equation 2.31. Figure 2.80 presents the attack on the 8 MSBs of the key based on this correlation between M_4 and M_6.

As shown in Figure 2.80, the 8 MSBs of the correct key (value 153) in AES is attacked successfully by identifying a significant peak using CPA. Further improvement on this analysis is also discussed by Ors et al. [177], which can be found in [177]. Tiri et al. [222] also used the CPA technique to impose an attack on a coprocessor which is executing AES. This attack of

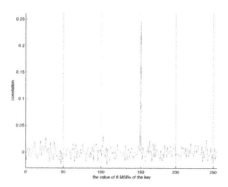

Figure 2.80: CPA attack in AES for 8 MSBs of the key [177]

Tiri et al. [222] is presented in Figure 2.81, which is the CPA trace of correlation coefficient against the number of power measurements clearly showing a higher correlation for the correct secret key guess. The correlation coefficients for the other key values (max and min) are drawn in gray.

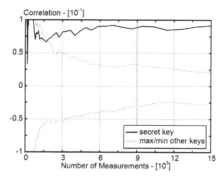

Figure 2.81: CPA attack in AES coprocessor for 8 MSBs of the key [222]

Recent research reveals that Correlation Power Analysis (CPA) is a preferred attack to demonstrate power analysis than Differential Power Analysis (DPA) on processor implementations because of its advantages over DPA [46]. However, Han et al. [101] claim that CPA causes an increase in computational complexity.

2.4.2 Big Mac Attack

Walter [238] presented the *Big Mac* attack on RSA, which is similar to DPA. The *Big Mac* attack identifies the secret key bit-by-bit by nibbling at sections of it in any order and the attack requires that a single k-bit multiplier performs RSA exponentiations in a digit sequential fashion [238]. The author investigated the attack on a simple k-bit multiplier using a simulation setup, counting gate switching in the combinational logic. RSA decryption computation "C^d mod M" involves a modular multiplication using the secret key d to decrypt the ciphertext C using a modulus M (explained in Section 2.1.3). Such modular multiplication can be performed using an m-ary method [238] by representing a number $X = \sum_{i=0}^{n-1} x_i r^i$, where $r = 2^k$ and n is the number of digits required. This allows the computation of modular product "(A×B) mod M" using the k-bit multiplier. Performing "(A×B) mod M" iteratively, yields the decrypted value of "C^d mod M" [238].

The *Big Mac* attack starts with a pre-computation by generating a random set of powers $\{C^{(1)}, C^{(2)},..., C^{(m-1)}\}$ using a variety of values for k and exponent base r. These inputs $C^{(i)}$ are used to simulate the pre-computation by multiplying with a random long integer B to create a trace tr_i for each $C^{(i)}$; a trace consists of vector of gate switch counts for each digit of $C^{(i)}$. The inputs $C^{(i)}$ are also fed into the chip performing RSA decryption to record corresponding power traces tr_s. Since the number of gate switches is proportional to the power magnitude, the power trace tr_s is substituted with its corresponding gate switch count. The trace tr_s is matched with the traces tr_i of each $C^{(i)}$, finding the Euclidean distance with every tr_i. Since this will give a measure of how close these traces are, the closest is chosen as the predicted i [238]. The correct value of i yields the secret exponent used.

Euclidean distance is the **ordinary** *distance between two points*
that one would measure with a ruler... – Wiki

This *Big Mac* attack of Walter [238] is not explained properly as the method raises so many questions, such as, how are the power samples extracted from the trace, what measures are used to find the distance, etc. Kaminaga et al. [118] also analysed and discussed *Big Mac* attacks. The authors state that the *Big Mac* attack uses a modular multiplication which has a structure of repeated multiple additions. Hence, averaging of multiple addition blocks will reveal the multiplier dependency from a single execution result [118].

2.4.3 Template Attacks

Chari et al. [55] proposed a template attack in RC4 [82], a popular stream cipher, which is used in many secure applications. Interested readers are referred to [124] for details and references in RC4, since the key concern here is not RC4, but the template attack. In template attacks, the adversary uses an experimental device which is identical to the device under attack, and performs rigorous analysis on the power measurements from the device to build templates corresponding to each possible value of the unknown key bits. Such templates consist of mean signal and noise probability distributions (refer to [55] for equations and definitions). Chari et al. [55] state that the adversary then uses the templates to classify the portion of concern in power sample S and limits the choices for the key bits to a small set. This step is repeated with a longer prefix of S involving more key bits. To classify a sample S with an unknown key, the probability of observing S in each template is computed using the mean signal of the template and the noise in sample S. The operation with the highest probability for a given template is predicted for the correct key guess (refer to [55] for detailed equations). According to the authors, RC4 is an ideal candidate for the template attack, which has substantial contamination (i.e., key dependent leakage over multiple cycles) from the secret key when processed. Chari et al. [55] proposed a pruning process to reduce the set of possible hypotheses to a very small number, while ensuring that the hypotheses with high probability are not discarded. The pruning process, which is referred to as the *ball approach*, keeps all hypotheses whose noise probability is at least $\frac{P_{max}}{c}$, where P_{max} is the maximum noise probability and c is a constant value.

RC4, officially termed as 'Rivest Cipher 4', is the most widely-used software stream cipher and is used in popular protocols such as SSL and WEP... – Wiki

The template attack experiment of Chari et al. [55] in RC4 uses 10 choices for the key byte. For each key byte, the mean of 2000 power samples are computed and 42 points are identified in each power sample (i.e., the same points) for statistical analysis and template comparison. The main measurements used for comparison are means and standard deviations of these points. Table 2.3 presents the results of classification experiments for the set of 10 key choices and their probability of correct hypothesis against the Ball Size (c). The average success rate is 99.29% when using the default probability distribution and it is improved proportionally with Ball Size using the *ball approach*.

Key Byte	Ball Size $c = 1$	Ball Size $c = c^6$	Ball Size $c = c^{12}$	Ball Size $c = c^{24}$
1111 1110	98.62	99.46	99.88	99.94
1110 1110	98.34	99.82	99.88	99.88
1101 1110	99.16	100.00	100.00	100.00
1011 1110	98.14	99.52	99.82	100.00
0111 1110	99.58	99.76	99.89	99.94
1111 1101	99.70	99.94	99.94	99.94
1111 1011	99.64	99.82	99.82	99.89
1111 0111	100.00	100.00	100.00	100.00
1110 1101	99.76	99.82	99.88	99.88
1110 1011	99.94	100.00	100.00	100.00
Average	99.29	99.81	99.91	99.95

Table 2.3: Percentage of correct hypothesis under different ball sizes [55]

Similar experiments with more points (such as 84 points) in the sample were also undertaken by the authors and the results (presented in [55]) proved that the increase in number of points in the sample for template generation further improved the percentage for the correct hypothesis. Chari et al. [55] identified a similar possibility of template attack in DES (refer Section 2.1.1 for details on DES) hardware in smart cards and also in EM signals observed from an SSL (Secure Socket Layer [237]) accelerator inside a closed server. However, the authors observed that a significant amount of effort is involved in creating templates and the requirement of having an identical experimental device is another weakness of this attack. Rechberger and Oswald [198] discussed the problems in the template attack of Chari et al. [55] on RC4 and came up with an improved version of the attack. The authors [198] claim that the method of Chari et al. [55] is computationally intensive and requires higher execution time and storage. Four main improvements stated by Rechberger and Oswald [198] are briefly as follows:

1. the programmable device is not only used for generating templates but also to perform trial classifications in order to improve the accuracy of the attack;

2. to efficiently find the n out of N points which has the most information for the template, first compute the vectors of means while building templates. Then compute the differences of each pair of the mean and add them together. Select the n points among the highest peaks;

3. instead of processing the template in the time domain, convert the template to the frequency domain using Fourier transformation before processing. The authors claim that this is a lucrative transformation;

4. apply an amplified template attack by adding up noise probabilities of every trace and apply the approach of maximum likelihood on the sum. [198]

The authors claim that even though the n highest points selection is not optimal in their experiment, the technique proposed is still better than the commonly used technique, Principal Component Analysis (PCA) [114]. The improved template attack explained here does have several advantages over Differential Power Analysis (DPA). The template attack does not need the adversary to know any details about the input or output of the used algorithm. Even if the samples are few, the template attack can still be successful using the amplified technique [198]. Aabid et al. [16] recently proposed a template attack in key schedule of DES algorithm using Principle Component Analysis (PCA [114]). According to the authors, the adversary gathers a large number of traces and computes the couple (μ_k, Σ_k) to represent a template for each set of trace (S_k) for a specific subkey value (k). The formula for the average μ_k and the covariance matrix Σ_k are shown in Equation 2.32. When the adversary observes a trace τ from the target system which is using the secret key executing DES encryption, the trace τ is projected and matched with the template set to find out which template it closely matches using Baye's rule [142] (detailed equations are shown in [16]). The closely matched template will yield its corresponding subkey, which will be guessed as the correct candidate.

$$\mu_k = \frac{1}{|S_k|} \sum_{t \in S_k} t \quad \text{and} \quad \Sigma_k = \frac{1}{|S_k| - 1} \sum_{t \in S_k} (t - \mu_k)(t - \mu_k)^T; \quad [16] \qquad (2.32)$$

Aabid et al. [16] conducted the template attack experiment on a DES key schedule using SecMat 0.13μm prototype academic circuit containing a DES coprocessor and using the IN-FINIIUM 54 855A oscilloscope from AGILENT, 1132A current probe for power measurements.

The authors also discussed performing template attacks using a Hamming weight model and a Hamming distance model [16]. Oswald and Mangard [179] proposed a template attack in a masked AES software implementation on an 8-bit microcontroller. Since the microcontroller used in the attack [179] precharges the bus lines, this causes leakage in Hamming weight of the data, which is claimed by the authors as common in smartcards. Templates are built for each instruction and all Hamming weights (HW). The masking approach on AES considered for the attack is shown in Figure 2.82 where the input and output of SubBytes are both masked by a random value m. The authors created 81 templates, one for each pair of $HW(m)$ and $HW(S(d_i \oplus k_j) \oplus m)$. The former instruction manipulates m at the beginning of the algorithm and the latter computes $S(d_i \oplus k_j) \oplus m$.

Figure 2.82: Part of masked AES round [179]

The result of the template attack on the masked AES implementation (shown in Figure 2.82) of Oswald and Mangard [179] is presented in Figure 2.83. As the result shows (left of Figure 2.83), the correct key has a probability of one whereas all other key hypotheses have probability zero. The right plot in Figure 2.83 clearly shows that the correct key is identified using around 15 traces. Oswald and Mangard [179] also performed a successful attack by combining Second-order Differential Power Analysis (DPA) (explained in Section 2.3) with the template attack. According to this combination, the adversary should preprocess the trace using a Second-order DPA technique before implementing template attack. However, the authors concluded that this combination did not provide any improvement over the standard Second-order DPA.

The template attack of Chari et al. [55] (explained earlier) is expanded and discussed in the context of DPA by Agrawal et al. [19]. The authors [20] presented a similar template attack on masking schemes. Peeters et al. [188] also performed a template attack on masked hardware implementations, but with a relatively higher number of traces. Archambeau et al. [27] presented a template attack similar to the other techniques, but using a subspace of the traces in RC4 and AES implementations. Gierlichs et al. [92] also discussed and analysed

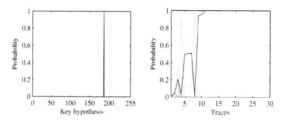

Figure 2.83: Attack (left) and Probability over no. of traces (right) [179]

the implementations of template attacks. Recently, there is a rapid increase in papers based on template attacks, which are equally popular to Differential Power Analysis (DPA) and Correlation Power Analysis (CPA).

2.4.4 Davies-Murphy Power Attack

Davies and Murphy [75] discovered an imbalance in the DES algorithm, where several subkey bits are shared for different SBOX accesses. Figure 2.84 shows such a scenario in DES where 4 bits are shared between SBOXes S_1 and S_2. Biham and Biryukov [35] also suggested an improved version of how such an imbalance can be used for cryptanalysis.

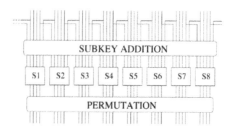

Figure 2.84: Shared subkey bits for SBOXes in DES [75]

Kunz-Jacques et al. [136] used this imbalance in DES proposed in [75] for power analysis (called the Davies-Murphy Power Attack). The authors use the Hamming weight model to predict data using the power measurements. The underlying idea of this attack is to predict the Hamming weight of the outputs from the adjacent SBOXes using the power consumption curves and to identify the shared subkey bits used based on the theoretical model developed using the algorithm. A brief description of the Davies-Murphy attack [136] is given as follows:

1. the adversary observes whether the distribution $(H(y_i \oplus R_i, H(y_{i+1} \oplus R_{i+1}))$ is biased for most constants R_i, R_{i+1}. H refers to the Hamming weight of the data after the SBOX access and y is the input (a portion of the plaintext). For example, the output places at SBOXes S_1 and S_2 as shown in Figure 2.84;

2. an empirical distribution of $(H(y_i \oplus R_i, H(y_{i+1} \oplus R_{i+1}))$ is built by encrypting a set of randomly chosen plaintexts. The power consumption is monitored while the smartcard is executing the software implementation of the DES program. Portions of the power consumption curves W_i and W_{i+1} are identified;

3. the resulting empirical distribution is matched with the theoretical results. Two different inner rounds in DES are used for comparison at the adjacent SBOXes.

Interested readers are referred to [136] for more details and results on the Davies-Murphy attack. The authors conclude that the power consumption for adjacent SBOXes is biased even for randomly chosen plaintexts.

2.4.5 Power Analysis Attacks on FPGA

The usage of Field Programmable Gate Arrays (FPGAs) [141] is rapidly increasing because of their advantages over the Application Specific Integrated Circuits (ASICs). Even though almost all the power analysis attacks explained in this section can be implemented in FPGAs (i.e., as far as the adversary can gather the power traces during secure execution, it is simply applying the technique), the author presents here a separate description dedicated to only FPGAs, considering how FPGAs can be attacked using power analysis exploiting their implementations and design. Standaert et al. [218] presented an investigation on how practical it is to perform power analysis in FPGAs, which the authors claim is the first experiment on FPGAs for power analysis. The authors used a VIRTEX-ARM board with Xilinx Virtex 1000 FPGA attached to it. A resistance was inserted next to the source supplying the Virtex and the unnecessary devices were undersupplied. The power analysis setup required a voltage source, a waveform generator, an oscilloscope (Tektronix 7140 with 1 GHz) and computer software to generate the FPGA programming files and to process the data. Figure 2.85 shows the experimental setup of Standaert et al. [218], and the necessary components are labelled.

Standaert et al. [218] show that the power consumption observed at the attached resistance

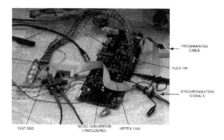

Figure 2.85: Experimental setup in FPGA board [218]

is strongly correlated with the internal bit switches of FPGA. This is proved in their experiments as shown in Figure 2.86, where the encryption rounds in DES are clearly identified from the power trace.

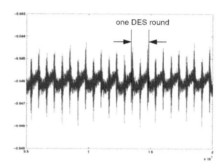

Figure 2.86: Power trace for DES encryption from FPGA [218]

However, the authors [218] identify certain critical limitations on performing power analysis in FPGAs: (1), since the application board has several components attached to it connecting the grounds together, isolating the FPGA consumption signal is difficult when the power consumption is measured at the ground pin; (2), since the working frequencies of the FPGAs are increasing to much faster rates, it involves very high sampling rates for measurements; and (3), compared to smartcards, where the data is managed by 8-bit registers, FPGAs deal with all the bits at once. This dilutes the effects of the bit computations exploited for SPA and DPA attacks. Standaert et al. [216] (the same group but different co-authors) demonstrated a Differential Power Analysis (DPA) attack in DES using an FPGA. A DPA attack on Rijndael (AES) is presented in [215] using an FPGA. Recent papers show that most of the power analysis attacks are demonstrated in FPGAs, because they are less expensive and easy to implement. This gives rise to the question of the security of FPGAs in real life implementations of the device.

2.5 Summary

This chapter provides a detailed explanation of the power analysis attacks attempted in the past. The attacks are mainly categorised into Simple Power Analysis (SPA), Differential Power Analysis (DPA) and other power analysis attacks. SPA attacks are further divided into attacks using Hamming weights and attacks using conditional branching. DPA attacks are classified into attacks on block ciphers, attacks on public cryptosystems and DPA extensions. The other attacks that are explained in this chapter (which are different from standard SPA and DPA attacks) are Correlation Power Analysis (CPA), Big Mac attack, template attack, Davies-Murphy power attack and power analysis on FPGA. DPA attacks are the most popular amongst all the power analysis attacks explained. AES and ECC encryption programs have higher numbers of attacks attempted compared to the other programs (such as DES, RSA, Twofish, Blowfish, etc.). Electro Magnetic (EM) based side channel attacks are also emerging as one of the contenders for power analysis, due to their ease in capturing the samples from a device. Since the EM emmission has a linear correlation with the power consumption, the side channel attacks proposed for EM signals can be also adapted to power analysis (such as frequency based attacks [89]).

Chapter 3

Countermeasures for Power Analysis

The increasing number of power analysis attacks, exploiting various properties in the power trace as explained in Chapter 2, have a serious impact on the current research in the security of embedded systems. Most of the security groups worldwide endeavour to find effective countermeasures to combat power analysis. This chapter presents such previously proposed countermeasures. The most investigated countermeasures are masking, algorithm modification and hardware balancing, which are further expanded into subsections. Masking techniques are classified into data masking, table masking and the window method. The rest of the countermeasures discussed in this chapter are dummy instruction insertion, signal suppression, current flattening, non-deterministic processors, the handling clock and special instructions. Each countermeasure is explained in detail, presenting its benefits and drawbacks.

3.1 Masking

An adversary is able to figure out certain instruction signatures of the executed code using the power profile to attack confidential information such as secret keys. Adding noise into power lines during measurements [127] results in acquiring more power samples for a successful attack to eliminate the noise effect. Such a noise could be in random nature, injected into the proper execution of the code to confuse the adversary, masking the secure information. In this section, the author presents all the versions of Masking countermeasures proposed over the years.

3.1.1 Data Masking

Data Masking obfuscates a vulnerable computation or an intermediate result using random arbitrary values or functions combined with the actual data [156]. Itoh et al. [110] state that this data randomising technique (also called *blinding*) makes the intermediate data during the encryption unpredictable by transforming the actual computations into executions involving random values. One of the early works in *blinding* to prevent power analysis is from Messerges et al. [155]. The authors adapted the *blinding* approach used by Kocher [130], who used the signature blinding approach [56] presented in 1983, to prevent timing attacks. The data masking techniques are categorised here into countermeasures proposed for different cryptographic programs. To give a generic example for masking, consider the *whitening* process [152] used in most block ciphers (such as DES and AES) which performs XOR between the input data *INPUT* and the secret key at the beginning of the encryption. Figure 3.1(a) depicts the *whitening* process at line **A** during the start of the encryption algorithm $W1$. This *whitening* process can leak information about the secret key, when a straight XOR operation is performed.

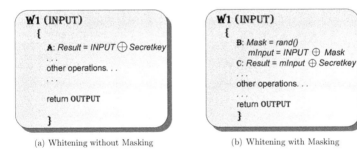

(a) Whitening without Masking   (b) Whitening with Masking

Figure 3.1: An Example for Data Masking [152]

Figure 3.1(b) shows the modified *whitening* process of the program $W1$ to prevent power analysis (i.e., data masking). A new random value *Mask* is generated each time the program is executed (line **B**) and XORed with the *INPUT* first. The intermediate result is then XORed with the secret key to compute the result as shown in line **C** of Figure 3.1(b). An adversary is left with only random information when line **B** and line **C** are exploited for power analysis.

3.1.1.1 Masking DES

Chari et al. [54] proposed a masking technique (called *encoding*) in XOR operations of DES, where the original computation of every bit is randomly split into k shares. For example, bit b can be encoded into k shares $b{\oplus}r_1, r_2, ..., r_{k-1}, r_1{\oplus}...{\oplus}r_{k-1}$. The r_i's are randomly chosen bits. Such splitting has to be performed only for sufficient number of rounds until the adversary has a very low probability of predicting bits [54]. According to the experiments of Chari et al. [54] in DES, only the first four rounds and the last four rounds have to be masked by splitting the XOR operations into k shares involving randomly chosen bits. The later rounds have to be also masked (encoded) if the adversary can observe the outputs [54]. Chari et al. [54] further stated that similar encoding can be applied to mask a byte of data. Equations and proofs related to the encoding scheme can be referred to in [54]. The authors theoretically proved that the encoding of an operation by splitting it into shares and computing it using random values does not leak significant information of a particular bit for the adversary to perform power analysis. However, this paper [54] does not present a real attack in DES to prove the practicality of the encoding technique. Chari et al. [54] also propose to randomise the order of SBOX executions in DES. Nevertheless, the authors observe that such random ordering should be done extensively throughout the execution, otherwise the adversary can realise the correct execution using fewer samples. Extensive random scheduling of the SBOX executions is impossible since the DES algorithm forces a causal ordering [54]. Such random ordering is also considered a possible countermeasure by some other security experts [241].

Messerges et al. [156] stated that data masking is an attractive countermeasure which generates a random mask and uses the mask to hide sensitive information. The authors denoted that the XOR operation ($\oplus$ – one of the reversible operations) could be used to mask the secret key d using a new random mask r, generated every time the DES cryptographic program is executed. The masked operation for such a scenario would be $d \oplus r$ for the secret data d [156]. The random mask r is generated at the start of the algorithm and the masked result is reversed to obtain the correct value at the later part of the algorithm using the same r [180]. Coron et al. [68] stated that the data masking using XOR operations as shown in Figure 3.1 is appropriate for DES, which uses XORs throughout the 16 rounds for encryption. However, these masking approaches in DES on the *whitening* process is proved vulnerable by Messerges [152] using second-order differential power analysis (explained in Chapter 2).

Akkar and Giraud [23] presented a slightly different data masking in DES, which is illustrated in Figure 3.2. The operations inserted for masking are represented by dotted lines. The author explains only the important parts in the figure related to masking. Interested readers are referred to [63] for more details on DES. According to Akkar and Giraud [23], the input message M is masked with a random value X using an XOR operation before the initial permutation IP.

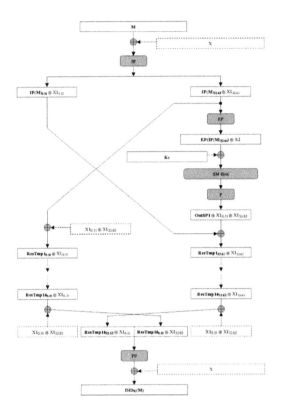

Figure 3.2: DES, with and without masking [23]

Since the SBOXes are non-linear in DES, they are replaced with modified SM-Box'es to include masking in the algorithm. $X1$ represents the intermediate result $IP(X)$ and $X2 = EP(X1_{32-63})$, where EP is the expansive permutation. To preserve mask $X1$ at the end of the round, the left part of the algorithm shown in Figure 3.2 is XORed with $X1_{0-31} \oplus X1_{32-63}$.

100

The correct ciphertext is obtained by unmasking the value after final permutation (FP) using the mask X. Akkar and Giraud [23] observed that creating the mask is also an important process, which should not reveal the values of X to the adversary. Hence, the mask X was created using a randomised bit-per-bit computation which was slow, but only at the start of each DES execution. The authors claim that, unlike other data masking methods, this method needs to know the mask value at a fixed step (whereas others need to consider masking at several steps in the algorithm) and the expected value is extracted at the end of the algorithm. This modified algorithm of DES presented in Figure 3.2 cost around 5X in runtime and 3X in memory space. The authors [23] conclude that their method performs operations using a random mask throughout the DES algorithm, masking the real intermediate results, thus preventing both Simple Power Analysis (SPA) and Differential Power Analysis (DPA). They further state that this masking solution prevents the attacks presented in [22] and [68]. Nevertheless, the authors realised that their technique would be still vulnerable to second-order DPA attacks [152] because of the general masking approach applied. This data masking technique in [23] does not completely prevent the attack on key scheduling in DES, where the subkeys are generated on-the-fly, creating a possibility for the adversary to predict the Hamming weight of each subkey [23]. According to Biham and Shamir [37], the *Skipjack* algorithm [36] can be used to prevent the attack on key scheduling in DES

SKIPJACK was designed using building blocks and techniques that date back more than forty years, to replace DES... – Wiki

3.1.1.2   Masking AES

Since AES [167] is also a block cipher, very similar to the nature of DES, the masking techniques proposed for DES can be adapted for AES. Chari et al. [53] stated that the masking proposed in [54] (explained earlier in this section) can be applied for XOR operations in AES. This technique divides a computation of a bit or a byte into k shares and performs the operations using randomly chosen values. Akkar and Giraud [23] proposed a data masking countermeasure for AES as shown in Figure 3.3, which is similar to their technique proposed for DES (illustrated in Figure 3.2). The operations related to the ith Round are highlighted, where the subkey for Round i is specified as K_i and X is the random mask value. ByteSub operation which involves SBOX accesses is modified for the masked version as shown in Figure 3.3 because of their non-linearity (more details on this modified ByteSub can be found in the paper [23] and in Section 3.1.2). $X1$ is the linear transformation computed using ByteSub for the mask X and $X2 = ShiftRow(X1)$, $X3 = MixColumn(X2)$. The same random mask is kept at each round and the expected correct value is produced at the end of each round using the random mask X.

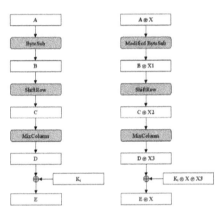

Figure 3.3: Round i in AES, with (right) and without (left) masking [23]

Akkar and Giraud [23] claim that the data masking presented in Figure 3.3 combats both Simple Power Analysis (SPA) and Differential Power Analysis (DPA) since all the operations throughout the AES algorithm perform computations with random values, thus masking the intermediate results. The implementation of this masking approach in a 128-bit AES cost around 3X in runtime and 2X in memory space. This data masking approach uses an additional multiplicative mask with the additive mask X in the Modified ByteSub operation shown in Figure 3.3, where the authors claim that all the intermediate values during the ByteSub operation are masked. Details on this ByteSub implementation using the multiplicative masks can be referred to in the paper [23] and explained in Section 3.1.2. Golic and Tymen [94] observed a weakness in the masking approach of Akkar and Giraud [23] where the multiplicative mask does not mask all-zero byte value of data (i.e., all-zero intermediate byte values remain unchanged after masking). Hence, Golic and Tymen [94] claim that the DPA attack (first-order) in the first round of AES using the SBOX output bits is still possible in the masking approach of [23] by targeting all-zero input bytes or the all-zero output bytes (also called as *zero attack* [232]).

Messerges [153] performed a thorough investigation of imposing data masking in the final five AES finalists, which are Mars [52], RC6 [199], Rijndael [72], Serpent [25] and Twofish [207]. Only the data masking technique on these algorithms are explained, but not the specifics of them. Interested readers are pointed to the paper [153] and also to specific references denoted for each algorithm. Messerges [153] presented two different masking methods called *Boolean* masking and *Arithmetic* masking as defined in Equation 3.1, where the word x is obfuscated using the random mask r_x to produce the masked value x'. The *Boolean* mask uses the bitwise XOR operator and the *Arithmetic* mask uses addition and subtraction modulo 2^n, where n is the word length ($n = 32$ in the experiments of [153]).

$$
\begin{aligned}
Boolean\ mask\quad &:\quad x' = x \oplus r_x; \\
Arithmetic\ mask:\quad &\quad x' = (x - r_x) \bmod 2^n;\quad [153]
\end{aligned}
\tag{3.1}
$$

The data masking strategy of Messerges [153] makes sure all the operations in AES algorithms work with masked input data and produce a masked output result, thus obfuscating all the intermediate values. This technique randomly masks the input data and the key prior to the algorithm execution. Messerges [153] states that all the operations except addition and multiplication can be obfuscated using *Boolean* masking, whereas the *Arithmetic* masking is used for addition and multiplication. The author realised the importance of converting *Boolean* to *Arithmetic* masking and vice versa, since most of the AES algorithms combine both. One way for such a conversion is to unmask the data and remask it using the other approach. According to the masking approach of Messerges [153], the table lookups are obfuscated by modifying the SBOXes such that masked inputs are fed in and masked data outputs are produced. All the other operations in the AES algorithms are obfuscated using *Boolean* and *Arithmetic* masking approaches defined in Equation 3.1, depending on whether they involve addition, multiplication or any other operation. Table 3.1 depicts the experimental results on masking in all the AES finalists, revealing cycle count information for performace decisions and RAM, ROM consumption to decide on the storage space of the algorithms in the smartcard. The Security Cost metric is just the division of the Masked result by the Unmasked result. Algorithms that use multiplication operations, such as Mars and RC6, have the worst cost in performance. Messerges [153] concluded that Rijnadael and Twofish are the best candidates suited for random data masking, based on the results in Table 3.1, where they provide less performance and storage space overheads compared to others.

Cycle Count	Mars	RC6	Rijndael	Serpent	Twofish
Unmasked	9,425	5,964	7,086	15,687	19,274
Masked	72,327	46,282	13,867	49,495	36,694
Security Cost	7.67	7.76	1.96	3.16	1.90

RAM (bytes)	Mars	RC6	Rijndael	Serpent	Twofish
Unmasked	116	232	52	176	60
Masked	232	284	326	340	696
Security Cost	2.00	1.22	6.27	1.93	11.60

ROM (bytes)	Mars	RC6	Rijndael	Serpent	Twofish
Unmasked	2,984	464	1,756	2,676	1,544
Masked	7,404	1,376	2,393	9,572	2,656
Security Cost	2.48	2.97	1.36	3.58	1.72

Table 3.1: Data Masking implementation results [153]

Coron and Goubin [68] observed that the *Boolean* to *Arithmetic* masking conversions and the *Arithmetic* to *Boolean* masking conversions proposed in Messerges [153] (maskings defined in Equation 3.1) were still vulnerable to DPA attacks. Such a vulnerability is mainly caused due to the availability of the original intermediate result during the unmasking (i.e., original data is revealed) before the conversion. The authors [68] defined a DPA attack on such a weakness, nevertheless they did not implement it. Coron and Tchulkine [67] proposed a new DPA free *Arithmetic* to *Boolean* masking conversion approach, which uses precomputed tables instead of any unmasking in between conversions. However, Ng [169] discovered that such a precomputation approach [67] would be a benefit only when the precomputation had to be performed at the start of the algorithm. Thus, the author presented an improved step-wise method for *Arithmetic* to *Boolean* masking conversion. Messerges et al. [156] state that data masking is an attractive solution to prevent power analysis attack on AES cryptosystems.

Trichina [229] states that the actual data should not be revealed during masking, when operations like AND and XOR had to be performed between the masked values. Revealing the original data at any stage creates vulnerability for Differential Power Analysis (DPA). The author realises that the XOR operation on two masked data bits does not need the unmasking of values before the operation, because it is a bit-wise linear operation. Hence, the XOR operation between two values a_i and b_j using masks x_i and y_j respectively, can be interpreted as follows: $(a_i \oplus x_i) \oplus (b_j \oplus y_j) = (a_i \oplus b_j) \oplus (x_i \oplus y_j)$. This proves that after XORing the masked values $((a_i \oplus x_i) \oplus (b_j \oplus y_j))$ the result using the correct XOR $(a_i \oplus b_j)$ can be produced from the intermediate value by unmasking with the same random masks. Unlike the XOR operation, the AND operation needs to be performed differently to make sure the correct value is produced without unmasking the data values during the operation. Trichina [229] defined the secure way of performing the AND operation as presented in Equation 3.2. The components $\tilde{a}$ and $\tilde{b}$ are the masked values of a_i and b_j using the masks x_i and y_j, where $\tilde{a} = a_i \oplus x_i$ and $\tilde{b} = b_j \oplus y_j$. As per the secure AND operation, the "mask correction" $(x_i \cdot \tilde{b})$ $\oplus (y_j \cdot \tilde{a}) \oplus (x_i \cdot y_j)$ to unmask the actual result at the end of the AES algorithm, can be carried out without compromising the actual data values. Figure 3.4 depicts the gate diagram of the secure AND operation based on Equation 3.2. Another extra random mask z is used to provide more robustness to the technique.

$$\tilde{a} \cdot \tilde{b} = (a_i \cdot b_j) \oplus (x_i \cdot \tilde{b}) \oplus (y_j \cdot \tilde{a}) \oplus (x_i \cdot y_j); \quad [229] \tag{3.2}$$

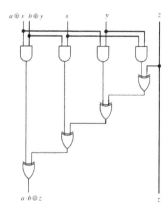

Figure 3.4: Masked AND [231]

Using the above designs of XOR and AND mask corrections, and the SBOX masking for the SubBytes operation explained in Section 3.1.2, Trichina et al. [231] developed a masked AES coprocessor. However, the authors did not perform a power analysis attack to justify the security of the masked coprocessor. Blömer et al. [41] presented the masking in AES, as a whole, using the previously proposed solutions and proved that the masking is secure using a formal model. Figure 3.5 shows the schematic diagram of the masked implementation of AES by Blömer et al. [41], where a true random number generator (TRNG) is used to create the random masks r_i and key k is protected against read access. The mask generation and the computation with masks are protected against manipulation, thus preventing the adversary in realising the mask operations [41].

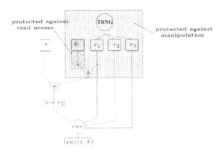

Figure 3.5: Schematic view of Masked AES [41]

Herbst et al. [103] state that almost all the data masking techniques are vulnerable to higher-order Differential Power Analysis (DPA) attacks (explained in Chapter 2). Hence, the authors propose to combine the masking approach in AES with a randomisation of executions. The randomisation in [103] utilises the feature that the 4×4 blocks in AES are processed independently, when the processing of these blocks is randomly scheduled. In addition to this random scheduling, the authors propose to insert dummy blocks of instructions at the start of each round. Such instructions are executed from a different memory area in the smartcard, but with the base addresses having the same Hamming weight for both dummy and real states. The sequence of MixColumns and ShiftRows operations are changed to facilitate the randomisation. This masked and randomised implementation of Herbst et al. [103] in AES on an 8-bit smartcard processor is roughly two times slower than the best unmasked implementation (the implementation in [23] is seven times slower). The runtime is increased by a factor of 3 compared to the unmasked AVR based implementation when no additional blocks are added in randomisation [103]. Figure 3.6 denotes the second-order DPA correlation traces performed on the masked implementation of AES by Herbst et al. [103]. The first column access in the first round of the masked AES is attacked using the method proposed in [180]. As shown in the left trace of Figure 3.6, the correct key guess still produces a significant peak (emphasised in black) while all the other key guesses (shaded in gray) produce a much lower variation. Similarly, the correlation trace shown in the right part of Figure 3.6 shows a higher coefficient value for the correct key guess (emphasised in black) after around 5000 samples. Hence, based on these traces, Herbst et al. [103] concluded that their masked and randomised AES implementation is still vulnerable to second-order DPA, but requires a large number of measurements. However, the authors stated that this technique is resistant against Simple Power Analysis (SPA), template attacks and first-order DPA attacks.

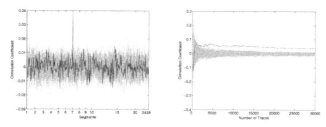

Figure 3.6: DPA traces for key guesses (left), for No. of samples (right) [103]

Rostovtsev and Shemyakina [200] presented a masking technique to randomly schedule the isomorphisms in the AES computations, to prevent the adversary from extracting necessary power values for the attack. This technique is similar to the randomisation method proposed in [103] (explained above).

Isomorphism is a one-to-one correspondence between all the elements of two sets such that any operation returns the same result on either set ... – Wiktionary

All of the data masking techniques for AES presented here are vulnerable to second-order or higher-order Differential Power Analysis (DPA) attacks. Saying that, it is indeed very hard to perform a successful higher-order DPA attack in a real implementation where the adversary needs to identify the footprint of mask operations in the power profile [180]. The higher-order DPA attacks are discussed in Chapter 2.

3.1.1.3 Masking RSA

The exponentiation process in RSA (i.e., encrypting message M using secret key d, and public modulus N: M^e mod N) is attacked by Messerges et al. [155] using Differential Power Analysis (DPA) as explained in Chapter 2. The Authors proposed a data masking countermeasure in RSA (called *blinding*) to mask the exponentiation based on the solution proposed in [130]. The blinding approach of Messerges et al. [155] is explained as follows:

1. blind the message M: $\hat{M} = (v_i M)$ mod N; where v_i is the random value, the public modulus $N = pq$;

2. blind the exponent e: $\hat{e} = e + r\phi(N)$; where $\phi(N) = (p - 1)(q - 1)$ & r a random number;

3. perform exponentiation: $\hat{S} = (\hat{M}^{\hat{e}})$ mod N;

4. unblind the result: $S = (v_f \hat{S})$ mod N; where $v_f = (v_i^{-1})^e$ mod N.

The authors stated that another countermeasure to protect RSA could be to randomise the exponentiation algorithm by selecting a random starting point in the exponentiation. For example, the square and multiply algorithm [206] could be started at random points by triggering the loop from a randomly chosen bit. According to Messerges et al. [155], this randomisation prevents the attacker from performing Simple Power Analysis (SPA) which makes it harder for the adversary to discover the starting point of the exponentiation from a single power trace. Blinding in RSA is also explained by Boneh [43]. Itoh et al. [110] noted that blinding for RSA provides enough security. Kaminaga et al. [118] identified that the blinding proposed by Messerges et al. [155] for RSA (explained above) is still vulnerable to BigMac attacks [240] and Template attacks [55], which are explained in Chapter 2. The BigMac attack [240] performs an averaging over multiple executions where a conventional blinding is not adequate and the Template attack [55] can be prevented only when the calculated value itself is blinded [118]. Based on these vulnerabilities in the blinding approach, Kaminaga et al. [118] proposed an improved blinding approach by dividing the secret exponent and randomising the processing order, especially to prevent from template attacks.

Figure 3.7 depicts the masking algorithm proposed by Kaminaga et al. [118]. Main points to note in the algorithm are the division of the secret exponent d into two separate components

```
Input: y, d, N
Output: y^d mod N
setup:
    w = rand; (< N)
    y'_j = y^j · w^{-3} mod N;   (j = 0, 1, 2, 3)
    d' = d + rand · φ(N)
    d_0 = rand; (≤ d')
    d_1 = d' - d_0;
    v = rand; (L(v) = L(d'), H(v) = L(v)/2)
main:
    u_0 = u_1 = L(d_0)/2 - 1;
    S_0 = S_1 = w;
    for (j = L(v) - 1 ; j ≥ 0 ; j = j - 1){
        S = S_{v[j]};      ······(2-1)
        S = S^4 mod N; or  { S = S^2 mod N;
                           { S = S^2 mod N;
        switch (d_{v[j]}[u_{v[j]}]){
            case 00: S = S · y'_0 mod N;
            case 01: S = S · y'_1 mod N;
            case 10: S = S · y'_2 mod N;
            case 11: S = S · y'_3 mod N;
        }
        S_{v[j]} = S;      ······(2-2)
        u_{v[j]} = u_{v[j]} - 1;
    }
    S = S_0 · S_1 mod N;
    S = S · w^{-1} mod N;
    return S;
```

Figure 3.7: Masked modular exponentiation [118]

d_0 and d_1 using a random value, and the usage of another random value v to randomise the processing order of S_0 and S_1, processes associated with d_0 and d_1 respectively. $H(x)$ denotes the Hamming weight of x and $L(x)$ indicates the bit length of x. The values d_0 and d_1 are padded with 0's to have equal bit lengths. The *switch* statement in Figure 3.7 executes different exponentiations decided using the random value v. Diving the exponent to prevent power analysis was already proposed by Clavier and Joye [62]. Kaminaga et al. [118] used this division method in their technique as shown in Figure 3.7, but realised that Clavier and Joye [62] did not explain the switching of processes in an actual implementation. Hence, Kaminaga et al. [118] implemented their improved blinding technique shown in Figure 3.7 on an AE45C microcontroller with switching methods between processes S_0 and S_1, which are securely mapped in the memory. For a 1024-bit modular exponentiation, the implementation cost double in processing time compared to the unmasked approach (without any countermeasure applied). The template attack on the unmasked and masked implementations are presented in Figure 3.8. The implementation without any countermeasure successfully reveals the exponent value, where the second template from the top is matched with the waveform taken from the target chip. The masked implementation of the algorithm explained in Figure 3.7 does not allow the adversary to create templates with unique variations, when the templates are indistinguishable for different exponents as shown in Figure 3.8(b).

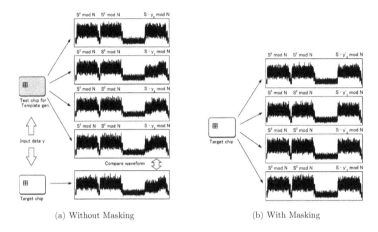

(a) Without Masking   (b) With Masking

Figure 3.8: Template attack on the implementations [118]

As shown in Figure 3.8, the template attack fails in the masked approach of Kaminaga et al. [118]. However, the authors claimed that they would not be able to verify their technique against BigMac attacks [240]. Mentens et al. [150] designed a Public Key Cryptography (PKC) coprocessor and implemented it in the XC3S5000 FPGA, including the masking approach presented above.

3.1.1.4   Masking ECC

Power analysis during the computation $Q = dP$ in Elliptic Curve Cryptography (ECC) is exploited to predict the secret component d as explained in Chapter 2. One of the first masking countermeasures on this ECC vulnerability is by Coron [65], who applied data masking using random numbers into the computation of $Q = dP$. Three main countermeasures are proposed by the author as follows:

1. **randomisation of the private exponent:**

   In a computation $Q = dP$; d is the private exponent, P is a point in an ECC curve. $\#\mathcal{E}$ is the number of points in the curve.

   (i) select a random number k of n bits.

110

(ii) compute $d' = d + k.\#\mathcal{E}$.

(iii) compute the point $Q = d'P$.

The required point $Q = dP$ is still obtained since $\#\mathcal{E}P = \mathcal{O}$, where $\mathcal{O}$ is the point at infinity. This technique prevents the adversary from realising the secret exponent because d' changes for each execution.

2. **blinding the point** P:

This method is influenced by the signature blinding technique proposed in [57] for RSA.

(i) select a secret random point R and precompute $S = dR$. S and R are stored inside the card and refreshed for each execution, computing $R \leftarrow (-1)^b 2R$ and $S \leftarrow (-1)^b 2S$, where b is a random bit generated at the start of each execution of the ECC program.

(ii) compute the scalar multiplication $Q = d(R + P)$.

(iii) subtract $S = dR$ to extract the required value $Q = dP$.

This technique prevents power analysis since the point $P' = P + R$, which is multiplied by d, is not known to the adversary.

3. **randomise Projective Coordinates:**

Projective coordinates [8, 148] are used in addition and doubling in ECC, where a point $P = (x, y)$ is defined using projective coordinates (X,Y,Z) as; $x = \frac{X}{Z}$ and $y = \frac{Y}{Z}$. The projective coordinates are not unique because, $(X,Y,Z) = (\lambda X, \lambda Y, \lambda Z)$, for every $\lambda \neq 0$. Hence, the projective coordinates of P are randomised with a random value λ for every execution of $Q = dP$. This makes the power analysis infeasible.

Coron [65] further states that all the above countermeasures to protect ECC are easy to implement and do not cost much in efficiency. However, the author realises that it cannot be guaranteed that these countermeasures could prevent all types of power analysis attacks. It seems that none of the countermeasures of Coron [65] are implemented and proved as secure. Okeya and Sakurai [175] investigated the masking countermeasures proposed by Coron [65] (explained above) for weaknesses and vulnerabilities. According to the authors, the randomisation of the private component (computing $d'P$) assumes that the inside scalar multiplication algorithm is secure for Simple Power Analysis (SPA). If this assumption is not true, the adversary can perform an attack by observing the execution order of the additions and doublings on the inside scalar multiplication which computes $d'P$. Similar vulnerability is also found in the *blinding of point* P solution of Coron [65], where this countermeasure requires an SPA immune algorithm [175]. Okeya and Sakurai [175] further performed an attack on this countermeasure exploiting the fact that the random point R has less number of candidates, and thus has a limited number of possibilities for R after many executions. The *randomising the project coordinates* solution is also identified as vulnerable as it requires an SPA immune algorithm and the performance of this countermeasure is significantly low compared to other methods [175]. Based on these drawbacks and vulnerabilities of the countermeasures from Coron [65], Okeya and Sakurai [175] presented an improved masking scheme for ECC using a faster scalar multiplication algorithm. The improved algorithm uses projective coordinates, as used by Coron [65], which are applicable to any Montgomery-like scalar multiplications. The Montgomery-form elliptic curve performs one addition and one doubling, without regarding whether the specific bit is 0 or 1 [173]. Interested readers are referred to [161] for more details on Montgomery multiplication and the definitions of Montgomery scalar multiplications can be found in [173]. The masking algorithm of Okeya and Sakurai [175] is presented in Figure 3.9, where a faster scalar multiplication dP is performed. The operations on the elliptic curves are done in projective coordinates, by choosing a random value for k every time the algorithm is executed. Another main point to note in the algorithm is the *Substitute m for 2m* part which refers the substitutions of the pair of points $(mP,(m+1)P)$ by the pair $(2mP,(2m+1)P)$.

INPUT a scalar value d and a point $P = (x, y)$.
OUTPUT the scalar multiplication dP.

1. Generate a random number k.
2. Express the point $P = (kx, ky, k)$ using projective coordinates.
3. $i \leftarrow |d| - 1$
4. Calculate the point $2P$ from the point P.
5. $m \leftarrow 1$
6. If i is equal to 0 then go to 15. Otherwise go to 7.
7. $i \leftarrow i - 1$
8. If d_i is equal to 0 then go to 9. If it is equal to 1 then go to 12.
9. Calculate the point $(2m+1)P$. That is, add the point mP and the point $(m+1)P$.
10. Calculate the point $2mP$. That is, double the point mP.
11. Substitute m for $2m$, and go to 6.
12. Calculate the point $(2m+1)P$. That is, add the point mP and the point $(m+1)P$.
13. Calculate the point $(2m+2)P$. That is, double the point $(m+1)P$.
14. Substitute m for $2m + 1$, and go to 6.
15. Output the point mP as the scalar multiplication dP.

Figure 3.9: Masked faster scalar multiplication [175]

Okeya and Sakurai [175] claim that their masking scalar multiplication algorithm, shown in Figure 3.9, performs addition first and then doubling for all the cases, making the execution order of the operations invariant. Since the scalar value has no correlation with the execution order, the authors argue that their technique is resistant to power analysis, especially DPA. The technique of randomising the projective coordinates prevents the adversary from correlating the intermediate values with the expressions, because the point P is randomised right from the start of the algorithm as shown in Figure 3.9. Okeya et al. [174] further improved this algorithm to reduce the computational cost. The improved scalar multiplication algorithm using the randomised projective coordinates [174] computes an operation of points with randomised expression and points without randomised expressions, thus reducing the computational cost while maintaining the same degree of security against power analysis. This scalar multiplication using projective coordinates in Montgomery form [174] is claimed as the fastest technique compared to the countermeasures [65, 116, 117, 139] proposed for power analysis on the other type of Elliptic Curves.

Hasan [102] presented masking countermeasures to prevent Koblitz curve [125] scalar multiplication $Q = kP$ from Differential Power Analysis (DPA) attacks. Koblitz Curves (KCs) [125], defined as $y^2 + xy = x^3 + ax^2 + 1$, are a special class of Elliptic Curves (ECs) where the definition of ECs ($y^2 + xy = x^3 + ax^2 + b$) is substituted by $b = 1$. Three countermeasures are proposed by Hasan [102] for masking KCs. Detailed explanations on these countermeasures can be referred in the paper [102]. The countermeasures are briefly as follows:

1. **Key Masking with Localised Operations (KMLO):**

   Due to the nature of KCs and by changing the value of a in the equation $y^2 + xy = x^3 + ax^2 + 1$, the secret symbol k can be given a window of values. For example, for $a = 1$, the symbol k_i (secret component k of size n is replaced with $k(\mathrm{mod}\ \tau^n - 1)$) can be given in the range of [-2,2] where,

   $$Q = \left(\sum_{i=0}^{n-1} k_i \tau^i \right) P \equiv \left(\sum_{i=0}^{n-1} \hat{k}_i \tau^i \right) P, \text{ and } \hat{k}_i = k_i \pm 2.$$

2. **Random Rotation of Key (RRK):**

   Let $P' = \tau^r P$, where r is a random integer. Hence,

   $$Q = kP = \left(\sum_{i=0}^{n-1} k_i \tau^i \right) P = \left(\sum_{i=0}^{n-1} k_{(r-1-i)\ \mathrm{mod}\ n} \tau^i \right) P'$$

   P' is computed before the start of the program execution without revealing r against power analysis.

3. **Random Insertion of Redundant Symbols (RIRS):**

   The main idea of this method is to insert redundant symbols k_i at random locations in the secret key sequence, making sure they collectively nullify their own effects. An N bit random number is generated for the implementation and there are a total of n' redundant symbols which are paired. Then these redundant pairs are inserted at the location of 1's in N.

Hasan [102] claimed that these countermeasures are less complex to implement in Koblitz curve based cryptosystems [125], nevertheless, the author failed to experiment with the countermeasures against a real power analysis attack. Möller [159] states that the countermeasures of Coron [65], blending random values into various components in the point multiplication (i.e., $Q = dP$), prevents the system from DPA, however, they will not provide sufficient protection in ECC algorithms when SPA is possible. Joye and Tymen [117] presented masking countermeasures in ECC by exploiting the isomorphic nature of Elliptic Curves (ECs). The masked scalar multiplication $Q = kP$ is computed as shown in Equation 3.3, where φ is a random isomorphism of an Elliptic Curve.

$$\mathbf{Q} = \varphi^{-1}(k(\varphi(\mathbf{P}))); \quad [117] \tag{3.3}$$

Figure 3.10 depicts the scalar multiplication algorithm of Joye and Tymen [117] which uses the random isomorphisms $E'(\mathbb{K})$ of an Elliptic Curve $E(\mathbb{K})$ to prevent power analysis. As illustrated in Figure 3.10, a random point $\mathbf{P'}$ is chosen and the point $\mathbf{Q'}$ in the Elliptic Curve $E'(\mathbb{K})$ is computed by multiplying with k. The point $\mathbf{O}$ is the *point at infinity*. The authors claim that this algorithm is faster since a point with Z-coordinate equals to 1 is chosen, as shown in Step 2 of the algorithm in Figure 3.10. Joye and Tymen [117] further extended this technique by randomising both the x and y coordinates of point $\mathbf{P}$ and developed a scalar multiplication algorithm using *randomised isomorphic fields*. Interested readers are referred to the paper [117] for more information.

Blake et al. [40] proposed a signed windows algorithm to express k, which is used to multiply the fixed point P (i.e., kP) using a lookup table of the point multiples; $P_i = [2i + 1]P$. Equation 3.4 shows the conversion of k into a pair of metrics $b_i \in \{-2^{R-1} + 1, -2^{R-1} +$

```
Input:   A point P = (x₁, y₁) ∈ E(K) with E/K : y² = x³ + ax + b.
         An integer k.
Output: The point Q = kP.
1. Randomly choose an element u ∈ K*;
2. Form the point P' ← (u⁻² x₁, u⁻³ y₁);
3. Evaluate a' ← u⁻⁴ a;
4. Compute Q' ← kP' in E'(K) with E'/K : y² = x³ + a'x + b';¹
5. If (Q' = O) then return Q = O and stop. Otherwise set Q' ← (x'₃, y'₃);
6. Return Q = (u² x'₃, u³ y'₃).
```

Figure 3.10: Scalar multiplication using randomised isomorphisms of ECC [117]

$3,...., 2^{R-1} - 3, 2^{R-1} - 1\}$ and $e_i \in \mathbb{Z}_{\geq 0}$.

$$k = \sum_{i=0}^{d-1} b_i 2^{e_i}; \quad [139] \tag{3.4}$$

Liardet and Smart [139] analysed this window algorithm of Blake et al. [40] and realised that it uses a fixed window length for k, where $e_{i+1} - e_i \geq R$. Hence, the authors [139] presented a randomised Signed Window Method as presented in Figure 3.11, which receives a number k as an input and generates a sequence of pairs for (b_i, e_i). The only difference of this randomised algorithm with the traditional one from [40] is line 5, where $\leftarrow R$ denotes a random assignment to the variable r from the set on the right. The authors claimed that the randomised window algorithm in Figure 3.11 would provide a more difficult target for power analysis attacks. However, this technique is not implemented in a real attack.

Signed m-ary Window Decomposition

```
INPUT:   An integer k = ∑_{j=0}^{ℓ} k_j 2^j, k_j ∈ {0,1}, k_ℓ = 0.
OUTPUT: A sequence of pairs {(bᵢ, eᵢ)}_{i=0}^{d-1} .

1.    d ← 0, j ← 0.
2.    While j ≤ ℓ do:
3.        If k_j = 0 then j ← j + 1.
4.        Else do:
5.            r ← _R {1, ..., R}.
6.            t ← min{ℓ, j + r - 1}, h_d ← (k_t k_{t-1} ⋯ k_j)₂.
7.            If h_d > 2^{r-1} then do:
8.                b_d ← h_d - 2^r ,
9.                increment the number (k_ℓ k_{ℓ-1} ⋯ k_{t+1})₂ by 1.
10.           Else b_d ← h_d.
11.           e_d ← j, d ← d + 1, j ← t + 1.
12.   Return the sequence (b_0, e_0), (b_1, e_1), ..., (b_{d-1}, e_{d-1}).
```

Figure 3.11: randomised Signed Windows Algorithm [139]

Oswald and Aigner [178] argued that the randomisation and blinding countermeasures presented above for ECC require additional parameters to be stored or to perform additional operations. The authors analysed the survey by Gordon [95] on efficient implementations to perform scalar multiplications of elliptic curve points using the binary algorithm. Based on their analysis, Oswald and Aigner [178] proposed a countermeasure for power analysis to randomise the binary algorithm itself. Figure 3.12 shows an example of the randomisation of the binary algorithm [178] which takes a path from one state to the other (states are represented in circles) based on a random value e. The randomised paths in Figure 3.12 are drawn in dash-dotted lines and all the multipliers are designed to have only one double or one double and one add (or subtract). The authors state that due to randomisation, the intermediate values that are attacked are computed at different times or not calculated at all, thus preventing DPA. However, Oswald and Aigner [178] realise that this technique is vulnerable to SPA, if there exists a distinction between double and add (or subtract). This randomisation of the binary algorithm [178] required 9% in the additional number of operations regardless of the keylength.

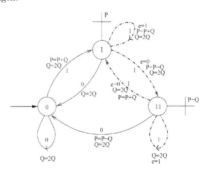

Figure 3.12: randomised Binary Algorithm [178]

The randomised binary algorithm of Oswald and Aigner [178] is attacked by Shi and Zhang [209, 251] exploiting the difference between the doubling and the addition operations in the power profile. An SPA is used for the attack to identify the bits computed based on the operations sequence. Walter [239] stated that *key blinding* in the ECC proposed by Coron [65] (explained earlier in this section) only helps if more than one decryption power profile is required for key recovery. The *message blinding* countermeasure for the ECC of Coron [65] is also realised as only helpful against chosen ciphertexts [239].

As can be seen from the above explanations of the masking countermeasures, ECC is the most popular encryption program addressed using masking techniques. More algorithmic modifications in ECC to protect against power analysis are presented in Section 3.3.

3.1.2 SBOX Masking

SBOX is a fixed or a dynamic mapping table which returns values for cipher text based on the plain text and decides the strength of a symmetric encryption algorithm. Most of the Differential Power Analysis (DPA) attacks utilise the SBOX accesses in the power profile (DES SBOX [86, 127], AES SBOX [44, 94]), because they provide enough power variations of different data values for key prediction. For example, Figure 3.13 presents a brief introduction in performing Differential Power Analysis (DPA) using SBOX accesses, where the inputs are fed into the system and the power traces are collected. Using the inputs and guessing a possible key value, the cryptographic algorithm in use is simulated and the output values from an SBOX are computed. Based on one of the bit values of the output (it is the least significant bit b in Figure 3.13) the power traces are placed in two different sets: Set 0, input and key generating bit $b = 0$ and Set 1, input and key generating bit $b = 1$. The highest peak produced using the mean difference between these two sets is identified as it corresponds to the correct key guess. Hence, the operations performed in SBOXes are visible for the adversary in the power profile to experiment such a DPA attack. More details on DPA can be found in Chapter 2.

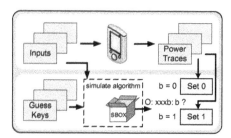

Figure 3.13: Differential Power Analysis using SBOX access

Masking the SBOX accesses in the power profile combats many DPA attacks. The author presents the masking techniques proposed for Data Encryption Standard (DES) and Advanced Encryption Standard (AES) block ciphers, since they are the most popularly used symmetrical algorithms in embedded systems. Similar countermeasures can be also applied to other block ciphers.

3.1.2.1 Masking DES SBOX

The first SBOX masking technique is proposed by Goubin and Patarin [97] in DES (called the *Duplication method*), where the inputs and the outputs of the SBOX are masked by dividing the standard SBOX into two different SBOXes. Figure 3.14 depicts a standard SBOX (S) access in DES which reveals the input v and the output $v' = S(v)$, providing sufficient signatures for the adversary in the power profile at those instances. According to Goubin and Patarin [97], these predictable values v and v' appear in RAM (Random Access Memory) at some point of time in the DES program execution.

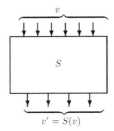

Figure 3.14: The Standard SBOX access in DES [97]

The standard SBOX access in DES uses 6 bits input and produces a 4 bits output as shown in Figure 3.14. Goubin and Patarin [97] modified this vulnerable SBOX (S) implementation into two SBOXes as shown in Figure 3.15. The modified SBOXes (S_1' and S_2') are designed to output 4 bits each by taking in a 12 bits input. As illustrated in Figure 3.15, the modified implementation does not reveal the proper input $v = v_1 \oplus v_2$ and the proper output $v' = v_1' \oplus v_2'$. S_1' uses a randomly chosen secret transformation $A(v_1, v_2)$. Since the modified SBOX access involves random values, the authors claim that there will not be any correlation between the actual operation and the power profile, thus preventing DPA. Further, the computation $v_1 \oplus v_2$ is also avoided with the use of two SBOXes [97].

Goubin and Patarin [97] realised that the modified SBOX implementation shown in Figure 3.15 consumes too much memory (except if it is implemented in DES hardware), and thus is not suitable for smartcards. Hence, the authors proposed another SBOX masking implementation, which is presented in Figure 3.16. This improved SBOX masking approach uses two SBOXes (S_1' and S_2') which receive a 6 bits common input $v_0 = \varphi(v_1 \oplus v_2)$ and produces 4 bits outputs ($v_1' = A(v_0)$ and $v_2' = S(\varphi^{-1}(v_0)) \oplus A(v_0)$). φ is a bijective and a secret function

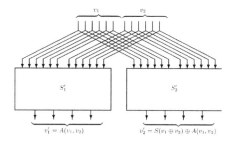

Figure 3.15: The first modified implementation of the SBOX [97]

from 6 bits to 6 bits and A is a random and a secret transformation from 6 bits to 4 bits. Suitable candidates for φ are discussed in the paper [97]. The proper input v and the proper output v' as in the standard SBOX lookup presented in Figure 3.14 are also not revealed in the improved version shown in Figure 3.16.

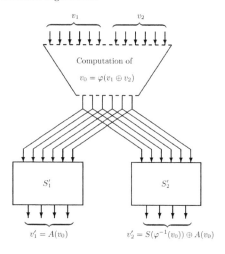

Figure 3.16: The second modified implementation of the SBOX [97]

bijection *is a function f from a set X to a set Y with the property that, for every y in Y, there is exactly one x in X such that f(x) = y... – Reference.com*

119

Both the SBOX masking approaches (shown in Figure 3.15 and Figure 3.16) prevent the DES encryption from Differential Power Analysis (DPA). Goubin and Patarin [97] performed a DPA attack (defined in the paper) on the second (i.e., improved) masked SBOX implementation presented in Figure 3.16. Figure 3.17 depicts the DPA traces on the masked SBOX implementation, where Figure 3.17(a) refers to an incorrect key guess and Figure 3.17(b) is produced for the correct key guess. As from these two traces and from the other 62 traces (i.e., altogether 64 traces for a 6 bits subkey guess) the authors conclude that the trace corresponding to the correct key guess is not *very special* compared to the others, thus the masked SBOX implementation combats DPA.

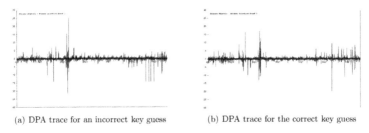

(a) DPA trace for an incorrect key guess   (b) DPA trace for the correct key guess

Figure 3.17: DPA attack on the Masked SBOX implementation [97]

Daemen et al. [70] investigated the *Duplication* method of Goubin and Patarin [97], presented above, for limitations and weaknesses. The authors [70] observed that the *Duplication* method does not guarantee decorrelation between operands and intermediate state values. According to Daemen et al. [70], chosing a random function A, as presented in Figure 3.15, is very unlikely to cause decorrelation between the bits of v'_1, v'_2 and v. Peeters et al. [188] considered an SBOX masking approach as shown in Figure 3.18, where the standard SBOX S performs a lookup using a random value r XORed together with the input b and the key k. Another precomputed SBOX S' is used such that $S(b \oplus k \oplus r) = S(b \oplus k) \oplus S'(r, b \oplus k \oplus r) = S(b \oplus k) \oplus q$. The precomputed SBOX S' takes in the random value r and the input fed to the standard SBOX S and outputs q as illustrated in Figure 3.18. Hence, the output q is combined with the output of the standard SBOX to produce the standard output $S(b \oplus k)$. The authors performed a second-order DPA on this SBOX masking countermeasure and successfully attacked the secret key k (the attack is discussed in Chapter 2). Karlof and Wagner [119] also performed a DPA attack on the SBOX masking countermeasure presented in Figure 3.18.

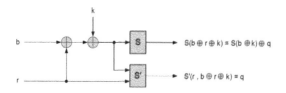

Figure 3.18: Masking of SBOX access [188]

Gebotys [86] proposed an SBOX masking countermeasure for DES (called *table* masking). Figure 3.19 depicts this masking countermeasure, where the left half shows DES without the masking countermeasure. The *table* masking countermeasure [86] works as follows: a masked SBOX table $S'[x] = S[x] \oplus r[x]$ is generated by combining the standard SBOX table $S[x]$ and a random data $r[x]$ which is different for each table address x. A corresponding mask table $M[x]$ is used to store the corresponding masks for each address, such that the XOR of random data and the mask table value is a fixed value $m = r[x] \oplus M[x]$. However, the author articulates that the m is always split into two values $r[x]$ and $M[x]$, and is never computed, thus avoiding first-order DPA.

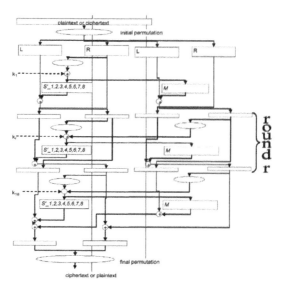

Figure 3.19: Table masking in DES [86]

121

The *table* masking [86] shown in Figure 3.19 uses the masked SBOX tables S'_1,2,3,4,5,6,7,8 providing both SBOX substitution and P-box permutation (refer to [63] for more details on DES and note that there are 8 SBOXes in DES). The oval shapes in Figure 3.19 represent the permutations and the rectangular boxes refer to the inputs and outputs of each round. A single mask table M is used. It is assumed, in the experiments of Gebotys [86], that the round key k_1 is masked and the L and R boxes to the right of Figure 3.19 are filled with zeroes at the start. This *table* masking [86] employs dynamic updation on the masking tables using random values and the masking tables $S'[x]$ and $M[x]$ are refreshed for each DES execution. The author performed first-order DPA attacks on an ARM7TDMI evaluation board, executing DES encryption with and without the masking countermeasure. Figure 3.20 presents these first-order DPA plots against possible round key guesses, produced by attacking the SBOX lookup at the store operation of the first round in DES. As shown in Figure 3.20(a) the correct key guess is identified (a significant peak) when no masking is implemented. The DPA trace when *table* masking is implemented, as shown in Figure 3.20(b), does not reveal a significant peak at the correct key guess, thus preventing DPA.

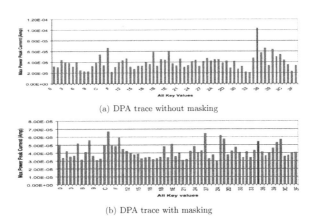

(a) DPA trace without masking

(b) DPA trace with masking

Figure 3.20: DPA attack on table masking in DES [86]

From the DPA traces shown in Figure 3.20, Gebotys [86] concludes that the *table* masking countermeasure presented in Figure 3.19 combats DPA attacks, costing less energy overheads compared to the other solutions.

3.1.2.2 Masking AES SBOX

The SubBytes operation in the AES cryptosystem (explained in [167]) involves SBOX lookups, which receive inputs and produce outputs based on a mapping table in the SBOX. Messerges [153] proposed an easier way of masking an SBOX by using an input mask r_{in} and an output mask r_{out}. The author derived a boolean masked SBOX (table) T' in terms of the standard SBOX T, the random masks r_{in} and r_{out} as shown in Equation 3.5. An input is masked with r_{in} and fed into the masked table T', which produces the masked output using r_{out}. According to the author, the random values r_{in} and r_{out} can be generated at the start of the AES execution and the masked table is constructed then stored in RAM (Random Access Memory).

$$T'[x] = T[x \oplus r_{in}] \oplus r_{out}; \quad [153] \tag{3.5}$$

Trichina [229] claims that the SBOX masking of Messerges [153] shown in Equation 3.5 consumes too much space for the precomputed tables and requires a significant amount of precomputation time. Hence, Trichina et al. [232] proposed an algorithm to perform the table generation on-the-fly, which is also stated as time consuming since it has to be performed 16 times per round [229]. Itoh et al. [109] also presented a similar SBOX masking scheme in AES (called *random value masking*) as shown in Figure 3.21, where random values RK_i are created and the masked SBOX is updated using the masked input RIN. The *RandomSboxUpdate* operation also uses a random number generator to produce random output masks $ROUT$ (refer to Equation 3.5). As Figure 3.21 depicts, the *ByteSub_RM* operation performs table lookups from the masked SBOXes stored inside RAM.

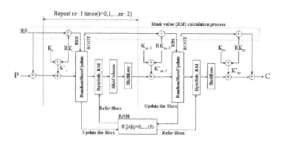

Figure 3.21: Random value masking in AES SBOX [109]

Itoh et al. [109] also argued that the random value masking in SBOX (presented in Figure 3.21) incurs a high processing overhead for the SBOX updation in each round. An excessive memory consumption in RAM is also observed in the random value masking approach to store the masked SBOXes [109]. Gebotys [86] states that the masking approach of Itoh et al. [109] uses the same random mask input RIN for a masked SBOX. Hence, the author in [86] proposes a better SBOX masking countermeasure (called *table* masking, similar to the one presented for DES as explained earlier), which exercises different random masks for each addressed data in the table. Figure 3.22 depicts the *table* masking countermeasure in Rijndael (i.e., AES) proposed by Gebotys [86], where a masked SBOX table Si' ($S'[x] = S[x] \oplus r[x]$) and a separate masked table Mi ($m = r[x] \oplus M[x]$) are created for each SBOX (note that there are four SBOXes in AES [167]). $r[x]$ is a random value and m is a fixed value. The round key rk_i is XORed at the end of the segment. Gebotys [86] proved that this *table* masking countermeasure in AES (shown in Figure 3.22) is secure against Differential Electro Magnetic Analysis (DEMA). Consequently, the author claims that the *table* masking is also immune to Differential Power Analysis (DPA), since the electro magnetic emmission from a chip is proportional to the power consumption. Interested readers are referred to [86] for the DEMA technique and its traces.

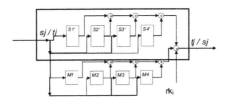

Figure 3.22: Partial Rijndael implementation with table masking [86]

The data masking countermeasures for AES presented in Section 3.1.1 attempt to mask the actual data throughout the algorithm, thus not revealing the expected intermediate values to the adversary in the power profile. However, performing such a complete masking in the SubByte operation of AES [167] involves certain modifications in the SBOX lookup process. A SubByte transformation in AES involves an inversion of data in GF(2^8) then an affine transformation to produce the SBOX output.

A Galois field (GF) or Finite field is a field that contains only

finitely many elements... - PlanetMath.org

A masked value using a random mask $X_{i,j}$ on an input $A_{i,j}$ to a SubByte transformation has to also go through an inversion in $GF(2^8)$ and then the affine transformation f, as shown in Figure 3.23. The main problem for masking to solve here is to obtain $A_{i,j}^{-1} \oplus X_{i,j}$ without compromising the 8-bit value $A_{i,j}$ using a modified inversion in $GF(2^8)$. This is solved using a multiplicative masking method as presented in Figure 3.24, where another non-zero random mask $Y_{i,j}$ is included in the computation. $\otimes$ represents multiplication of two numbers and $\oplus$ represents XOR between two values.

Figure 3.23: SubByte transformation with masking [23]

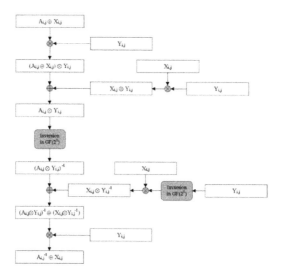

Figure 3.24: Modified inversion in $GF(2^8)$ with masking [23]

Golic and Tymen [94] observed a weakness in the masking approach of Akkar and Giraud

[23] where the multiplicative mask shown in Figure 3.24 does not mask all-zero byte value of data (i.e., the all-zero intermediate byte value remains unchanged after masking). Hence, Golic and Tymen [94] claim that the DPA attack (first-order) in the first round of AES using the SBOX output bits is still possible in the masking approach of [23] by targeting the all-zero input bytes or the all-zero output bytes (also called a *zero attack* [232]). Based on such a vulnerability of multiplicative masking for DPA, the authors in [94] proposed an improved multiplicative masking approach (which they call an approximate, nonideal solution), which maps the zero intermediate value to a random value. Trichina et al. [232] proposed an improved solution of the same idea of Akkar and Giraud [23] (presented in Figure 3.3) by reducing the number of field operations while maintaining the security against *zero attack*. Wolkerstorfer et al. [243] presented an ASIC (Application Specific Integrated Circuit) implementation of masked AES SBOXes. Oswald et al. [181] analysed all these above SBOX implementations in AES, which use multiplicative masking, and proposed a better countermeasure to prevent *zero attack* [232] with a relatively smaller implementation than the previous explained techniques. The authors use additive masks to all the intermediate values as well as the input and the output for the inversion in the SubByte operation in AES (gate level details of this implementation are referred to in the paper [181]). Figure 3.25 depicts the comparison performed by Oswald et al. [181] with respect to the area-time (AT) product of the SBOX implementations quoted above.

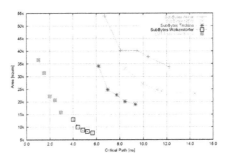

Figure 3.25: Comparison of different SBOX implementations [181]

Based on the SBOX comparisons in Figure 3.25, Oswald et al. [181] claim that their approach (denoted as SubBytes NEW) is better than the design of Akkar and Giraud [23] (denoted as SubBytes Akkar), but less efficient than the design of Trichina et al. [232] (denoted as **SubBytes Trichina**). However, the SubBytes NEW technique is immune to *zero attack* [232], whereas **SubBytes Trichina** is not. The LUT based design analysed in Figure 3.25 refers to the SubBytes implementation using Look-Up-Tables (LUTs). An optimised hardware implementation of SBOX in AES is presented in [205], where the authors used the Itoh-Tsujii algorithm [111] for computing the multiplicative inverse in the finite field. Oswald et al. [182] analysed these multiplicative inverse approaches and proposed an easier, linear SBOX masking scheme by reducing the inversion of AES SBOX to GF(4). Oswald and Schramm [183] realised that previous SBOX masking countermeasures either required a huge space for lookup tables or consumed many operations. Hence, the authors presented a masking scheme for the AES software implementation that required relatively less tables and less operations. The proposed countermeasure of Oswald and Schramm [183] works on the fact that a non-zero element in a finite field can be inverted by computing the logarithm and exponentiating again with the negated logarithm. A Differential Power Analysis (DPA) is performed on the SBOX masking approach of Oswald and Schramm [183] implemented in a smartcard based on the 8-bit RISC (Reduced Instruction Set Computer) architecture, which proved that the implementation combats DPA. Corresponding DPA traces can be found in the paper [183].

Well known RISC families include DEC Alpha, ARC, ARM, AVR, MIPS, PA-RISC,
Power Architecture (including PowerPC), and SPARC... - Wiki

Courtois and Goubin [69] observed that all the previous SBOX masking techniques decomposed the inverse operation for the SBOX lookup (shown in Figure 3.23) into simpler operations. The authors proposed an algebraic masking method to perform the inversion in the SubByte operation of AES as a whole using a group of homographic transformations over the projective space. Interested readers are referred to the paper [69] for more details on this solution, since it involves several mathematical terms which are not related to this book.

3.1.3   Window Method

Itoh et al. [110] claimed that the exponent splitting for RSA [62] costs two times the normal computation. The authors also observed that the masking countermeasures proposed for Public Key Cryptosystems (PKCs) failed to address both RSA and ECC most of the time. For example, randomising the projective coordinates for ECC [65, 117, 174] cannot be applied to RSA. Hence, Itoh et al. [110] presented three DPA countermeasures to secure PKCs based on the window method [168]. According to the window method, a modular exponentiation can be carried out by dividing the exponent into certain sizes of windows and performing the exponentiation in iterations per window [168]. Figure 3.26 depicts the Overlapping Window Method (O-WM) of Itoh et al. [110], where the top part of the figure explains the algorithm and the bottom part explains the overview. As shown in the O-WM algorithm, the table is precomputed at the start using the input a, public modulus n and the bit size of the system k. The next step in O-WM is to create random numbers for the number of windows q and the bit length h_i between consecutive windows as shown in Figure 3.26. h is set a fixed value to protect against Simple Power Analysis (SPA), having multiplication and squaring in the square-and-multiply algorithm repeated in a constant pattern. d is the secret key and $u = log_2 d$. Random window values w_i are created using q and h_i. The final step in the O-WM algorithm is to perform the modular exponentiation using the precomputed table tab and the randomly chosen window w_i. An overview of the algorithm is presented in the bottom part of Figure 3.26.

The O-WM algorithm presented in Figure 3.26 masks the intermediate data by randomly choosing the windows in the encryption which use modular exponentiation. A key feature of the O-WM is the overlapping of random windows during computation. The second countermeasure of Itoh et al. [110] is called the randomised Table Window Method (RT-WM) which uses random values when precomputing tables. Another method called the Hybrid randomising Window Method (HR-WM) is proposed by combining O-WM and RT-WM. Interested readers are referred to the paper [110] for more details about these window masking techniques. Figure 3.27 illustrates the DPA attack performed by Itoh et al. [110] on normal window method ($4 - ary$: 4 bit d) and the Overlapping Window Method (O-WM) by guessing w_3 window with 20000 inputs and corresponding power measurements.

As the DPA attack in Figure 3.27 explains, the correct guess of w_3 shows significant visible

```
1: /* pre-computed table data making */
2: for (i = 0; i < 2^k; i + +) tab[i] = a^i  (mod n);
3: /* window w_i and overlapping length h_i making */
4: /* generate random number q and 0 < h_0, h_1, ..., h_{q-2} < k
5: which satisfy q × k + (h_0 + h_1 + ... h_s) = u.
6: For securing against SPA, h_i are recommended to be
7: the fixed value h ≥ k/2. */
8: (h_i, q) = GenRandom(); u' = u - k; dt_{q-1} = bit(d, u - 1, ... u');
9: for (i = 0; i < q - 1; i + +) {
10:    w_i = (Random number, max(0, dt_i - 2^{h_i} + 1) ≤ w_i ≤ dt_i);
11:    dt_{i+1} = (dt_i - w_i) × 2^{k-h_i} + bit(d, u' - 1, ..., u' - (k - h_i));
12:    u' = u' - (k - h_i);
13: }
14: w_{q-1} = dt_{q-1};
15: /* modular exponent process */
16: v = tab[w_0]; i = 1;
17: while (i < q) {
18:    v = v^{2^{k-h_i}}  (mod n); v = v × tab[w_i]  (mod n); i = i + 1;
19: }
20: Return(v);
```

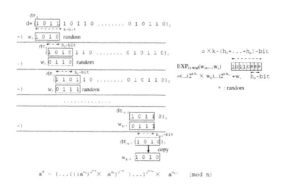

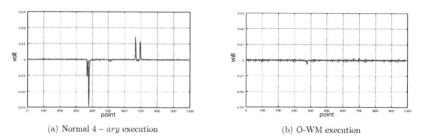

Figure 3.26: Overlapping Window Method (O-WM) [110]

(a) Normal 4 − *ary* execution (b) O-WM execution

Figure 3.27: DPA when guessing w_3 [110]

spikes in the DPA trace for the normal window method (Figure 3.27(a)). There are no such significant spikes observed from the DPA trace attacked on the O-WM countermeasure, as presented in Figure 3.27(b), proving that it is immune to DPA attacks. The authors conclude that their window method countermeasures (such as O-WM, RT-WM and HR-WM) cost 105%

in RSA and 119% in ECC for computation time compared to the normal window methods [168], but do not require any additional parameters like Coron's method [65] and are 13% faster than Messerges's countermeasure [155]. An SPA protection, by having constantly repeated square and multiply operations, is also an advantage in these window techniques [110].

3.2 Dummy Instruction Insertion

One of the earliest countermeasures to prevent power analysis, proposed by Kocher et al. [127], is to randomise the execution time. Chari et al. [53] claimed that countermeasures involving random delays (i.e., dummy instructions can be used to provide random delays in an execution) should be performed extensively, otherwise they can be undone and re-ordered, causing a successful attack. Daemen and Rijmen [71] consider the insertion of dummy instructions based on some modifying parameter to change the sequence of program execution every time. However, the authors realise that this desynchronisation could still be unfolded and it does not prevent Simple Power Analysis (SPA). Daemen and Rijmen [71] state that inserting dummy instructions is not an appropriate solution when each instruction has its own power profile and synchronisation is possible. Clavier et al. [61] name the dummy instruction execution to produce mismatch in the corresponding operation cycles to prevent Differential Power Analysis (DPA) as Random Process Interrupts (RPIs). RPIs are meant to cause random time shifts by not executing all the operations sequentially. According to the authors, these time shifts are just added noise in the normal execution increasing the samples needed for power analysis, but not making the attack theoretically infeasible. Clavier et al. [61] performed a successful DPA attack (called the Sliding Window DPA (*SW-DPA*) explained in Chapter 2) on a system using RPIs, nevertheless no details were provided on how the RPIs can be implemented (such as the type of dummy instructions used, consideration of pipelines, etc.). Coron and Goubin [68] addressed the countermeasure random time shifts stating that it is crucial to make sure that no statistical method will eliminate the dummy insertions. Mangard [144] also states that the countermeasure of random disarrangement in execution time could still be vulnerable to power analysis, where the adversary can approximate the random delays based on a software model of the countermeasure.

Brier and Joye [47] considered the double-and-add algorithm in ECC which proved vulnerable to SPA (explained in Chapter 2) due to the variation in execution based on a bit value.

The authors quoted the dummy operation insertion proposed by Coron [65] as a countermeasure for this vulnerability, where a dummy addition is suggested to be inserted for execution when no addition is performed (thus executing double and add all the time). Messerges et al. [156] specified that random delays causing random time shifts are feared to still be vulnerable for power analysis because of the possibility of removing the randomisation by the adversary. Gebotys and Gebotys [88] presented a redundant operation insertion technique to prevent power analysis attacks in a DSP processor core (SC140) executing Elliptic Curve implementations. The double-and-add algorithm in ECC is vulnerable to SPA, when the adversary identifies the secret key bits based on distinguishable power patterns for double and add (sum) operations (SPA attacks are explained in Chapter 2). Gebotys and Gebotys [88] observed that such a sum operation takes twice the number of clock cycles than the double operation. Hence the authors divided the sum operation into two sum operations *sum1* and *sum2*. This makes the operations *double*, *sum1* and *sum2*, have the same number of clock cycles. The authors realised that having the same number of clock cycles for all the operations was not enough to protect against power analysis, where the adversary can predict the operations based on different patterns they produce in a power profile by executing a different instruction sequence. To achieve this, redundant dummy instructions are added in each operation, when needed, to maintain the same operation sequence in *double*, *sum1* and *sum2*. Figure 3.28 shows the modified operations *double*, *sum1* and *sum2*, with dummy instructions inserted (variables starting with ___ or an underscore) to execute the same instruction sequence matching each line.

Based on the modified fixed instruction sequence for the operations *double*, *sum1* and *sum2*, Gebotys and Gebotys [88] claimed that the adversary would not be able to differentiate these operations from the power profile. This is proved in the power profile observed by the authors with and without the countermeasure as illustrated in Figure 3.29. The power trace without the countermeasure clearly reveals the double (*D*) and sum (*S*) operations, as shown in Figure 3.29(a), producing different patterns. Figure 3.29(b) depicts the power profile generated from the implementation with the fixed instruction sequence countermeasure (instructions shown in Figure 3.28) applied, where the patterns for double *D* and sum *S* (i.e., *sum1* and *sum1*) appear the same. Hence, this prevents the adversary from identifying the secret key bits by realising the operations executed in the power profile.

Double	Sum1	Sum2
b1 = y ^2	z2s = z2 ^2	hs = h ^2
e1 = z ^2	z1s = z1 ^2	om = j ^2
b2 = b1 * b1	z2c = z2s * z2	al = th * hs
b = b2<<3	__al=y2<<3	__th=y2<<3
__z2=y2 * x2	f = z1s * x2	la = h * hs
z31 = y * z	g = z2s * x1	th = la * i
e2 = x - e1	__th=x1-z1s	x3 = om - al
e3 = x + e1	__ga=x1+z1s	__be=al + om
e = e2 * e3	z1c = z1s * z1	z3 = ga * h
z12 = z31<<1	__om=g<<1	__al=hs<<1
c1 = e<<1	__ga=z1c<<1	__be=z3<<1
c = c1 + e	th = f + g	__om=be+z3
f1 = b1<<2	__al=z2s<<2	__ga=hs<<2
a = f1 * x	ga = z1 * z2	la = hs * g
f3 = a<<1	__la=ga<<1	__al=la<<1
d1 = c * c	i = y1 * z2c	__be=om*om
x12 = d1 - f3	__al=i-la	om = la -x3
y31 = a - x3	h = f - g	__ga=om-al
y32 = y31 * c	om = y2 * z1c	al = om * j
y12 = y32 - b	j = om - i	y3 = al - th

Figure 3.28: Redundant instruction insertion for fixed instruction sequence [88]

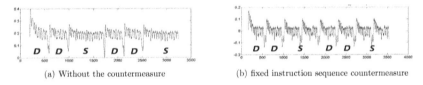

(a) Without the countermeasure   (b) fixed instruction sequence countermeasure

Figure 3.29: Power Traces in ECC double-and-add [88]

A similar dummy instruction insertion technique of Gebotys and Gebotys [88] is also investigated by Trichina and Bellezza [230], and Batina et al. [32] in ECC to execute a homogeneous
group of operations for double and add. Barbosa and Page [30] realised that creating such
indistinguishable functions, containing a fixed instruction sequence by hand is laborious and
error prone when the complexity of the algorithm increases. Hence, the authors proposed an
approach to automatically construct the indistinguishable functions using dummy instructions
to protect against Simple Power Analysis (SPA). Chevallier-Mames [59] presented a similar
dummy instruction insertion technique to prevent the square-and-multiply algorithm in RSA,
which has a similar SPA vulnerability to ECC (SPA attacks in RSA are explained in Chapter 2). Aciiçmez et al. [17] also emphasises that dummy operations can be inserted in RSA to
prevent SPA. Herbst et al. [103] discuss the possibility of inserting random dummy operations
which randomise the execution of the AES algorithm and prevent power analysis on a smart
card. According to the authors, the designer has to be very careful in choosing the dummy

instructions when they should not be distinguished from real operations. Herbst et al. [103] suggest adding additional rounds with dummy instructions at the beginning and at the end of the encryption algorithm.

David et al. [74] patented a random instruction injection technique, where a random number of *pseudo shift* instructions are injected within the SBOX lookup operations in DES to destroy the signatures and time patterns of the original program. Figure 3.30 depicts the block digram of the methodology of the random instruction injection proposed by David et al. [74]. A CPU fetches the instructions from ROM and RAM contains the data values. SP1 to SP8 denote the 8 SBOXes used in DES. The RIM control flag, which is connected to the CPU, as shown in Figure 3.30, is used to control the instruction injection and is set using a special instruction in the source code. The CPU is halted at random times when the RIM control flag is set and the pseudo dummy shift instructions are injected. The execution of the pseudo random shift instructions does not change the original data values in the program, when the program counter register is halted disabling the register updates in response to computations. There are two random number generators used, as shown in Figure 3.30: (1), a 1-bit generator, which is used to control the interval of instruction injection; (2), a 32-bit pseudo random generator, which is used to inject pseudo random shift instructions into a CPU. A multiplexor (MUX) is attached to switch between proper instructions from ROM and the pseudo random shift instructions. Another special instruction is used to stop the random instruction injection by clearing the RIM control flag.

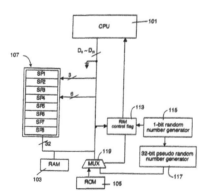

Figure 3.30: Block Diagram of Random Instruction Injection [74]

David et al. [74] claim that their random instruction injection technique, shown in Figure 3.30, thwarts Differential Power Analysis (DPA) attacks in DES. However, this random instruction injection [74] needs modification of the source code to indicate where to insert random instructions and to modify shift operations (for example, instead of shifting 8 places, use a loop to shift 1 place at a time and inject random instructions and then shift the other until you shift 8 times). This technique focuses only on shift operations, avoiding adversaries from detecting shifts. It also increases the code size by a significant amount if all of the shift operations need to be masked and there is a possibility that the adversary could still detect the other parts of the encryption block which are not masked.

Almost all the dummy instruction insertion methods emphasised in this section, except the ones from Gebotys and Gebotys [88] and David et al. [74], were just proposals and not implemented. Barrantes et al. [31] presented a randomised instruction set emulator to prevent against binary code injection attacks [176], where the byte code is individually scrambled using pseudo random numbers seeded with a random secret key. This technique can also be adapted to prevent power analysis attacks.

3.3   Code/Algorithm Modification

Public Key Cryptosystems like RSA and ECC have been severely attacked using Simple Power Analysis (SPA), which is explained in Chapter 2, mainly because of the conditional branching in the encryption. Such vulnerabilities in the program can be prevented by modifying the implementation or replacing it with a new algorithm to perform the same task. This section presents the algorithm modification techniques proposed to generate a power analysis immune code.

3.3.1   Constant Execution Path

When Kocher et al. [127] presented the power analysis in 1998, the authors observed that SPA can be prevented by avoiding routines which use secret intermediates or keys for conditional branching. Chari et al. [53] stated that the code execution path should be independent of the key and data to prevent the smartcard from SPA. Figure 3.31 depicts the presentation of Coron [65] on two different versions of the double-and-add algorithm used for ECC (Elliptic Curve Cryptography) encryption. The SPA vulnerable version of the double-and-add implementation is shown in Figure 3.31(a), where a conditional branching (the *if* statement) is performed based on the secret key bit values. Such conditional branches produce significant patterns in the power profile, thus revealing the bits to the adversary (a detailed explanation of SPA based on conditional branches can be found in Chapter 2). Coron [65] proposed to modify this code, which has conditional branches, into a constant path execution SPA immune code, as presented in Figure 3.31(b). Since there are no conditional branches and both double and add are performed independently of the key bits, the adversary will not be able to correlate the patterns in the power profile to predict the secret key.

input P
$Q \leftarrow P$
for i from $\ell - 2$ to 0 do
    $Q \leftarrow 2Q$
    if $d_i = 1$ then $Q \leftarrow Q + P$
output Q

(a) SPA vulnerable code

input P
$Q[0] \leftarrow P$
for i from $\ell - 2$ to 0 do
    $Q[0] \leftarrow 2Q[0]$
    $Q[1] \leftarrow Q[0] + P$
    $Q[0] \leftarrow Q[d_i]$
output $Q[0]$

(b) SPA immune code

Figure 3.31: Simple Power Analysis in Conditional Branching [65]

Several researchers [30, 102, 178] have emphasised the use of the constant path execution code, shown in Figure 3.31, to prevent the double-and-add algorithm from SPA. Huiping and Zhigang [105] proposed a similar constant path modification in RSA encryption to prevent the square-and-multiply algorithm from SPA (explained in Chapter 2). Chevallier-Mames [59] illustrated a slightly different modification to avoid conditional branching in square-and-multiply algorithms for RSA. Figure 3.32(a) represents the unprotected version of square-and-multiply algorithm for RSA, where a conditional branch (the *if* statement) is performed in each iteration based on the secret key bit d_i. The SPA resistant approach of Chevallier-Mames [59] is shown in Figure 3.32(b), which avoids a conditional branch by performing constant path iterations a greater number of times.

A similar constant path execution for RSA, as shown in Figure 3.32, is also considered by Giraud [93] for SPA resistance. Page and Stam [184] discussed the possibility of using the constant path execution algorithm, explained above for the XTR [138], a contender for ECC. The XTR encryption [138] is claimed as more efficient in terms of processing and requires less bandwidth compared to ECC, and thus is a better candidate for smart cards [184].

Input: $x, d = (d_{m-1}, \ldots, d_0)_2$	Input: $x, d = (d_{m-1}, \ldots, d_0)_2$
Output: $y = x^d$	Output: $y = x^d$
$R_0 \leftarrow 1$; $R_1 \leftarrow x$; $i \leftarrow m - 1$	$R_0 \leftarrow 1$; $R_1 \leftarrow x$; $i \leftarrow m - 1$
while $(i \geq 0)$ **do**	$k \leftarrow 0$
$R_0 \leftarrow (R_0)^2$	**while** $(i \geq 0)$ **do**
if $(d_i = 1)$ **then** $R_0 \leftarrow R_0 \cdot R_1$	$R_0 \leftarrow R_0 \cdot R_k$
$i \leftarrow i - 1$	$k \leftarrow k \oplus d_i$; $i \leftarrow i - k$
endwhile	**endwhile**
return R_0	**return** R_0
(a) SPA vulnerable code	(b) SPA immune code

Figure 3.32: Conditional Branching in Square-and-Multiply [59]

XTR is surprisingly efficient and can be used to all discrete logarithm based

public key algorithms... – EmailPrivacy.info

3.3.2 Replacing New Algorithms

Elliptic Curve Cryptography (ECC) and RSA have been modified in different ways in the recent past to prevent against power analysis attacks. Only brief descriptions of such modified algorithms are presented and the interested readers are referred to respective papers for more details. One of the main weaknesses in ECC for power analysis is the double-and- add algorithm used for point multiplication [30]. Miyaji et al. [158] proposed efficient point multiplication algorithms compared to the standard double-and-add algorithm. The authors also state that the Jacobian coordinates [60] perform slower addition and faster doubling, which is suitable for ECC. Torii and Yokoyama [228] state that the Schoof's algorithm [208] is used to randomly generate an ECC curve and you can choose the one which is secure based on the requirements. The authors [228] further improved the Schoof's algorithm by changing different parameters in the curve to make ECC more efficient as well as secure. Brier and Joye [47] presented the Montgomery version of the point multiplication (kP), as shown in Figure 3.33, replacing the standard double-and-add algorithm. The Montgomery approach is based on the hypothesis that the sum of two points, whose difference is a known point, can be computed without the y-coordinates of the two points. There is always a fixed sequence of instructions executed in the Montgomery version, as shown in Figure 3.33, thus preventing SPA.

Input: $\mathbf{P}$, $k = (k_{l-1}, \ldots, k_0)_2$
Output: $x(k\mathbf{P})$
1. $\mathbf{R}_0 = \mathbf{P}$; $\mathbf{R}_1 = 2\mathbf{P}$
2. for $i = l - 2$ downto 0 do
3.   if $(k_i = 0)$ then
4. $x(\mathbf{R}_1) \leftarrow x(\mathbf{R}_0 + \mathbf{R}_1)$; $x(\mathbf{R}_0) \leftarrow x(2\mathbf{R}_0)$
5.   else [if $(k_i = 1)$]
6. $x(\mathbf{R}_0) \leftarrow x(\mathbf{R}_0 + \mathbf{R}_1)$; $x(\mathbf{R}_1) \leftarrow x(2\mathbf{R}_1)$
return $(x(\mathbf{R}_0))$

Figure 3.33: Montgomery approach for Modular Multiplication [47]

Joye and Quisquater [116] investigated the Hessian parametrisation in Elliptic Curves (ECs), where a single procedure is used for all addition, doubling and subtraction of points to prevent power analysis and also to improve performance by 33%. The Hessian parametrisation [116] uses 12 multiplications to process addition (two different points), doubling and subtraction indifferently. Liardet and Smart [139] emphasised the Jacobi form of Elliptic Curves for more efficient computation while maintaining the same level of security. Instead of using special Elliptic Curves as in [116] and [139], Möller [159] uses conventional point multiplication and proposes a uniform way of performing addition and doubling in a fixed pattern. Such a fixed execution of addition and doubling produces no difference in the power profile, thus preventing power analysis. Figure 3.34 presents the uniform approach of Möller [159] where the point multiplication eP is performed, converting the secret key e into 2^w-ary digits; $e = \sum_{i=0}^{k} b_i \cdot 2^{wi}$. The precomputation stage of the algorithm performs operations to store the intermediate values P_{b_j}. The evaluation stage, which performs doubling and addition, as shown in Figure 3.34, executes both operations in a fixed pattern. However, the author observed that this uniform approach required more addition than the standard approach.

Möller [160] further extended the uniform double and addition algorithm by avoiding the table lookup using a parallel approach. This technique reduces the information leakage to the adversary and also improves performance. Similar to the double-and-add algorithm in ECC, the square-and-multiply algorithm for modular multiplication in RSA has also been modified to prevent power analysis. Walter [239] quoted a Montgomery Modular Multiplication (MMM) algorithm which is attacked by the author using power analysis, exploiting the imbalance caused by a conditional subtraction performed at the end of the algorithm. Clavier and Joye [62] proposed a SPA immune exponentiation approach for RSA, named the

---

Algorithm 1 Compute $\left[\sum_{i=0}^{k} b_i \cdot 2^{wi}\right] P$

{*Precomputation stage*}
$P_1 \leftarrow P$
for $n = 2$ to $2^w - 2$ step 2 **do**
  $P_n \leftarrow [2]P_{n/2}$
  $P_{n+1} \leftarrow P_n + P$
  {$P_n = [n]P,\ P_{n+1} = [n+1]P$}
end for
$P_{-2^w} \leftarrow -[2]P_{2^{w-1}}$
{$P_{-2^w} = [-2^w]P$}

{*Evaluation stage*}
$A \leftarrow P_{b_k}$
for $j = k - 1$ down to 0 **do**
  $A \leftarrow [2^w]A$
  $A \leftarrow A + P_{b_j}$
end for
return A

Figure 3.34: Uniform Addition and Doubling [159]

universal exponentiation algorithm. This algorithm performs a multiplication of values from two registers at each iteration (i.e., no conditional branching) using a precomputed register sequence.

3.3.3 Software Balancing

The software code can be modified in such a way that complementary events are coded to negate the effects of the actual computations. Chari et al. [54] argued that such balancing fails to prevent power analysis in high resolution and a large number of samples, where the adversary would be able to enlarge the slight differences between the balancing operations for a successful attack, by changing the operation conditions (such as supply voltage and frequency) inside the smart card. Daemen and Rijmen [71] stated that software balancing can be a possible countermeasure for power analysis by modifying the program to process words containing both the data bits and their complements. According to the authors, this balancing approach will diminish the correlation between the original data bits and power magnitudes. Sakai and Sakurai [202] also stated that software balancing in ECC is a reasonably better countermeasure for power analysis attacks.

3.4 Hardware Balancing

In recent few years there has been a significant increase in hardware balancing techniques, where the logics are balanced at the gate level by placing complementary logics together with the original logics. Evidently, balancing at the gate level is the most appropriate solution to prevent power analysis, since the power is consumed/dissipated depending on the switching activities in gates. This section presents hardware balancing techniques, discussing the pros and cons of each.

3.4.1 Dual Rail Logic

In Dual Rail Logic, two wires are used to carry each bit of the circuit [236]. Figure 3.35 depicts the dual rail implementation of an OR gate from a standard logical OR gate, where logic 0 in the standard logic is represented as (0,1) and logic 1 as (1,0). The AND gates labelled as "C" are special gates which act as standard AND gates when the output is 0 and perform OR when the output is 1 [133]. Similarly, all the other standard gates can be encoded into dual rails [236]. More details on dual rail circuits can be found in [123, 212].

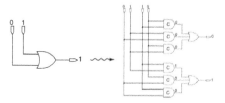

Figure 3.35: Dual Rail implementation of an OR gate [236]

Plana et al. [189] stated that the dual rail circuits which use two wires to represent one signal in the normal logic, as shown in Figure 3.35, can be used to prevent power analysis since the symmetry between 0 and 1 is preserved. However, the authors realised that the dual rail still has a vulnerability to power analysis because the change in the output is still observable. Dhem and Feyt [76] and Moore et al. [163] also suggested that dual rail can be used to defeat power analysis, keeping the overall power consumption constant by using two complementary bits for each bit. Saputra et al. [204] designed special instructions which used dual rail logics to counter power analysis in DES (Data Encryption Standard Encryption Program), however, they claimed that the power consumption was doubled. Another loophole in dual rail logic is a small imbalance in the design causing significant leakage of useful information in the dissipated power [164]. Researchers have utilised these dual rail circuits and designed several Dual Rail Precharge (DRP) logics, such as Sense Amplifier Based Logic (SABL), Wave Dynamic Differential Logic (WDDL) and Dual-Spacer, to achieve constant power consumption by charging and recharging the wires in dual rail when needed.

3.4.1.1 Sense Amplifier Based Logic: SABL

The dual rail logic do not reveal any power consumption when the inputs are (0,0) and (1,1), but trigger outputs for combinations (0,1) and (1,0). Similarly, CMOS (Complementary Metal Oxide Semiconductor) logics create an asymmetry in power consumption, costing no power for transitions 0-0 and 1-1, as shown in Figure 3.36. The 0-1 transition consumes energy from the power supply and 1-0 transition releases the energy stored in the output capacitance as illustrated in Figure 3.36. Such an imbalance of the power consumption for different transitions is claimed vulnerable for DPA by Tiri et al. [221].

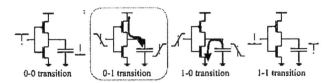

0-0 transition   0-1 transition   1-0 transition   1-1 transition

Figure 3.36: CMOS logic output transitions [221]

To eliminate the imbalances in the power consumption for different transitions, Tiri et al. [221, 224] propose the Sense Amplifier Based Logic (SABL) which charges in every clock cycle with a constant value. This results in a fixed amount of energy consumed for every transition, preventing power analysis. Figure 3.37 depicts the SABL logic design for a generic n-gate, where DPDN (Differential Pull Down Network) is used to connect the input nodes to the output nodes and an M1 transistor guarantees that all internal nodes are discharged. When the clock goes high, the same capacitances are charged, thus providing independent power consumption of the inputs at every cycle.

As shown in the SABL design, the gate switches its output every time and loads a constant capacitance to produce a fixed power consumption. Even though the experiments of Tiri et al. [221] proved that SABL is immune to power analysis, the area increase is 80%. Hwang et al. [107] state that SABL dissipates the same dynamic power regardless of any bit transition (0 → 0, 0 → 1, 1 → 0, 1 → 1). Kulikowski et al. [134, 135] used the SABL design to implement balanced logics. Yang and Yuan [245] presented the Current Balanced Logic (CBL) and the Enhanced Current Balanced Logic (ECBL), which are claimed as superior to SABL in terms

140

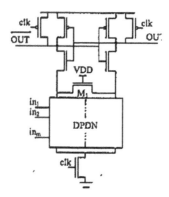

Figure 3.37: SABL generic n-gate [221]

of area and power reduction, by Khatibzadeh and Gebotys [122]. The CBL and ECBL [245] use an extra transistor (called the equalising transistor) attached to the logic to compensate the current drained from the source, thus balancing the power consumption.

3.4.1.2 Wave Dynamic Differential Logic (WDDL)

Tiri and Verbauwhede [225] realised that SABL uses a completely new standard cell library with a modified design and characterisation from regular libraries. Hence, the authors proposed Wave Dynamic Differential Logic (WDDL), which contains two complementary gates, one computing the true output using true inputs while the other produces the false output with false inputs. Figure 3.38 depicts the WDDL AND gate and WDDL OR gate, which use a precharge logic to set the inputs to 0 and the outputs to 0 in the precharge phase (clock-high). The evaluation phase (clock-low) computes the differential output, where true inputs are given to the normal logic and inverted inputs are given to the balancing logic to produce complementary outputs, as shown in Figure 3.38. The precharge circuit is also balanced for when the output out does not switch the differential output $\overline{out}$ switches.

The WDDL prevents power analysis and is claimed to be superior to SABL since the standard libraries can be still used. However, the library needs modification to add balancing logics next to the original logics [225]. Further descriptions on WDDL can be found in [222, 223, 226, 227]. Hwang et al. [106] designed an AES based Differential Power Analysis (DPA) resistant secure coprocessor using WDDL. The authors state that WDDL requires more area

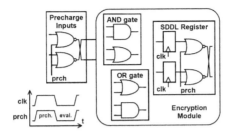

Figure 3.38: WDDL Gates [225]

and power than a fully customised DPA resistant library. Correlation analysis and DPA are performed in the coprocessor [106] as shown in Figure 3.39, where no peaks are observed at the correct key guess, masking the secret key.

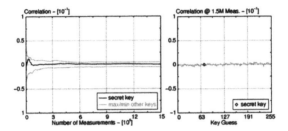

Figure 3.39: DPA in WDDL coprocessor [106]

Yu and Schaumont [250] found out that implementing WDDL in FPGA would still be vulnerable to power analysis because of the asymmetry in routing. Hence, the authors proposed DWDDL (Double WDDL), which used two WDDL circuits placed next to each other with balanced routing. The area cost of DWDDL is 10X and the increase in clock delay is 5 times of the normal WDDL implementation.

Sokolov et al. [73] realised that dual rail logics at the gate level are not symmetric because they use only a (0,0) state (also called a *spacer*) to represent the absence of data. The switching happens on a particular rail from the all-zero *spacer* to an intermediate value and then back to the *spacer*. The authors proposed a Dual Spacer Dual Rail technique which uses both an all-zero *spacer* and an all-one *spacer*. An input to the Dual Spacer Dual Rail produced switching in both rails, where the flips are forced from the all-zero *spacer* to the all-one *spacer* through the intermediate state and backwards. Since this provides symmetrical balancing at

142

the gate level, by having all the gates inside the dual rail firing all the time, the Dual Spacer Dual Rail circuit is more resistant to power analysis [73].

3.4.2 Masked Dual Rail Precharge Logic: MDPL

Even though the Dual Rail Precharge (DRP) logic styles (SABL, WDDL and Dual Spacer Dual Rail, explained above) guarantee constant power consumption by charging and discharging the wires in every clock cycle, current Electronic Design Automation (EDA) tools place and route automatically which does not guarantee the provision of equal capacity load for both wires [191]. Popp and Mangard [191] claim that such a problematic place and route can still be performed manually, but with significant design cost. Hence, the authors propose a Masked Dual Rail Precharge Logic (MDPL) to randomise the power consumption rather than trying to balance the bitflips. The basic idea of MDPL is to represent a logic value d as $d_m = d \oplus m$ (where m is a mask value and $\oplus$ operation is addition modulo 2), instead of representing d using two complementary signals d and $\bar{d}$. Similar to Dual Rail Precharge (DRP) logics, the MDPL also contains the complementary signal $\overline{d_m}$ for each signal d_m in the circuit. A schematic of the MDPL AND gate is presented in Figure 3.40, where the majority (MAJ) circuit is shown on the left. The outputs in the MDPL AND gate shown on the right part of Figure 3.40 are produced using the equations: $q_m = ((a_m \oplus m) \wedge (b_m \oplus m)) \oplus m$ and $\overline{q_m} = ((\overline{a_m} \oplus \overline{m}) \wedge (\overline{b_m} \oplus \overline{m})) \oplus \overline{m}$; where $\wedge$ is a logical AND. All signals are precharged to 0 before the next evaluation phase in MDPL, similar to WDDL (explained above). A new mask m is created using a pseudo random number generator for every clock cycle.

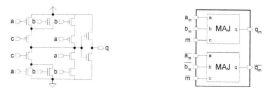

Figure 3.40: CMOS MAJ gate (left) and MDPL AND gate (right) [191]

Similar to the MDPL AND gate, shown in Figure 3.40, all the other fundamental gates can be designed using MDPL. The MDPL has the benefit of using standard cell libraries as opposed to SABL [221] and also does not require any routing constraints unlike WDDL [225] with automatic place and route. However, Popp and Mangard [191] pointed out that MDPL involves additional compilation of the MDPL synthesis cell library, causing extra effort, as the masked and dual rail logics cannot be synthesised using state of the art synthesisers. The area overhead of MDPL is 4X compared to the normal CMOS implementation and the speed is halved in the worst case scenario. Popp et al. [190] performed DPA in normal CMOS logic, Dual Rail Precharge (DRP) logic, and Masked Dual Precharge Logic (MDPL) chips exploiting the MOV operation. Figure 3.41 depicts the DPA plots of these three logics with time against correlation, where the correct data guess is plotted in black and the other wrong guesses in gray. As shown in Figure 3.41, all the logics produce significant peaks in correlation with the correct data guesses. However, the Normal CMOS logic reveals much higher correlation values compared to the DRP and MDPL implementations. The number of samples needed to visualise the peaks at the correct data guesses are also much higher for the latter implementations.

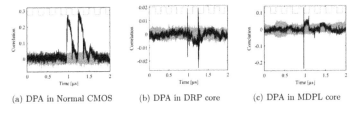

(a) DPA in Normal CMOS   (b) DPA in DRP core   (c) DPA in MDPL core

Figure 3.41: DPA using MOV operation on balanced logics [190]

Even though the attacks, using MOV operation, on all three logic implementations, shown in Figure 3.41, revealed the correct data by producing significant correlation values at the correct guess, the DPA attack on the AES coprocessor implementation of Popp et al. [190] failed to reveal significant peaks at the correct key guess for both DRP and MDPL cores, even over one million samples. The authors claim that such a situation is possible mainly because of the difference in the implementation of the AES module compared to the MOV operation implementation. An improved version of the MDPL is also proposed by the authors which can be referred to in the paper [190]. Bucci et al. [50] proposed a randomised logic style similar to MDPL, but by randomising the pre-charge logic.

3.5   Signal Suppression Circuit

Daemen and Rijmen [71] suggested having a built-in hardware module inside the chip to blend noise to the power consumption, reducing the Signal-to-Noise Ratio (SNR) to prevent the adversary from differentiating the power profile. Fruhauf et al. [84] presented a circuit to randomise the current dissipated by the chip. Such designs cannot guarantee security against power analysis where the noise could be averaged over a huge set of samples. Kessels et al. [121] proposed a power reduction chip design in a smart card by using asynchronous circuits instead of synchronous circuits. This design does not address power analysis, nevertheless it is quite obvious that this technique can also be used to prevent power analysis, as the adversary receives only the suppressed current consumption. Rakers et al. [195] proposed an Isolation circuit, as illustrated in Figure 3.42, attached to the chip to make the current path independent of the digital circuitry. As Figure 3.42 depicts, the current supply MP1 is independent of the digital circuitry. However, Rakers et al. [195] realised that the ground path had still some dependency (around 66 dB of isolation) increasing the number of samples needed for power analysis by 2^{22} times.

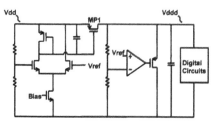

Figure 3.42: Isolation Circuit [195]

A similar suppression circuit is also proposed by Ratanpal et al. [196] to reduce the information leakage through the power supply pin. This suppression circuit is claimed to have an advantage over the circuit of Rakers et al. [195] in that it can be attached to the existing hardware, and thus does not affect the algorithm implementation. Muresan et al. [166] proposed a power smart system-on-chip architecture for embedded cryptosystems where the current variation is reduced by up to 80% by using an extra suppression circuitry, but where total power consumption is increased by 20%. A block diagram of the power smart architecture of Muresan et al. [166] is presented in Figure 3.43. The current sensor module measures the supply current of the processor core in real-time. A filter module is used to extract the sensed current I_{sense}. As shown in Figure 3.43, the power smart control block drives the activity of the current injection, voltage regulator and clock frequency modules. The key aim of this architecture is to maintain the current consumption of the system to a constant level I_{ref}. The

I_{ref} is compared with the I_{sense}, and, based on this comparison, the current controlled voltage regulator will bring down the power supply of the system to $V_{DD-regulated}$, thus reducing the current consumption to I_{ref}. The current injection module used in the power smart architecture, shown in Figure 3.43, injects extra current into the system when the sensed current I_{sense} is less than the constant current needed I_{ref}. The current controlled voltage regulator and the clock frequency module are used to scale the clock when required, to compensate delays.

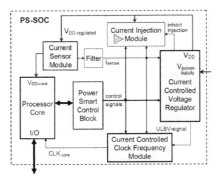

Figure 3.43: Power Smart Architecture [166]

All the above signal suppression circuits failed to flatten the current but suppressed the variation in the signals as much as possible. However, none of these techniques underwent experiments for power analysis to show that the suppression successfully prevents the attack. Because a smaller variation in the power magnitude might be enough for the adversary to perform a successful attack.

3.6 Current Flattening

Muresan and Gebotys [165] observed that a program charges the capacitor producing variations in power consumption based on the instruction types and the parallelism within the program. The authors proposed to insert *nops* (dummy instructions which do not alter the state of the program) in the program to extend the execution time and increase the discharge time when a higher current consumption is predicted, thus attempting to flatten the current signal. This balancing is possible because all the instructions consume more current than the *nop* instruction. Hence, executing several *nops* provides discharge, reducing the current. Each instruction is analysed for its current consumption to determine the number of *nops* and the places of *nops* to be inserted to flatten the current signal. The balancing is performed in blocks and each block is balanced based on a reference value.

NOPs are often involved when cracking software that checks for serial numbers, specific hardware requirements, presence of hardware dongles... – Wiki

The current flattening technique of Muresan and Gebotys [165] considers a parallelised program, where *nops* are added when necessary based on the instantaneous current consumption measured. A software implementation is initially proposed by the authors initially, and then a hardware implementation is considered. Figure 3.44 depicts the current flattening module of Muresan and Gebotys [165] which has a two issue pipeline unit. The instantaneous current is measured using another circuit (not shown here) to produce two feedback signals CC (Cut Current, when the current is higher than the limit) and IC (Increase Current, when the current is less than the limit) to control the current consumption. Based on these control signals, the MUX decides the instructions to be placed in the dispatching unit for execution, as shown in Figure 3.44. The proper instructions are taken from the instruction fetch unit and two different kinds of dummy instructions (I_{min} and I_{max}) are triggered for CC and IC control signals using the table shown in Figure 3.44. I_{min} represents a *nop* instruction which consumes minimal current and I_{max} represents an instruction which consumes high current (such as "OR dn,dn").

As Figure 3.44 depicts, whenever the measured instantaneous current is higher than the reference current, the MUX will receive the CC control signal set, thus injecting 2 *nops* (i.e., I_{min}) to provide discharge in order to reduce the current. If the instantaneous current is less than the reference value, the MUX receives the IC signal set, and I_{max} instructions will be injected to increase the current consumption. Though this technique is referred to as one of the better countermeasures to prevent power analysis based side channel attacks, the runtime overhead is 70% which is quite significant for an embedded application. Another drawback of

147

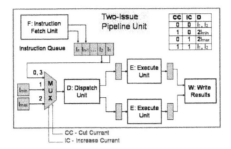

Figure 3.44: Current Flattening Module [165]

this current balancing of Muresan and Gebotys [165] is that it flattens the current for local individual blocks considering different reference values, hence failing to balance the whole program.

3.7   Non-deterministic Processors

May et al. [145] proposed a non-deterministic processor design, where the independent instructions are identified and executed out-of-order, in a random choice, by the processor. This infringes the conventional attack rule, removing the correlation between multiple executions of the same program, thus preventing the adversary from comparing different runs for power analysis. The authors presented a random instruction selection unit to chose independent instructions (i.e., instructions which do not depend on a result which is not yet available and do not overwrite any results which are going to be used by the other instructions). A block of logic is used to determine conflicting instructions and to derive the independent instruction set. An instruction is randomly selected from this set using a random number generator and scheduled for execution. The random instruction selection logic [145], shown in Figure 3.45, splits the instruction into separate components including the registers inside the instruction register. Each operand is then checked into defined-by and used-by tables to read the masks, indicating whether the source operand registers of the instruction are the result of a previous instruction and whether the destination register may overwrite a value used by previous instructions. As Figure 3.45 depicts, the Random Issue Buffer is updated with the instructions and their corresponding dependency bits. The Random Selection Unit chooses an instruction randomly from instructions which have all dependency bits cleared (i.e., value of zero). The

148

scheduled instructions are updated in the Instruction Table to be executed by the processor.

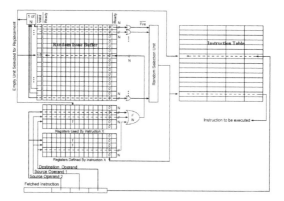

Figure 3.45: Random instruction issue unit [145]

May et al. [145] stated that the random issuing, illustrated in Figure 3.45, can be used for both pipelined and superscalar processors (refer [113] for more information on superscalar processors).

A superscalar processor executes more than one instruction during a clock cycle by simultaneously dispatching multiple instructions to redundant functional units on the processor... – Wiki

A Differential Power Analysis (DPA) performed by May et al. [145] on a standard processor and their non-deterministic processor executing DES encryption, is shown in Figure 3.46. As Figure 3.46(a) depicts, the standard processor reveals significant peaks on the correct subkey guess in DES. On the other hand, the non-deterministic processor produces a DPA plot where the significant peaks disappear showing a noise like variation as presented in Figure 3.46(b).

The DPA analysis in Figure 3.46 proves that the non-deterministic processor design of May et al. [145] combats DPA, where no significant peaks are revealed for the correct subkey guess. May et al. [145] realised that one suitable way of removing more dependencies in a code is by

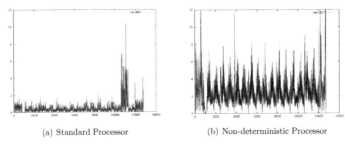

(a) Standard Processor   (b) Non-deterministic Processor

Figure 3.46: DPA plots for DES [145]

renaming the registers used in instructions. This results in more possible random schedules (because of the increased independency in the code), further boosting the immunity of the processor from Differential Power Analysis (DPA). Figure 3.47 depicts an example of register renaming used by May et al. [146] on a code segment which implements A = B and C = D. The actual assembly code shown in Figure 3.47(a) uses a single register R0, which is used to hold and store both variables B and D. The third instruction of loading D cannot be executed before the store instruction of A. A register renamed version is shown in Figure 3.47(b), where R1 is replaced for R0. This will result in executing the program in parallel, assigning A=B and C=D simultaneously.

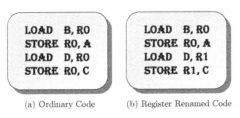

(a) Ordinary Code   (b) Register Renamed Code

Figure 3.47: An Example in Register Renaming [146]

Considering the register renaming approach illustrated in Figure 3.47(b), May et al. [146] further investigated the suitability of performing a random register renaming at runtime to weaken Differential Power Analysis (DPA) attacks. The authors proposed a non-deterministic register renaming circuitry (not shown here) which uses a random selection unit to randomly rename the registers at runtime. May et al. [146] combined their register renaming circuitry with the non-deterministic processor, explained in Figure 3.45, and claimed that it was more secure than a non-deterministic processor alone. Irwin et al. [108] proposed to have an extra pipeline stage in the non-deterministic processor design presented in Figure 3.45, where random calculations were fused into the actual algorithm at runtime to obfuscate the original behaviour. This technique is named the Instruction Stream Mutation, which places a mutation pipeline stage in front of the execution stage in the processor. A software approach to create a table of flags specifying the liveliness (i.e., used or unused) of each register before an instruction execution, is considered by inserting additional instructions in the source code. Whenever the mutation stage finds a register is unused, it creates a random instruction and performs the operation to update that register, thus maintaining the state of the processor while adding a random nature at runtime [108]. The instruction mutation technique [108] involves too much software modification and increases the source code significantly. Though non-deterministic processors provide unsynchronised power profiles to prevent power analysis, they do not obfuscate a highly dependent code segment which cannot be executed out-of-order.

3.8   Handling Clock

Different ways of handling clock signals to prevent power analysis have been proposed in the past, since clock signals are analysed by the adversaries to identify certain significant instruction executions in the power profile. Sprunk [213] proposes a random clock generation circuitry as shown in Figure 3.48 where the clock frequency is continually randomly changed. A random modulation source is used to create random values using an LFSR (Linear Feedback Shift Register). The random value is then used in the variable frequency source to create random frequency signals, as illustrated in Figure 3.48, which will be used as the clock to drive the crypto processor to execute cryptographic programs. Such a random clock will produce out of sync. power profiles for different runs, preventing the adversary from direct correlation. However, this random clock generation will not prevent power analysis where synchronisation could still be possible with less effort since only the width of the power signal is randomised to be different but the power magnitude is not.

Kocher et al. [128] stated that such random clock signals shown in Figure 3.48 makes the attackers work harder to identify the points of interest within the collected power profiles. The authors proposed another way to achieve this feature by using *clock skipping* [128], which utilises an internal clock separate from the normal clock to drive only the cryptographic operations in the processor. Daemen and Rijmen [71] surmised that having instructions to

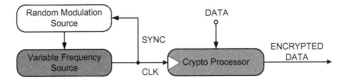

Figure 3.48: Random Clock Generation [213]

vary the number of cycles and having cycles with varying length will prevent power analysis. Benini et al. [33] discussed a randomised clock gating technique to scramble the power profile without increasing the power consumption (refer to [34] for more details in clock gating). A random circuit is used to randomly gate the clock, thus producing an unpredictable power profile. Similar clock countermeasures are also proposed in [9, 234]. However, Chari et al. [54] concluded that it is very easy to negate the random delays (generated from the above explained randomisation in clock signals) using signal processing techniques.

clock gating, which is used in Pentium 4 processors, refers to activating the clocks in a logic block only when there is work to be done... – Webopedia.com

3.9 Special Instructions

Goubin and Patarin [97] claim that power analysis can be prevented by replacing critical instructions with assembly instructions whose power signature is difficult to analyse. Saputra et al. [204] designed special secure instructions, which replace the normal instructions in the code. For example, the standard load and store instructions are replaced with secure load and store instructions in the code. These special instructions use two complementary logics producing complementary switching activities in parallel to mask the data dependent operations in the power profile (these complementary logics are explained in Section 3.4). Whenever a secure version of the instruction is executed, both the normal and complementary circuits in the processor are activated [204]. The authors claim that their technique reduces overall energy consumption, compared to the hardware balancing techniques presented in Section 3.4, by triggering the complementary logic using special instructions (replacing these in the code when needed). However, the energy consumption for special instruction execution costs double the normal execution. Though using special instructions appears to be a better countermeasure for power analysis based side channel attacks, there are only very few researchers looking into this area [233]. Interested readers are referred to [81, 98, 219, 220] for more details on extensible instruction sets for cryptographic programs.

3.10 Summary

This chapter analyses various countermeasures proposed to combat power analysis based side channel attacks over the years. These countermeasures are categorised into masking, instruction injection, code modification, hardware balancing, signal suppression, current flattening, non-deterministic processors, handling clock and special instructions. The majority of the countermeasures fall under masking, code/algorithm modification and balancing. Masking techniques are proved vulnerable against multi-order DPA attacks, even though they protect against standard DPA. Code modification techniques have significant performance overhead and require software instrumentation. The balancing techniques, which are considered as the most appropriate countermeasures, consume substantial amount of area and power overheads.

Chapter 4

RIJID: Random Code Injection to Mask Power Analysis*

This chapter presents a countermeasure (called **RIJID**) to prevent power analysis. **RIJID** is a hardware software randomised instruction injection method which injects random instructions, random number of times, at random places during the encryption. Such randomisation scrambles the power wave so that the adversary is unable to identify specific segments such as encryption rounds within the entire power wave. A random generator is attached to the processor to chose random number of instructions from an instruction pool that contains instructions which do not change the state of the processor. The system identifies the encryption by having two special instructions around the encryption routine (at the start and, at the end). *RIJID* index, a simple mathematical formulation, is introduced based on cross correlation that measures the scrambling provided by **RIJID**.

4.1 Overview

Each instruction has its unique functionality, thus creates its own signature in the power profile [71]. This results in similar patterns in the power profile for the same sequence of instruction execution (for example, loops executing the same instruction sequence in iterations produce similar patterns). A typical attacker would observe the patterns occurring in the

---

*This work is presented in the Design Automation Conference (DAC'07) held at San Diego, USA.

power waveform as depicted in Figure 4.1. This figure shows six TripleDES SBOX[1] lookup rounds. All power waves for the shown rounds appear similar in Figure 4.1. By correlating power values of identified segments with guessed secret keys as explained in Chapter 2, the adversary tries to identify the correct secret key using fewer power samples than if brute force were to be applied.

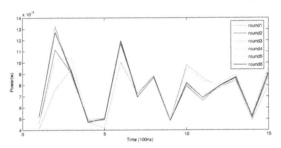

Figure 4.1: TripleDES Rounds

The secret key of a system is usually revealed by analysing the differences in magnitudes of power values between differing rounds [143, 127, 197]. For example, in Figure 4.1, multiple peaks (at approximately 250ns) show differing numbers used in an XOR instruction. SPA attacks will only be successful when instructions executed have an obvious and simple relationship with the secret key [39, 147, 155, 172]. DPA attacks are much more powerful than SPA attacks, as statistical analysis is used on the observed power wave to find secret keys [180, 127]. For both SPA and DPA to be successful, it is imperative that the adversary is able to identify the power waveform with encryption rounds. If one can foil the identification of the power waveform, then the system becomes more secure against power wave based side channel attacks.

In this Chapter, the author introduces a hardware software Randomised Instruction inJectIon methoD, *RIJID*, which scrambles the power wave so that the adversary is unable to identify specific segments such as encryption rounds within the entire power wave. *RIJID* prevents both SPA and DPA attacks by foiling the adversaries' attempts to identify power waves corresponding to encryption rounds. It is worth noting that *RIJID* uses *real* instructions at random places (and NOT dummy instructions like NOP at fixed places) for the injection.

---

[1] a fixed or a dynamic mapping table which returns values for cipher text, based on the plain text and decides the strength of the encryption algorithm

156

Figure 4.2 depicts the power sequences when injecting dummy and real instructions. There are six repeating templates (circled and numbered in Figure 4.2(a)) in a power waveform denoting six in-lined loops without any injection applied. The dissipated power wave when dummy instructions (NOPs) are injected is shown in Figure 4.2(b). As the figure shows, the injections are distinguishable in the power wave as significant troughs, while the rest of the patterns remain the same as the original. Simple time shifting can be deployed [61] to eliminate these insertions of dummy instructions, to predict the original power wave. Since dummy instructions do not perform operations in all pipeline stages (only the fetch stage), such instructions will cause only minor changes on the power profile of neighbouring instructions.

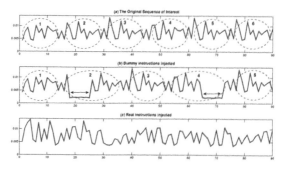

Figure 4.2: Dummy Vs Real Instruction Injection

Figure 4.2(c) shows the dissipated wave when real instructions are injected using *RIJID*. No patterns or significant troughs prevail in the power wave, hence the insertions cannot be spotted. *RIJID* uses random operands and random registers (note that the usage of random registers and operands lead to differing amounts of bitflips, further obfuscating the power waveform). Since these are real instructions (such as ADD, SUB etc.), they will also change the power dissipated by neighbouring instructions due to the pipeline in the processor. Time shifting cannot be applied to predict the original sequence, because the dissipated sequence (shown in Figure 4.2(c)) appears as some other random sequence.

Since the processor has a pipeline, the power waveform at any point in time will be contributed to by a number of instructions. Even if the adversary somehow can remove the points in the power waveform corresponding to inserted instructions, it would be impossible from the resulting waveform to find out what the original power waveform would have looked like. Since the random bit flips within the random instructions would have corrupted the waveform to such an extent that statistical correlation for DPA is not possible. In fact it is even difficult to find the segments corresponding to the sbox rounds in the waveform.

To observe how close is the obfuscated sequence to a random sequence the author has defined a new index called the *RIJID* index which uses cross-correlation to give us a measure of obfuscation. This measure allows us to quickly find the level of obfuscation needed. To be absolutely certain, one must take electrical power measurements and try to perform DPA on it, which would take a very long time indeed.

4.2   Contribution

In general, data masking techniques have been vulnerable to second order DPA attacks [115, 180, 235]. The table masking methods [86, 97] are algorithm specific approaches (works for the algorithms which use an *sbox*) and they successfully prevent DPA. However, masking techniques require a high degree of manual intervention and they fail to scramble the power patterns since the instructions executed remain unchanged. The dummy operation insertion techniques proposed for ECC systems [30, 88] are application specific and needs significant human intervention. Non-deterministic processors [145] are not feasible in highly dependent software code, which cannot be executed *out-of-order*. The techniques proposed using non-deterministic processors [108, 146] have complex circuitry but do not have their overheads reported, as none have been implemented to the best of the author's knowledge. The circuitry level solutions [196, 222] cost significant area and energy overheads. The signal suppression technique [196] does not completely prevent DPA, but tries to make the attack more difficult. Balancing bit flips is also a costly solution which increases the size of the components used (e.g. in [204], bus size is doubled to balance the bit flips). The current flattening technique, which is considered the most appropriate countermeasure for power analysis based SCAs increases execution time by up to 75%, and flattens locally, based upon basic blocks. More details on these countermeasures are presented in Chapter 3.

As opposed to the pitfalls from previous methods, *RIJID* provides a generalised solution with little human intervention compared to the masking methods [54, 68, 86, 97, 217], allowing the processor to take care of masking. On a Simplescalar processor, the additional area cost is just 1.98% compared to the area cost of constant logic chips [222] and the cost of balancing techniques [204], with an average energy cost of 27.1% and an average runtime cost of 29.8%

compared to current flattening [165], for six industry standard benchmarks. *RIJID* confuses the adversary without flattening the current [165], but scrambling the patterns in the power wave. It can be applied to any vulnerable segment (and is not algorithm dependent like masking techniques [86, 217]). Dummy instruction insertions can be eliminated using simple time shifting [61], whereas *RIJID* injects real instructions at random places a random number of times. Hence the adversary will observe different power profiles on different tries.

4.2.1 Limitations

1. *RIJID* needs compiler support;

2. *RIJID* is proposed as a design time technique, since *RIJID* needs hardware changes; and,

3. the author assumes that the system is self contained with memory on chip.

4.3 RIJID Framework

In this section, the hardware architecture is presented for the *RIJID* framework and the software instrumentation, which is necessary for starting and stopping the randomisation process.

4.3.1 Software Instrumentation

The software instrumentation for *RIJID* is performed at compile time. Figure 4.3 shows the encryption block of a cryptographic application which has several similar instruction segments (*sbox* rounds). Two flag instructions (*SET-FLAG* and *RESET-FLAG*) are inserted at the start and the end of the block as shown in Figure 4.3, to indicate to the processor the points to start and stop inserting random instructions at random places. When the processor fetches a *SET-FLAG* instruction, it starts generating random instructions and stops when it reads the *RESET-FLAG* instruction.

Multiple occurrences of a loop containing a set of instructions, which causes a repeat power sequence template, is a potential place for flag instruction insertion. Recent SPA and DPA attacks reveal that the encryption block which has *sbox* rounds, is the most critical block [180], which is selected for random instruction injection. Programmers decide the blocks upon

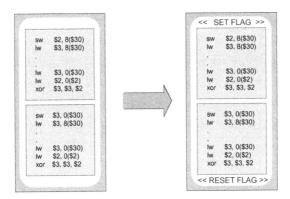

Figure 4.3: Software Instrumentation at Compile Time

which to apply flag instructions. However, instrumentation can be automated for any given code, by having a parser which identifies encryption loops.

4.3.2 Hardware Architecture

Figure 4.5 shows a block diagram of the hardware architecture of **RIJID** framework. When the processor fetches the *SET-FLAG* instruction, a special register (*Flag*) is set. The dotted box in Figure 4.5 shows the hardware component added for **RIJID** framework. When *Flag* is set, the Random Generator component(R/G) sends a hold (*PC Hold'*) signal to the Program Counter (PC) and starts generating random instructions at random intervals. *PC Hold'* from the R/G is *Multiplexed* with the *PC Hold* signal from the controller (*CONTR.*) before it is connected to the *PC*. The random instruction generation performed by R/G is limited by a pair of boundary values, which are set by the *SET-FLAG* instruction. This pair, which is called the *injection pair* represents: (1) the maximum number (N) of random instructions to be injected between two regular instructions when the flag is set; and (2) the maximum number (D) of regular instructions to be skipped before each injection. Figure 4.4 depicts several possible instruction sequences when an injection pair of (3,4) is injected ('x' denotes an injected instruction).

PC Hold' signal from R/G is switched between on and off for random intervals based on the *injection pair*. When *PC Hold'* is high, the random instructions (R/I) generated by R/G are sent to the data port of the instruction register (*IR*). During hold, instruction which is

Inst. Seq.	ABCAABCDEFGAABBCDEF
ABxxCAABxxCDExFGxxxAABBxxCDExF
ABCAxxxABCxDEFxxGxAxxABBxxCDxxxEF
ABCAxABCxDxxEFxxGAAxxxBxBCxxDEF
AxxBCxxAAxBCxDExFxxGAxxxABxxBCxDxEF

Figure 4.4: Instruction sequence possibilities for Injection Pair (3,4)

pointed to by the PC is refetched from the instruction memory; however, this instruction is not written into the *IR*.

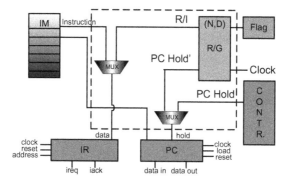

Figure 4.5: Random Instruction Injection

Since, execution of an instruction will generally affect the state of the processor, creating any random instruction will overwrite or edit effective data values. Therefore, only a limited set of instructions is selected such that, a random register is used and computed with the *zero* register and the result is written onto the same random register. Since the *R/G* selects random instructions from a specific set, it is called a pseudo random generator. For example, a randomly selected ADD instruction adds the value in the random register and the zero register and writes the result back to the same random register. Three different schemes of inserting random instructions were tried: (1), instructions with zero registers; (2), instructions with *zero* and a fixed register; (3), instructions with *zero* and a randomly selected register. The insertions from (1) and (2) can be identifiable on the power wave, when same instructions are scheduled due to the lower amount of bit flips, which causes low power variation. The third scheme (use of random registers for consecutive random instructions) was the most appropriate for *RIJID* as it caused higher power variation due to bit flips in registers [146].

4.4   Design Flow

This section presents the software design flow and the hardware design flow of the *RIJID* implementation.

4.4.1   Software Design Flow

Figure 4.6 depicts the software design flow of the *RIJID* framework. The source code of a cryptographic application is compiled with the front-end of a compiler to generate the assembly version of the application (*.s files*). Critical blocks (blocks with encryption activities) in the assembly code are instrumented as explained in section 4.3.1. The resulting assembly file is assembled and linked to generate the binary of the application (iBinary in Figure 4.6). Even though the instrumentation process here is performed manually, it is possible to write a software parser to perform this automatically.

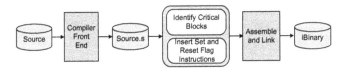

Figure 4.6: Software Design Flow

4.4.2   Hardware Design Flow

Figure 4.7 depicts the generation of a processor model which implements the *RIJID* framework. An additional flag instruction, which is used as a tag to enable and disable randomisation, is combined into the instruction set architecture (ISA) of the target architecture. The new instruction is designed such that it sets and resets a flag when it is executed. This flag is used by the randomised instruction injector to manage the start and stop of random instruction injection as explained in section 4.3.2. Combined ISA is then passed into an automatic processor design tool (*ASIPMeister* [10]) to generate the *RIJID* processor model.

The output of ASIPMeister is a synthesisable VHDL processor model, which was enhanced by the R/G component (functional unit) as explained in section 4.3.2. R/G component is designed separately and then is combined with the processor.

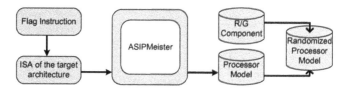

Figure 4.7: Hardware Design Flow

4.5   RIJID index

In the *RIJID* framework, $RIJID$ index is used as a measure to evaluate the randomisation provided by random code injection to scramble a repeating pattern (*template*) in a power sequence. This is a simple mathematical method, where the vulnerability of a power sequence can be quickly predicted using $RIJID$ index instead of taking practical measurements and analysing the electric waves. The *RIJID* framework: (1), analyses the original power sequence and extracts a template; and (2), uses $RIJID$ index as a measure to compute the randomisation provided in the scrambled power sequence.

Figure 4.8 depicts an example of how $RIJID$ index is computed using cross-correlation [186]. When a single occurrence (the template as shown in Figure 4.8(a)) of a repeating sequence is cross correlated with the original sequence (as shown in Figure 4.8(b)), significant peaks will appear in the output at places where the template matches with the original sequence [186]. Figure 4.8(e), which shows the cross-correlated sequence of the template and the original sequence, has two significant peaks, because two templates of Figure 4.8(a) exist in the original sequence shown in Figure 4.8(b). Figure 4.8(c) depicts the obfuscated sequence, which is the scrambled sequence using *RIJID*. The cross-correlation between the template and the obfuscated sequence is shown in Figure 4.8(f). Figure 4.8(d) depicts a random sequence which does not have such templates. Therefore the cross-correlation between the template and the random sequence does not produce a significant peak as shown in Figure 4.8(g).

When the significant peaks (two peaks) are removed from the cross correlated wave (called top elimination) in Figure 4.8(e), the resulting mean is moved by a certain amount as shown by dotted lines in Figure 4.8(e). Such mean movement for the cross-correlated sequences between the template and both the obfuscated sequence (Figure 4.8(f)) and the random sequence (Figure 4.8(g)) is less compared to the movement in original sequence, because there are no significant peaks. Since the random sequence does not have any correlation with the

template,

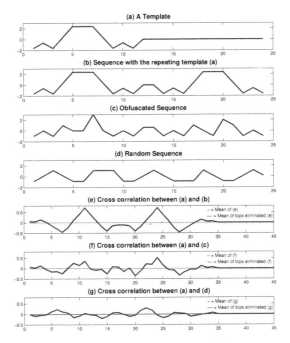

Figure 4.8: An example RIJID Index calculation

The number of significant peaks are decided based on the number of occurrences of the template. For example, TripleDES has 16 rounds within an encryption block. Therefore, when the template is correlated with a sequence of an encryption block, there will be 16 significant peaks in the cross-correlated wave. Thus the number of significant peaks are 16.

Similar cross-correlation curves are taken for both random sequence and the obfuscated sequence with the same template. The same number of significant peaks (decided using the template and the original sequence) are removed in all three sequences (Original, Random, Obfuscated) and the mean movement differences will be used to find the *RIJID* index. *RIJID* index will give us a measure of how much the vulnerable sequence with template is obfuscated compared to a random sequence.

When the mean movement on obfuscated sequence reaches the movement produced by the random sequence, the vulnerability of the obfuscated sequence reduces (that is, the scrambling imposed on the original sequence increases). Hence, *RIJID* index is defined in Equation (4.4) using the mean movements of Original, Obfuscated and Random sequences based on a specific template from the original sequence.

$$\Psi_{f,g} = \frac{\sum_{i=1}^{2N-1}(f \star g)_i}{(2N-1)} \tag{4.1}$$

$$\varphi_{f,g,T} = \frac{\sum_{i=1}^{2N-1}(f \star g)_i - \sum_{1}^{T} TopT}{(2N-1) - T} \tag{4.2}$$

$$\Delta_f = \Psi_{f,g} - \varphi_{f,g,T} \tag{4.3}$$

Equation (4.1) gives the mean of the cross correlation sequence of two sequences f and g. The number of points in the cross correlated sequence are $2N - 1$, where N is the maximum number of points within the sequences which cross correlate. Equation (4.2) gives the mean value of the resulting cross correlation sequence with a number of peaks or maximum values removed. $TopT$ represents T number of maximum values in sequence $(f \star g)_i$. Equation (4.3) defines the mean movement (difference between the mean before and after top elimination) of a sequence f.

$$RIJID\ index = (\Delta_o - \Delta_z)/(\Delta_o - \Delta_r) \tag{4.4}$$

RIJID index ($0 \leq$ RIJID index ≤ 1), as defined in Equation (4.4), uses the mean movements of the Original (Δ_o), Obfuscated(Δ_z) and Random(Δ_r) sequences. The original sequence is used to form a related measure, where mean movement differences between the original sequence with obfuscated and random sequences are used. RIJID index reaches the value of one when the mean movement of the obfuscated sequence equals the mean movement of the random sequence. Such case gets the best scrambling from the *RIJID* processor, where the dissipated power sequence appears as a random sequence (that is, no expected templates exist). The higher the RIJID index of a power sequence, the higher the masking.

4.6   Experimental Setup

In this section, the main components used for experimentation and the process of randomisation measurement is explained. The *RIJID* framework is implemented in a processor with

PISA (Portable Instruction Set Architecture) instruction set (as implemented in SimpleScalar tool set with a six stage pipeline) processor without cache. Figure 4.9 shows the process of measuring *RIJID* index, using the original and scrambled code. Programs in C are compiled using GNU/GCC cross compiler for the PISA instruction set. Original binary (oBinary) is produced from the original code of the program, which does not have the randomisation technique applied. Instrumented binary (iBinary) is produced as explained in Section 4.4.1. ASIP Meister[10], an automatic ASIP design tool is used to generate synthesisable VHDL description of the processor as explained in Section 4.4.2.

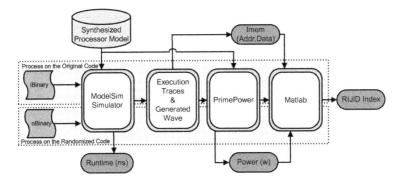

Figure 4.9: The Process of Measurement on Randomisation

The same set of operations are performed for both the original processor with the non instrumented original binary (oBinary) and the *RIJID* enabled processor using the instrumented binary (iBinary). Corresponding binaries and synthesised processor models (Synopsys Design Compiler is used for synthesis) are simulated together in ModelSim hardware simulator, which generates the stimulus wave with switching information. Using ModelSim simulator, the execution trace is verified and extracted for future use. The runtime of each execution is also measured using ModelSim simulator. The power values are measured using PrimePower, which gives the measurements in watts(W). The address (*Addr*) and instruction opcode (*Data*) of instruction memory (*Imem*) are extracted from the execution trace as shown in Figure 4.9. Perl scripts are used to combine the Imem(Addr,Data) and power values(*Power*) taken from PrimePower, which helps to map the power values for each instruction of the program execution. Matlab is used to analyse and plot the combined data. *RIJID* index from the power sequences is calculated by implementing necessary functions in Matlab.

The experiments demonstrated in this work are performed for the cryptographic applications implemented in C language. A detailed explanation of the experiment on the TripleDES application is presented and the results of other applications are tabulated. Dissipated power waves are observed by running the encryption programs for specific keys and different data.

4.7 Results

This section presents the experimental results on the *RIJID* implementation, highlighting the appropriate number of instructions for injection and the overheads.

4.7.1 RIJID index Vs Runtime Overhead

Figure 4.10 shows the variation of RIJID index and runtime overhead for TripleDES program, when the *injection pair* (N,D) is varied. As expected, the runtime increases for each case when N increases, and decreases when D increases for each N.

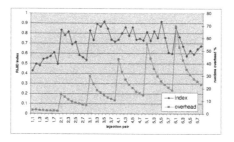

Figure 4.10: RIJID index and runtime overhead on TripleDES

The maximum RIJID index values from Figure 4.10 are produced for the injection pair (3,5) and (5,5) of values 0.9158 and 0.9157 with runtime overheads of 14.5% and 25.9% respectively. When the (N,D) pair is small, the possible combinations of injections are small and similar patterns may start to appear after several tries. Therefore the author decided to have (N,D) = (5,5) as the most suitable injection pair as it will produce more permutations than (N,D)= (3,5).

Equation 4.5 shows the lower bound of the power pattern permutations of a single TripleDES round (which has the original size of 115 instructions, and six is the number of available instruction types which are randomly injected). The lower bound number is due to the fact that the random register values and random registers used in the injected instructions are not taken into account.

$$C = (\sum_{k=1}^{N} \frac{6!}{(6-k)!})^{\frac{115}{D}} \qquad (4.5)$$

The possible number of waveforms for a single round of TripleDES is approximately 2^{240} when using (N,D)= (5,5) and 2^{170} when using (N,D)= (3,5). The other injection pairs ((N,D) > (6,8)) are not tested since they will increase overhead without providing far greater scrambling.

4.7.2 RIJID on other cryptographic applications

RIJID is applied to different encryption programs and the results are tabulated in Table 4.1, where column 1 and 2 gives the N, D pair, Columns 3, 5, 7 gives the *RIJID* index for RSA, IDEA, and RC4 algorithms, and columns 4, 6, 8 refer the runtime overheads. The results show that RSA gets the highest *RIJID* index when using (N,D)= (3,3) with a runtime overhead of 32.97% as injection pair, and (5,5) for IDEA and RC4 with a runtime overhead of 12.16% and 26.45%, respectively. Only the injection pairs of interest (from (3,3) to (6,6)) are shown in Table 4.1.

N	D	RSA		IDEA		RC4	
		index	% OH	index	% OH	index	% OH
3	3	0.9998	32.97	0.7204	8.5	0.9908	24.67
4	4	0.9896	15.88	0.7475	10.6	0.9523	26.25
5	5	0.9511	6.38	0.9738	12.16	0.9998	26.45
6	6	0.9607	11.76	0.7571	12.58	0.9364	24.80

Table 4.1: Runtime Overheads and *RIJID* index for cryptographic programs

The injection pair of (5,5) is considered to be the best choice to implement *RIJID* in all of these three applications, since it scrambles sufficiently, without too much overhead.

4.7.3 Energy Overhead

The average energy values for the original and scrambled (with Injection Pair 5,5) encryption blocks for different encryption programs are tabulated in Table 4.2. Since the maximum scrambling takes place using an Injection Pair value of (5,5) as presented in Table 4.1, the average energy values are calculated for (5,5) and the overheads are decided with the values of original encryption block.

In all cases energy increases slightly, attributable to the increase in runtime.

	RSA (μJ)	RC4 (μJ)	IDEA (μJ)	T-DES (μJ)	Rijndael (μJ)	Blowfish (μJ)
Original	0.96	23.0	5.8	13.1	20.7	475.7
Obfuscated(5,5)	1.08	30.8	6.9	15.6	22.2	701.4
Overhead(%)	12.5	38.2	18.9	19.1	7.2	47.4

Table 4.2: Energy Overhead for Injection Pair (5,5)

4.7.4 Hardware Overhead

An additional functional unit is created for the random instruction generation (R/G as explained in Section 4.3.2). The *RIJID* processor costs an additional 1.98% area overhead when compared with the normal processor without *RIJID*, as shown in Table 4.3. The clock period remains the same for the *RIJID* processor as the original processor.

	Area (*cell*)	Clock Period (*ns*)
Normal Processor	111,188	41.33
RIJID Processor	113,393	41.33
Overhead(%)	1.98	0

Table 4.3: Hardware Overheads

RIJID provides less hardware overheads when compared to other hardware designs, such as the secure coprocessor proposed by Tiri et. al. [222] which costs three times increase in area.

4.7.5 Varying the Instruction Injection

Figure 4.11 depicts the variation of power values when using the same random instruction injection, but using: a) immediate operands in the random instructions which are set to zero; b) registers which do not change during the injection for a given random instruction (thus, injected ADD will always work with a fixed register); and c) random registers with random immediate operand in the injected instructions.

When similar instructions are injected next to each other (circled in the Figure 4.11) due to the values scheduled by the random generator, a constant power tends to be seen for the zero register and fixed register cases. This is because of insufficient bit flips inside registers to cause a significant change in the power consumption. The constant power is changed by using random register writes as shown in the figure and by causing random bit flips inside registers. This figure is a simple demonstration to show that the greater the randomisation the better.

169

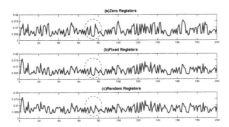

Figure 4.11: Register Types on Injected Instructions

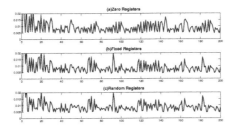

Figure 4.12: Register Types on Injected Instructions for different seed

Figure 4.12 shows the power profile for the same instruction segment as the segment shown in Figure 4.11 with a different seed value. As from the figures, the power profile significantly varies when changing the seed of the random generator for the random register case. The seed is designed to be changed every time the program executes. Therefore the adversary will observe different power profiles for different tries which makes it harder to determine the injected instructions.

4.8 Summary

This chapter presents a randomised instruction injection technique (*RIJID*) to prevent side channel attacks. Random number of real instructions at random places are injected during the runtime of the processor to scramble the power wave, so that adversaries cannot extract any useful information by observing the power wave leakage from the processor. Special instructions are added around the encryption routine in assembly (i.e., at the start and at the end) to trigger the instruction injection. Random generators are used to chose random instructions from an instruction pool, which do not change the state of the processor when executed.

A new pattern matching methodology is used to measure the degree of randomisation to identify suitable injection values. The *RIJID* processor consumes an area overhead of 1.98%, an average runtime overhead of 29.8% and an average energy overhead of 27.1%. *RIJID* can be used to prevent several side channel attacks such as Power Analysis (SPA and DPA), Electro magnetic analysis (SEMA and DEMA).

Chapter 5

ARIJID: A Smart Random Code Injection*

This chapter presents another secure processor, *A-RIJID*, which is an extension of the *RIJ-ID* processor (explained in Chapter 4). The *A-RIJID* processor automatically identifies the encryption routine and starts injecting random instructions, at random places, random number of times and stops the injection when the encryption is completed. A signature detection technique is utilised to identify signatures at runtime to capture the encryption routine from a program. The *RIJID* index is used to justify the obfuscation provided by *A-RIJID* in the dissipated power profile. A DPA attack is demonstrated in *A-RIJID* to prove its immunity against power analysis.

5.1   Overview

The unique signatures of critical segments (such as encryption block) in the power profile should be masked to prevent from power analysis based side channel attacks. To obfuscate the encryption block of a cryptographic program, the processor can be modified to apply masking when it detects such critical segments. This can be implemented in two ways: (1), Software instrumentation (explained in Chapter 4), where programmer specifies tags (special instructions) in the code, where critical segments are; or (2), Defining signatures of these critical segments to identify such signatures at runtime. Signatures, defined based on the instructions executed, takes away from the programmer the responsibility associated with adding instructions in method (1). Since nowadays, the software of an application is developed by multiple programmers working in different modules and combining them together, the

---

*This work is presented in the CODES+ISSS '07 Conference held in Salzburg, Austria.

author strongly believes that hardware modification does guarantee the secure feature been properly implemented.

Several researchers have implemented methodologies to find the frequently executed loops using signatures based on jump instructions [96, 151] for HW/SW co-design methods. Thus far, there has been no implementation of signatures to identify critical segments (such as encryption block) in a cryptographic program. Several secure operations could be automated by pre-defining such signatures inside the processor.

This chapter presents a hardware Automatic Randomised Instruction inJectIon methoD (*A-RIJID*), which scrambles the power wave so that an adversary is not able to identify specific segments such as encryption rounds from the entire power wave. For the first time, a signature based system is implemented to identify the critical segments for the instruction injection. *RIJID* index, a simple mathematical formulation explained in Chapter 4.5, is used to evaluate the scrambling provided by the random instruction injection. *A-RIJID* prevents both SPA and DPA attacks by foiling the adversaries' attempt to identify the power waves corresponding to the encryption rounds.

5.2 Contribution

As opposed to the pitfalls from previous methods, *A-RIJID* provides a generalised solution with no human intervention compared to masking, constant execution path and current flattening methods [30, 54, 68, 86, 88, 97, 165], allowing the processor to take care of masking. On a processor with PISA (Portable Instruction Set Architecture) instruction set (as implemented in SimepleScalar), the additional area cost is just 1.2% compared to the area cost of constant logic chips [222], with an average energy cost of 28.5% and an average runtime cost of 25% compared to current flattening [165], for industry standard benchmarks. *A-RIJID* confuses the adversary without flattening the current[165], but scrambling the patterns in the power wave. It can be applied to any vulnerable segment (and is not algorithm dependent like masking techniques [86, 217]). Dummy instruction insertions can be eliminated using simple time shifting [61] and the random instruction masking [74] injects random instructions at fixed places denoted in the source code, whereas *A-RIJID* injects real instructions at random places a random number of times. Hence the adversary will observe different obfuscated power profiles on different tries.

5.2.1 Limitations

1. *A-RIJID* is proposed as a design time technique, since it needs hardware changes;

2. the author assumes that the system is self contained with memory on chip; and,

3. more signatures need to be added when an entirely different encryption algorithm with different nature is introduced, compared to the ones considered in this chapter.

5.3 Signature and Concomitance

Signatures can be used to identify certain properties in a program at runtime. Such signatures should be defined using the instructions executed, allowing the processor to identify the pattern of instructions executed and respond accordingly. Cryptographic programs contain an encryption block which does secure computations using secret keys. The key aim of this section is to identify such encryption blocks by defining an appropriate signature.

Concomitance is a measure which shows how frequently instructions are executed, and how close together these instructions are executed using a trace. This measure can be used to define signatures for the encryption routines inside a program. The concomitance metric presented by Janapsatya et. al. [112] is used, and is slightly modified to support the analysis in this chapter.

As shown in Equation 5.1, self-concomitance $\sigma(b, T)$ of an instruction is a measure of how clustered consecutive executions of the instruction b are, in the execution trace (T). The distance between two consecutive executions $e(b)$ and $e'(b)$ of an instruction b is referred as d, which is the number of instructions executed in between $e(b)$ and $e'(b)$ including b.

A weight function called W is used to find the concomitance using d as presented in Equation 5.2. The W is used to give a decreasing significance to the two consecutive executions of the same instruction that are further apart in the sense of the above notion of distance. Thus, it is a non-negative real function that is decreasing, i.e., such that, if u, v are real numbers and $u \leq v$, then $W(u) \geq W(v)$. The self-concomitance is computed as a sum of all weights on instruction b in the execution trace (T) as shown in Equation 5.1. Figure 5.1 depicts the self-concomitance analysis on instructions in cryptographic programs.

$$\sigma(b,T) = \sum_{e(b)\epsilon T} W(d[e(b), e'(b)]) \tag{5.1}$$

$$W(d[e(b), e'(b)]) = 1/d[e(b), e'(b)] \tag{5.2}$$

$$\Upsilon(b,T) = \sigma(b,T)_{w.e}/\sigma(b,T)_{w.o.e} \tag{5.3}$$

The plotted values in Figure 5.1 are the ratio $(\Upsilon(b,T))$ of self-concomitances with $(\sigma(b,T)_{w.e})$ and without $(\sigma(b,T)_{w.o.e})$ the encryption blocks within cryptographic programs, computed using Equation 5.3. The self-concomitance ratio $(\Upsilon(b,T))$ values for the cryptographic programs in Figure 5.1 except RSA are much higher for *xor* instructions compared to other instructions. Even though some instructions provide a higher value similar to *xor* such as *or* in sha and *addiu, and* in seal, *xor* gives a higher value on all the tested programs, except RSA. This denotes that *xor* instructions are mostly used within the encryption block of cryptographic programs, giving a higher $\Upsilon(xor, T)$.

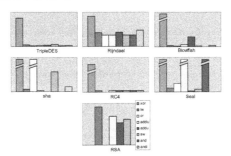

Figure 5.1: Self-concomitance

A threshold-concomitance is introduced to find the most appropriate distance between *xor* instructions such that all the *xor* instructions inside the encryption block can be included for concomitance. This is to make sure that none of the encryption part is left out without balancing. The weight function W is modified to W_t as shown in Equation 5.4 to find the threshold-concomitance by changing different c values. When distance d is greater than c, the weight added is zero in the summation. The self-concomitance values are computed for each c using the Equation 5.1, substituting weight W_t. This measure allows to predict the distance that would cover all the consecutive *xor* instructions inside the encryption block. Figure 5.2

depicts the threshold-concomitance analysis for *xor* instruction in cryptographic programs, where self-concomitance is computed, incrementing c by one starting from one until the value gets stabilised (note that the values are scaled to show the variation). The distance where the self-concomitance stabilises is referred as threshold-concomitance.

$$W_t(d[e(b), e'(b)]) = \begin{cases} 0 & \text{if } d[e(b), e'(b)] > c, \text{ where } c \in \mathbb{R}, \\ 1/d[e(b), e'(b)] & \text{if } d[e(b), e'(b)] \leq c \end{cases} \quad (5.4)$$

According to Figure 5.2, the maximum threshold-concomitance is for rc4 with 85, with 55 for blowfish, 45 for seal and 30, 21 and 12 for rijndael, sha and tripledes respectively. Therefore, 85 is considered as the appropriate choice for threshold-concomitance in all the analysed cryptographic programs (except RSA), where all the *xor* instructions inside the encryption blocks are included.

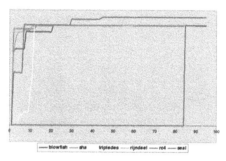

Figure 5.2: Threshold-concomitance for XOR

As presented in Figure 5.1, the RSA cryptographic program has zero $\Upsilon(xor, T)$ for *xor* instruction, which is the appropriate choice for signature in other cryptographic programs. A concomitance analysis is used to find any possible instruction combination to differentiate the encryption block within RSA from the rest of the program. Concomitance predicts how tightly interleaved the executions of two instructions are, in the execution trace. Equation 5.5 depicts the concomitance $\tau(a, b, T)$ of instructions a and b in the execution trace T. There should be at least one b instruction execution $e(b)$ between two a instruction executions, $e(a)$ and $e'(a)$: this is denoted by $b \in [e(a), e'(a)]$. The weight function W is computed from Equation 5.2.

$$\tau(a, b, T) = \sum_{b \in [e(a), e'(a)], \ e(a) \in T} W(d[e(a), e'(a)]) + \sum_{a \in [e(b), e'(b)], \ e(b) \in T} W(d[e(b), e'(b)]) \quad (5.5)$$

177

The concomitance analysis performed on RSA is presented in Figure 5.3. The concomitance ratios ($\Upsilon(a, b, T)$ as shown in Equation 5.6) are plotted, computing the concomitance with the encryption block ($\tau(a, b, T)_{w.e}$) and without the encryption block ($\tau(a, b, T)w.o.e$). As Figure 5.3 shows, the maximum ratio is produced when using *mult* followed by *div*. All the other possible instruction combinations except the plotted ones gave zero ratio ($\Upsilon(a, b, T)$=0). From this analysis, you can conclude that $mult-div$ instruction combination is the appropriate choice to detect the encryption block within RSA (where removal of the encryption block causes higher ratio on $mult - div$, compared to other instruction combinations).

$$\Upsilon(a, b, T) = \tau(a, b, T)_{w.e}/\tau(a, b, T)_{w.o.e} \tag{5.6}$$

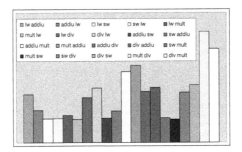

Figure 5.3: Concomitance on RSA

Threshold analysis is performed on RSA to decide two main distances: (1), the most appropriate distance between *mult* and *div* instructions; and (2), the most appropriate distance between $mult - div$ segments, for the signature definition. The concomitance equation shown in Equation 5.5 is slightly modified to Equation 5.7 for the threshold-concomitance analysis on RSA. Distances $d1$ and $d3$ separate *mult* then *div* and distance $d2$ separates two consecutive $mult - div$ segments.

$$\tau(a, b, T) = \sum_{e(a),e(b)\epsilon T} W_{rt}(d[e(a), e(b)]) + \sum_{e(b),e'(a)\epsilon T} W_{rt}(d[e(b), e'(a)]) + \sum_{e'(a),e'(b)\epsilon T} W_{rt}(d[e'(a), e'(b)])$$

$$= \sum_{e(a),e(b)\epsilon T} W_{rt}(d1) + \sum_{e(b),e'(a)\epsilon T} W_{rt}(d2) + \sum_{e'(a),e'(b)\epsilon T} W_{rt}(d3)$$

$$\tag{5.7}$$

$$W_{rt}(d1) = \begin{cases} 0 & \text{if } d1 > c, \text{ where } c \, \epsilon \, \mathbb{R}, \\ 1/d1 & \text{if } d1 \leq c \end{cases}$$

$$W_{rt}(d3) = \begin{cases} 0 & \text{if } d3 > c, \text{ where } c \, \epsilon \, \mathbb{R}, \\ 1/d3 & \text{if } d3 \leq c \end{cases} \tag{5.8}$$

$$W_{rt}(d2) = 1/d2$$

Figure 5.4(a) depicts the variation of the concomitance metric, when changing the distance between $mult$ then div instructions (referred as $d1$ in Figure 5.4(a)) using Equation 5.7 and Equation 5.8 in RSA. The value c is incremented by one starting from one, until the concomitance metric stabilises. When threshold value c is less than the distances, corresponding weights are assigned to zeros as shown in Equation 5.8. The concomitance metric stabilises at distances 5, 40, 60 and 70 as shown in Figure 5.4(a). To capture only the encryption block using $mult, div$ instruction combination, the threshold-concomitance of $five$ is considered as the appropriate choice, where only the encryption block has $mult$, div instructions separated by five instructions.

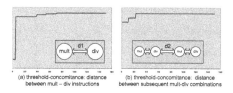

(a) threshold-concomitance: distance   (b) threshold-concomitance: distance
between mult – div instructions   between subsequent mult-div combinations

Figure 5.4: Threshold-concomitance for RSA

Figure 5.4(b) shows the threshold-concomitance analysis on RSA to find the appropriate distance between $mult - div$ segments using Equation 5.7 and Equation 5.9. The distance between two consecutive $mult - div$ segments (referred as $d2$ in Equation 5.9 and Figure 5.4(b)) is ignored ($W_{rt}(d2)=0$) if it is greater than the threshold distance c, which is increased from one upwards. As Figure 5.4(b) depicts, the concomitance stabilises at a distance of 25, hence having a threshold-concomitance of 25.

$$W_{rt}(d1) = 1/d1$$

$$W_{rt}(d3) = 1/d3$$

$$W_{rt}(d2) = \begin{cases} 0 & \text{if } d2 > c, \text{ where } c \in \mathbb{R}, \\ 1/d2 & \text{if } d2 \leq c \end{cases}$$

(5.9)

	Programs	xor hits	m hits	Inst.	% X	% M
G	Dijsktra	686	0	975333	0.00	0.00
E	JPEG	3	0	9167386	0.00	0.00
N	FFT	449	0	732776	0.06	0.00
E	QSORT	23	0	22684	0.10	0.00
R	BasicMath	8196	0	4489680	0.18	0.00
A	StringSearch	1125	0	300710	0.37	0.00
L	CRC32	51	0	11296	0.48	0.00
	Blowfish	26184	0	301753	8.67	0.00
C	SHA	1325459	0	13209078	10.03	0.00
R	Rijndael	265	0	13268	1.99	0.00
Y	SEAL	44279	0	1100640	4.02	0.00
P	RC4	312126	0	24882358	1.25	0.00
T	TripleDES	1060	0	30019	3.50	0.00
O	ECC	10288585	0	897392501	1.15	0.00
	RSA	1	8	7095	0.00	0.12

Table 5.1: Instruction hits on BenchMarks

As per the concomitance analysis, the XOR instructions (repeated within a window of 85 instructions) are mostly used in encryption blocks of a cryptographic program. A multiplication then the division within a window size of five is another signature which stands out in RSA. Table 5.1 shows the number of *xor hits* and Multiplication and Division hits for different benchmarks. The first column of Table 5.1 divides the benchmarks into general and cryptographic programs. The second column details the name of applications, the third column gives the number of XORs in the application, and the fourth gives the number of MULT and DIV instructions within five instructions of each other (*m hits*). The fifth column gives the total number of instructions in the trace of the program. The final two columns show the percentage of *xor* and *m hits* which occur in the trace. The total *xor* and the *m hits* were obtained using the SimpleScalar instruction set simulator.

The percentage *xor hits* (% X) for general programs (non- cryptographic programs) are much less than for the cryptographic programs as shown in Table 5.1. All analysed cryptographic programs, except RSA, have significant *xor hits* due to the usage of XOR instructions for encryption. As Table 5.1 depicts, SHA has the maximum *xor hit* percentage of 10%, while SEAL has 4%.

The *m hits* within a window of five instructions is analysed for the benchmarks as shown in Table 5.1. No other program except RSA has *m hits*. RSA has an *m hit* percentage of 0.12% on the total number of instructions executed.

Based on this analysis the author defines two different signatures: (1), to capture the encryption blocks which use XOR (such as Blowfish, SHA, Rijndael, SEAL, RC4 and TripleDES); and, (2), to capture the encryption blocks which use Multiplication followed by Division within a window size of five (for RSA).

5.3.0.1   Signature 1 - sigXOR

The first signature (*sigXOR*) is defined as shown in the diagram on the left side of Figure 5.5. When an XOR is executed for the first time, it is identified as the start of the signature. The signature expires when there is no more XORs seen before 85 instructions. The value of 85 is decided based on the concomitance analysis and, the research of Ross and Vahid [96].

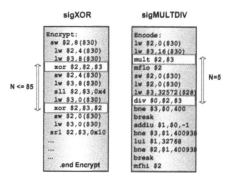

Figure 5.5: Signature Definitions

Therefore, an identification of an XOR instruction indicates the existence of a *sigXOR* signature. Multiple *sigXOR* detections are possible, where each new XOR occurrence after an expiry is considered the start of another *sigXOR*.

5.3.0.2 Signature 2 - sigMULTDIV

RSA algorithm is an exception which does not use XOR within its encoding block. Instead, it uses MULT and DIV instructions. Therefore a signature is defined as shown in the right side diagram of Figure 5.5, where the signature is detected when a MULT and DIV instructions are seen within five instructions. This signature is considered expired when no such signature is seen again before 85 instructions after the previous *sigMULTDIV* execution. According to the analysis, no program (in the tested set) other than RSA contains *sigMULTDIV* signature as shown in Table 5.2

Unlike *sigXOR* where the signature is started when XOR is executed, *sigMULTDIV* is started only when both MULT and DIV are seen.

5.4 A-RIJID Framework

The *A-RIJID* Framework is shown in Figure 5.6 which includes the Random Generation (R/G) component to perform signature analysis and instruction injection. When CPU executes the XOR instruction, a special flag register ($XORSEL$) is set. Based on the value in $XORSEL$, R/G uses a *counter* to identify the signature and sets the SEL flag. It also controls $XORSEL$ for reading and writing.

Two similar flags ($DIVSEL$ and $MULTSEL$) are used for MULT (Multiplication) and DIV (Division) instructions to identify the *sigMULTDIV* signature which is explained in Section 5.3. The R/G sets and resets SEL flag based on the values inside $DIVSEL$ and $MULTSEL$ which are set by CPU, when the corresponding instructions execute.

When SEL is set, R/G sends a hold (*pc hold'*) signal to the Program Counter (PC) and starts generating random instructions at random intervals. The *pc hold'* from R/G and the *pc hold* signal from *controller* are multiplexed together before they are connected to the PC. The generated random instruction (R/I) is multiplexed with the data bus (*Inst.*) from the Instruction Memory(IM). The multiplexers are selected by R/G based on the instruction injection.

The random instruction generation performed by R/G is limited by a pair of boundary values (Injection Pair:N, D), which are set inside R/G. N represents the maximum number of random instructions to be injected between two regular instructions. D represents the

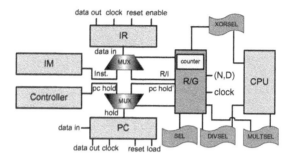

Figure 5.6: A-RIJID Architecture

maximum number of regular instructions to be skipped before each injection.

The *pc hold'* signal from R/G is switched between on and off for random times based on the *injection pair.* When *pc hold'* is high, the random instructions (R/I) generated by R/G are sent to the data port of the instruction register (IR). During hold, instruction which is pointed to by the PC is refetched from the instruction memory; however, this instruction is not written into the *IR.*

Since, execution of an instruction will generally affect the state of the processor, creating any random instruction will overwrite or edit effective data values. Therefore, only a limited set of instructions is selected such that, a random register is used and computed with the *zero* register and the result is written onto the same random register. Since the R/G selects random instructions from a specific set, it is called a pseudo random generator. For example, a randomly selected ADD instruction adds the value in the random register and the zero register and writes the result back to the same random register. The use of random registers for consecutive random instructions was the most appropriate for **A-RIJID** as it caused higher power variation due to bit flips in registers [146].

When one signature is detected ($sigXOR/sigMULTDIV$), the system does not detect the other. Hence this implementation avoids nested combinations.

5.5 Hardware Design Flow

This section presents the hardware design flow, describing how the **A-RIJID** framework is implemented in a pipelined RISC processor. Figure 5.7 depicts the generation of a processor model which implements the **A-RIJID** framework. The ISA is fed into an automatic processor design tool (*ASIP Design Tool* in Figure 5.7 - ASIPMeister[10]) to generate the *A-RIJID* processor model.

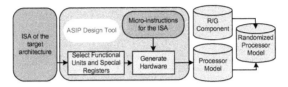

Figure 5.7: Hardware Design Flow

Necessary functional units and special registers for signature detection are selected. The micro-instructions and the functional units are combined to generate a hardware processor model. The output of ASIPMeister is a synthesisable VHDL processor model, which was enhanced by the R/G component (functional unit) as explained in Section 5.4. R/G component is designed separately and then is combined with the processor.

5.6 Experimental Setup

In this section, the main components used for experimentation and the process of randomisation measurement are explained. *A-RIJID* framework is implemented in a processor with PISA (Portable Instruction Set Architecture) instruction set (as implemented in SimpleScalar tool set with a six stage pipeline) processor without cache.

Figure 5.8 shows the process of measuring *RIJID* index (*RIJID* index is defined in Chapter 4.5), using the original and obfuscated processors. Programs in C are compiled using GNU/GCC cross compiler for the PISA instruction set and the binary is produced. ASIPMeister [10] is used to generate a synthesisable VHDL description of the processor as explained in Section 5.5.

The binary and synthesised processor models (Synopsys Design Compiler is used for synthesis) are simulated together in ModelSim hardware simulator, which generates the stimulus wave with switching information. Using ModelSim simulator, the execution trace is verified and extracted for future use. The runtime of each execution is also measured using ModelSim simulator. The power values are measured using PrimePower, which gives the measurements in Watts(w). The address($Addr$) and instruction opcode($Data$) of instruction memory ($Imem$) are extracted from the execution trace as shown in Figure 5.8. Perl scripts are used to com-

184

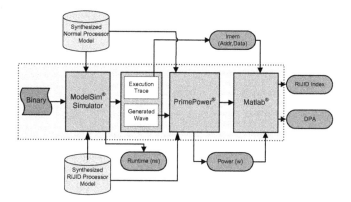

Figure 5.8: Measurement on Randomisation

bine the Imem (Addr,Data) and power values(*Power*) taken from PrimePower, which helps to map the power values for each instruction of the program execution. Matlab is used to analyse and plot the combined data. **RIJID** index from the power sequences is calculated by implementing necessary functions in Matlab. DPA is performed by analysing the source code and the extracted power values using Matlab.

Prior experimentation showed that an injection pair (see Section 5.4) of (N,D) = (5,5) provided sufficient obfuscation with a **RIJID** index which was above 0.7.

The experiments demonstrated in this work are performed for the applications implemented in C, which are taken from MiBench suite [100] and Sourcebank [6] suite. Evaluation is performed on these programs using four different processors: (1), **softRIJID processor** (explained as *RIJID* in Chapter 4), where tags are manually inserted in the assembly file to indicate the encryption block (this requires manual intervention, but allows a base processor to compare with); (2), **sigXOR processor**, identifying *sigXOR* signature; (3), **sigMULT-DIV processor**, identifying *sigMULTDIV* signature; and (4), a **combined processor (A-RIJID)**, identifying both *sigXOR* and *sigMULTDIV* signatures.

5.7   Results

This section presents the experimental results on the **A-RIJID** implementation, highlighting the overheads and the DPA plot.

5.7.1 Runtime & Energy

Table 5.2 depicts the runtime and energy overheads of *A-RIJID* processors for different benchmarks. The first column of Table 5.2 divides the benchmarks into General and Cryptographic programs. The second column details the name of applications, the third column gives the runtime of programs on *Normal* processor (a general processor without any signature recognition). The fourth, sixth and eighth columns show the runtime of programs when *sigXOR*, *sigMULTDIV* and *A-RIJID* applied, and the fifth, seventh and ninth columns depict respective runtime overheads of specified processors. The final column shows the energy overhead of each benchmark when *A-RIJID* is applied.

		Normal (μs)	sigXOR (μs)	% O.H	sigMULTDIV (μs)	% O.H	A-RIJID (μs)	% O.H	% Energy O.H
G	Dijsktra	549697	549706	0.00	549697	0.00	549706	0.00	5.7
E	JPEG	4234937	4234997	0.00	4234937	0.00	4234997	0.00	5.7
N	FFT	5725	5824	1.70	5725	0.00	5824	1.70	7.6
E	QSORT	3285	3307	0.67	3285	0.00	3307	0.67	6.5
R	BasicMath	179097	181879	1.50	179097	0.00	181879	1.50	7.4
A	StringSearch	48412	49333	1.90	48412	0.00	49333	1.90	7.8
L	CRC32	35	40	15.80	35	0.00	40	15.80	20.8
C	Blowfish	36397	59692	64.00	36397	0.00	59692	64.00	72.8
R	SHA	3076	3226	4.80	3076	0.00	3226	4.80	10.9
Y	Rijndael	1752	1896	8.20	1752	0.00	1896	8.20	14.5
P	SEAL	152392	206409	35.50	152392	0.00	206409	35.50	42.2
T	RC4	4504	4572	1.50	4504	0.00	4572	1.50	7.3
O	TripleDES	2902	3941	35.80	2902	0.00	3941	35.80	42.6
	RSA	160	165	3.10	175	9.40	180	13.10	9.0

Table 5.2: Runtime Overheads for A-RIJID processors

The runtime overheads when using sigXOR is much larger for cryptographic programs compared to non-cryptographic programs as shown in Table 5.2. Blowfish has the highest runtime overhead of 64%, and the lowest is RC4, costing 1.5%, amongst the cryptographic programs. Even though CRC32 (costs 15.8% in runtime) is not categorised as a cryptographic program, it can be considered a vulnerable program, as it computes checksums using XOR instructions. Note that despite just having 0.48% of XOR instruction in the trace of the CRC application, the overhead is high, due to the fact that the XORs are close to each other, and are frequently executed. RSA has 3.1% in runtime overhead, which gets just one XOR hit as shown in Table 5.1. This XOR is outside the encryption block, yet due to RSA's small size, a large overhead is observed. Table 5.2 shows that *sigXOR* does not significantly affect non-cryptographic programs (except CRC32) when *A-RIJID* is utilised. The maximum runtime overhead for non-cryptographic programs is for StringSearch with just 1.9%. The *A-RIJID* consumes 13.10% of runtime when applied to RSA as shown in Table 5.2. All other programs except RSA does not have any *sigMULTDIV* hits, hence have no runtime overhead.

The energy overheads for benchmarks proportionally increases with runtime overhead as shown in Table 5.2, due to the small variation in dissipated power. Blowfish gives the maximum energy overhead of 72.8%, while TripleDES and SEAL dissipating 42.6% and 42.2%.

5.7.2   Hardware Summary

Table 5.3 depicts the hardware overheads of *A-RIJID* processors. The first column of Table 5.3 denotes the types of processors used. The second column states the area of each processor. The clock period for each processor is listed in the third column. The area overheads are presented in the fourth column. The processor area is smaller for *sigXOR*, *sigMULTDIV* and *A-RIJID* compared to *softRIJID* as shown in Table 5.3 because of no special instruction usage.

The clock period does not have any significant difference when signature recognition is implemented. *A-RIJID* costs an additional area of 1.2% which is higher than *sigXOR* (with 0.8%) and *sigMULTDIV* (with 0.9%), due to the combinational circuit of both *sigXOR* and *sigMULTDIV*. *A-RIJID* provides reduced hardware overheads when compared to other hardware designs, such as the secure coprocessor proposed by Tiri et. al. [222] which costs three times increase in area.

Processor	Area (cell)	Clock (ns)	Area Overhead (%)
Normal	111,188	41.33	N/A
softRIJID	113,302	41.47	1.9
sigXOR	112,123	41.69	0.8
sigMULTDIV	112,200	41.69	0.9
A-RIJID	112,545	41.69	1.2

Table 5.3: Hardware Summary

5.7.3   Obfuscation and the RIJID Index

The higher the *RIJID* index (explained in Section 4.5), the higher the scrambling provided and lower the vulnerability of the power sequence. Table 5.4 depicts the *RIJID* indices of cryptographic programs and their loop size in number of instructions when imposed on *A-RIJID*. RSA, Blowfish and Rijndael provide *RIJID* indices of 0.9980, 0.9622 and 0.9495, while TripleDES and SHA, provide 0.7040 and 0.7096 respectively. Due to the enormous amounts of time taken for power simulations, only these five benchmarks were considered.

	Loop Size	RIJID index
TripleDES	14	0.7040
Blowfish	37	0.9622
Rijndael	109	0.9495
SHA	18	0.7096
RSA	36	0.9980

Table 5.4: RIJID index using A-RIJID

5.7.4 DPA and A-RIJID

Figure 5.9 shows the DPA performed on TripleDES, an attempt to prove that *A-RIJID* prevents DPA. TripleDES was chosen because it provides the lowest RIJID index, thus the most vulnerable amongst the programs shown above. Plots are provided for each selection bit where the last SBOX lookup of the 16th round is chosen as the attacking point. Figure 5.9(a) shows DPA plots on TripleDES without the *A-RIJID* implementation and Figure 5.9(b) shows using *A-RIJID* applied.

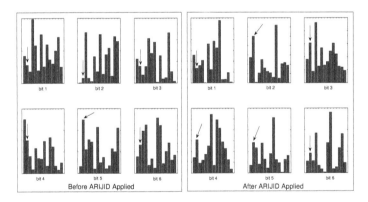

Figure 5.9: DPA before and after A-RIJID

Carefully chosen keys (just 14 out of the possible 2^{64}, including the correct one were chosen to demonstrate) were guessed such that DPA can be demonstrated using fewer power samples. Note that in a real implementation the adversary needs to consider all possible key guesses.

As Figure 5.9(a) depicts, the key is successfully predicted (place of the correct key is pointed to by arrows in each plot) when using *bit*5 (the second plot in the second row of Figure 5.9(a)) of the 6 selection bits used for SBOX lookup. All the other bits except *bit*5 (note that the bits are counted from the least significant bit - right to left) fail to give a peak at the correct key as shown in Figure 5.9.

The key cannot be predicted using any of the bits after *A-RIJID* is applied as shown in Figure 5.9(b), where no peaks appear on the correct key. This analysis demonstrates that DPA will not work even if the adversary manages to eliminate the injected instructions, identifying the proper places in the power sequence for the analysis.

5.8   Summary

This paper presents a random instruction injection technique (*A-RIJID*), an extension of *RIJID*, using dynamic signature detection to prevent side channel attacks. Two different signatures are defined to identify critical blocks (such as encryption blocks) in a cryptographic program. Random number of instructions at random places are injected during the runtime of the processor, based on the detected signatures, to scramble the power wave so that adversaries cannot extract any useful information by observing the power wave leakage from the processor.

The *A-RIJID* processor consumes an area overhead of 1.2%, an average runtime overhead of 25% and an average energy overhead of 28.5%. The downside of this approach is the small overhead, non-cryptographic programs can occasionally encounter.

Chapter 6

MUTE-DES: Multiprocessor Balancing for DES

This chapter introduces a multiprocessor balancing architecture (called *MUTE-DES*) to prevent power analysis based side channel attacks for DES algorithm. *MUTE-DES* contains two processors/cores which generally execute independent tasks. When one processor starts to execute the encryption algorithm, the second processor automatically starts the complementary version of the encryption program and execute in parallel (i.e., instruction-wise). Such algorithmic balancing obfuscates the useful information from the power profile. The complementary version of DES is deduced using the inverted secret key and the inverted data of the original. DPA attack is performed on the *MUTE-DES* to show that it does prevent power analysis. In addition to that, a Fast Fourier Transform (FFT) analysis is performed to justify that there is no critical information leakage in the power profile when data or key is changed.

6.1 Overview

Successful DPA attacks [127, 156, 177, 180, 188] prove that bit-flips caused by secret keys enforce significant variation in the dissipated power sequence. The author shows that executing a program with the inverted secret key and the inverted data will produce complementary bit-flips, with the original key and original data (e.g., bit-flip $1 \rightarrow 0$ will correspond to bit-flip $0 \rightarrow 1$). Therefore, if the same program can be executed simultaneously, but with the inverted secret key and the inverted data of the original, the information on the power profile due to bit-flips of the original key will cancel out. Note that the power profile itself will be additive of both processors. Specifically, it is the correlation between the critical information and the power profile that is obfuscated. Thus, it is not the author's intention to have a flat power profile, but a power profile which is absent of information containing the encryption key.

The plethora of embedded systems containing multiprocessors such as cell phones, PDAs, gaming consoles, audio players, video recorders and video cameras [12, 170, 242] motivated us to use one of the in-built processors to function as a balancing unit, countering the real effects caused by the secret key in the power profile.

The two processors generally execute independent tasks, but when one processor starts to execute the encryption algorithm, the second processor automatically starts the encryption program with inverted data and an inverted key. Note that the second processor is utilised for ordinary computation when encryption is not performed, thus resulting in minimal overhead.

6.2 Contribution

Several logic/circuitry level balancing techniques [73, 106, 107, 191, 225, 227] were proposed in the recent past. These techniques use a complementary logic or a modified secure logic to balance bitflips. For example, if the original logic flips from $0 \rightarrow 1$, the complementary logic is designed to flip from $1 \rightarrow 0$ at the same time as the original circuitry. Dual-Rail logic [73] (also known as Dual-Rail pre-charge (DRP) logic [191]) contains double the logic, one the original logic circuit and the other a similar logic but complementing the discharge from bitflips of the original [204]. This DRP design dissipates the same amount of power regardless of the data. Sense Amplifier Based Logic (SABL) [107] is designed to dissipate an unvarying amount of dynamic power for all bit transitions. The four possible bit transitions are $1 \rightarrow 0$, $0 \rightarrow 1$, $1 \rightarrow 1$ and $0 \rightarrow 0$. The Wave Dynamic Differential Logic (WDDL) is proposed by Tiri and Verbauwhede [225, 227] to dissipate power which is input independent. WDDL utilises a complementary gate in parallel to the original, which receives the inverted inputs of the original, thus producing inverted outputs of the original gate. This results in an unvarying balanced power for different inputs. The above mentioned circuit techniques are further improved in [106, 191]. Even though such circuitry level balancing techniques [73, 106, 107, 191, 225, 227] provide strong resistance to power analysis attacks, they also increase the chip area by 2X (some techniques require 4X), to accommodate the complementary logic. These additional logic circuits, which are permanently built inside the chip, are futile when no encryption is performed. WDDL techniques [225, 227] also require the routing of wires to be balanced, and the DRP logic [191] needs an additional compilation of special libraries.

MUTE-DES also requires manual intervention and it is algorithm specific at this stage, similar to masking techniques [68, 86, 156]. However, *MUTE-DES* is comparatively easy to generalise by examining the algorithm and is not vulnerable to second-order DPA. *MUTE-DES* does not need a complete software modification compared to current flattening [165] and it does not cause much runtime overhead. Compared to the hardware balancing methods [73, 106, 107, 191, 204, 225, 227], *MUTE-DES* consumes twice the hardware only when balancing is required, by utilising the already available processor. A miniscule amount of additional hardware is associated for the synchronisation and signature detection circuit in *MUTE-DES*. The second processor is borrowed in *MUTE-DES* only when an encryption/decryption part in a cryptographic program is executed by the first processor, and otherwise the second processor is left for normal processing of other tasks. *MUTE-DES* does not need any libraries to be modified or compiled as has to be done in [191]. Hence, *MUTE-DES* is an easily implementable system with reduced area overhead usage for switching and synchronising when no balancing is required.

6.2.1   Limitations and Assumptions

- *MUTE-DES* addresses only multiprocessor embedded systems with at least two identical processors.

- the author assumes that the system is self contained with separate memories for each of the processors.

- Caching is disabled during balancing.

- *MUTE-DES* has minimal or no operating system support.

- Both processors are clocked by a single source.

6.3   Algorithmic Balancing

The author demonstrates the methodology using DES [63], a popular embedded system encryption algorithm (note that DES is still being used in secure applications, for example, the transport cards in singapore [15]). Figure 6.1(a) depicts the original DES algorithm, where original data and original key are used. The algorithm contains 16 rounds. In the first round, as per the algorithm the input is passed through an initial permutation and then split into two parts, L_0 and R_0. XOR is applied to R_0 and the original sub key K_1 (which is 48 bits wide and is one of 16 subkeys). R_0 and K_1 are XORed and the output is used for SBOX look-up. An XOR operation is applied to the output from the SBOX and L_0 to produce the intermediate value a_1. This value a_1 is placed in R_1 and R_0 is placed in L_1. This completes the first round.

A similar procedure is continued for all rounds (16 rounds), as shown in Figure 6.1(a), and finally the output is generated using an inverted permutation. The point at which side channel power analysis occurs is the store operation of the intermediate result a_i in DES. Though differing places for exploitation have been tried by previous researchers, they have mostly succeeded when attacking a_i [86].

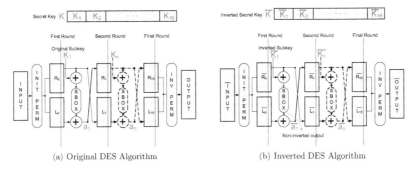

(a) Original DES Algorithm (b) Inverted DES Algorithm

Figure 6.1: Algorithmic Balancing in DES

The balancing effect in DES is accomplished by inverting both data and the key as shown in Figure 6.1(b). Similar to the original DES algorithm in Figure 6.1(a) the inverted DES algorithm in Figure 6.1(b) passes the inverted input through the initial permutation and then splits it into two parts, $\overline{L_0}$ and $\overline{R_0}$. XOR is again applied to the fragment of inverted data present in $\overline{R_0}$ and the inverted sub key $\bar{K}_1$. This results in the same output as applying XOR to non-inverted data and non-inverted key as shown in Figure 6.1(a). The output, which is the XOR of $\overline{R_0}$ and $\bar{K}_1$, is used for SBOX look-up, and the SBOX value produced will be the same as the one obtained with original data and original key. However, XOR is now applied to the output from the SBOX, and data $\overline{L_0}$, thus resulting in inverted output $\bar{a}_1$ being placed in $\overline{R_1}$. $\overline{R_0}$ is passed to $\overline{L_1}$; thus, $\overline{L_1}$ is complementary of L_1. The R_i and L_i in the original algorithm shown in Figure 6.1(a) are completely complementary to $\overline{R_i}$ and $\overline{L_i}$ of the inverted algorithm shown in Figure 6.1(b). This property of complementary execution will be preserved throughout all rounds of the DES algorithm. In this way a total complementarity of essential information is achieved between the processor performing the encryption with the real key and data with the processor acting on the inverted key and inverted data.

The attacking point (the place where DPA is performed) in DES is the store of a_i. Therefore having the same index for the SBOX lookup in both programs will not cause any vulnerability, since complementary outputs are stored. The following analysis proves that algorithmic balancing will provide an effective countermeasure against power analysis side channel attack for DES. To do this, the author considers a power model based on Hamming distance [45], as shown in Equation 7.1, where P is the power consumed, H is the Hamming weight function, k is the scalar gain and n is the noise term. H is given by $Y \oplus X$, where X is the previous value in the register and Y is the new value after the operation.

$$P = kH + n \tag{6.1}$$

As can be seen from Figure 6.1(a) and Figure 6.1(b), a_1 and $\bar{a}_1$ are complementary, and as such the Hamming weights between a_1 and $\bar{a}_1$ will be the number of bits in a_1. Likewise, a_2, a_3, etc. will be balanced by their corresponding complemented values as shown in Figure 6.1(b). Since the Hamming weights for $a_i \oplus \bar{a}_i$ is always 48, the attack point is no longer vulnerable, since k and n are constants, and now H is constant, thus making P a constant value. Similar to Brier et al. [45], the author assumes that the initial value $X = 0$.

6.4 MUTE-DES Framework

This section details the main components in the *MUTE-DES* framework; the base architecture, balancing control, switching, interrupts and the *MUTE-DES* architecture.

6.4.1 Base Architecture

Figure 6.2 depicts the schematic diagram of the base dual core processor taken for the design. As depicted, the processor has two identical cores with separate instruction and data memories for each core.

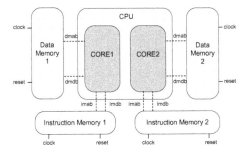

Figure 6.2: The Base Dual Core Processor with Memory Modules

6.4.2 Balancing Control

In this implementation, the author uses a flag register to indicate the encryption program execution and to start the balancing. This flag register can be set in one of these three ways: (i), using the operating system when scheduling the encryption program to the core; (ii), detecting the memory location accesses where the data and key for the encryption are stored; or (iii), using a special instruction to set the flag register. Termination of balancing, by clearing the flag register, can be performed in a similar fashion by using the operating system which can clear the flag register when the scheduled encryption program is completed; or by inserting a special instruction in the source code to clear the flag.

For the experiments, balancing is triggered and terminated by two special instructions which are instrumented in the source code (i.e., the first, *startBal*, and the last, *stopBal*, instructions of the encryption program A as shown in Figure 6.3).

The execution of the *startBal* instruction indicates the CONTROLLER that an encryption program is scheduled in the core. An External Interrupt is given to CORE2. This is a maskable interrupt which will trigger after all the pipelines are flushed. Necessary registers (Registerfile, LO, HI and Program Counter) of CORE2 are saved in the stack as shown in Figure 6.3. After the registers are saved, the CONTROLLER sends the program counter (PC) values to CORE1 and CORE2 at the same clock cycle (i.e., PC values of Encrypt in programs A and $\overline{A}$). Both the original and complementary programs are executed in parallel by CORE1 and CORE2 respectively. When the encryption is finished, the *endBal* instruction in program A will be

196

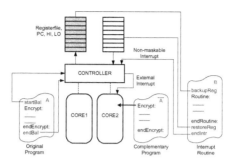

Figure 6.3: Switching and Synchronising

executed by CORE1, which will send a signal to the CONTROLLER indicating the completion of encryption. The CONTROLLER restores the saved registers from the stack. CORE2 will resume its execution and CORE1 will be scheduled with the next available program.

6.4.3 Switching and Interrupts

An External Interrupt is supplied by the CONTROLLER to one of the cores to service an interrupt while the balancing is in progress. This interrupt is serviced after the pipelines are flushed, thus the registers are updated with proper values. Each interrupt routine (e.g., program B) will have three code segments: one, *backupReg*, to save the registers into the stack; two, *restoreReg*, to restore the registers from the stack; and three, *endIntr*, to end the interrupt. The *endIntr* instruction sends a Non-maskable Interrupt (NMI) to the CONTROLLER as shown in Figure 6.3. An NMI request will force the controller to change the PC of both cores to their original places to resume balancing. This is done at the same clock cycle inorder to preserve synchronisation. When a CORE receives an interrupt during balancing, the other CORE is put on hold till the interrupt is serviced. However, the other CORE can be also allowed to execute the next program in the queue, but with careful modification in the controller to maintain synchronisation for balancing. Table 6.1 lists the additional resources used for balancing. The Program Counter (PC) is saved into *PC_backup* at the fetch stage of the *external* interrupt and saved in the stack at the memory stage. The *switch* register is set and cleared by the *startBal* and *endBal* instructions.

Resources	Names
Instructions	startBal, endBal, endIntr
Interrupts	external (masked), NMI
Registers	PC_backup, switch

Table 6.1: Additional Resources for Balancing

6.4.4 The MUTE-DES Architecture

Figure 6.4 presents the *MUTE-DES* architecture, where the second processor (CORE2) executes the same program as the first (CORE1) (shown in Figure 6.1(a)), in parallel, but using the inverted secret key and inverted data as shown in Figure 6.1(b) (when not encrypting, both processors run independently and execute different programs). CORE1 uses the proper key (K) and proper data (D), while CORE2 uses the inverted key (K') and inverted data (D').

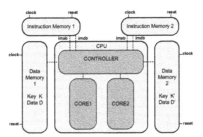

Figure 6.4: MUTE-DES Architecture

Each core fetches instructions from its corresponding instruction memory. The balanced DES program is stored in a part of CORE2's Instruction Memory. The CONTROLLER handles switching and interrupts for balancing as explained above.

The interrupts from one processor to another can be also handled by operating systems using software interrupts [77, 203]. Note that the caches are disabled during balancing, since having a cache will not allow the synchronising of processors. But if this results in excessive performance penalties, a scratchpad memory could be used for the encryption program.

6.5 Hardware Design Flow

Figure 6.5 depicts the hardware design flow of the processor architecture. An automatic processor design tool called *ASIPMeister* [10] is used to generate identical processors (CORE1 and CORE2) based on an Instruction Set Architecture (ISA).

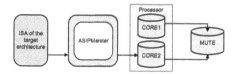

Figure 6.5: Hardware Design Flow

The processor architecture is designed by combining the processors (CORE1 and CORE2) generated by ASIPMeister as shown in Figure 6.5, and the CONTROLLER and interrupt logic with necessary registers.

6.6 Experimental Setup

The framework is implemented in a processor with the PISA (Portable Instruction Set Architecture) instruction set (as implemented in SimpleScalar tool set with a six stage pipeline [187]) without cache. The experimental setup for the power analysis implementations of a Normal Dual Processor (used as a base processor) and the *MUTE-DES* processor is outlined in Figure 6.6. The DES program in C is compiled using the GNU/GCC cross compiler for the PISA instruction set, and binaries are produced. ASIPMeister [10] is used to generate synthesisable VHDL description of the processor as explained in Section 6.5.

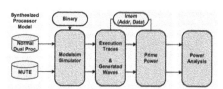

Figure 6.6: Experimental Setup

The synthesisable VHDL versions of the Normal Dual Processor and the *MUTE-DES* processor are synthesised using the Synopsys Design Compiler. ModelSim hardware simulator is used to simulate the program binary with the synthesised processor to generate the stimulus wave with switching information. The execution trace is extracted for future use from ModelSim after simulation. Power measurements are performed using PrimePower in watts (W). As shown in Figure 6.6 the address ($Addr$) and instruction opcode ($Data$) of instruction memory ($Imem$) are extracted from the execution trace. Perl scripts are used to reannotate the power values to the execution trace. DPA is implemented in a separate C program, and the execution extracts the necessary instruction power values from the trace.

6.7 Results

In this section the author presents the experimental results including differential power analysis plots, hardware and runtime analysis.

6.7.1 Hardware Summary

Table 6.2 shows the hardware details of the *MUTE-DES* architecture, generated by Synopsys Design Compiler. The *MUTE-DES* architecture consumes very little additional hardware (around 0.1%) compared to the standard dual processor. The clock period is slightly increased for *MUTE-DES*, because of the switching and synchronising of the cores.

	Normal Dual Processor	MUTE-DES
Area (*cell*)	221842	222242
Clock (*ns*)	41.63	49.61

Table 6.2: Hardware Summary

MUTE-DES is implemented on Virtex-II Pro Development System (XUP2VP: xc2vp30ff896-7) to analyse *MUTE-DES* on FPGA as shown in Figure 6.7(a). Embedded Development Kit (EDK) 8.2i is used to configure the FPGA, which has two in-built PowerPCs. EDK8.2i allowed us to configure PowerPCs and setup the BlockRAMs as program memory and instruction memory for each PowerPC. Each memory is allocated 64kBytes. Two separate buses were created for each PowerPC to communicate with its own data memory and program memory. Figure 6.7(b) shows the block diagram produced by EDK8.2i of *MUTE-DES* implementation. The LED and RS232 components are used to debug PowerPCs separately.

Table 6.3 depicts the device utilisation of *MUTE-DES* on XUP2VP FPGA, produced by EDK8.2i. The first column of Table 6.3 categorises the components into used, available and used percentage. The second column upto the eighth, lists the component details for specified categories. As shown in Table 6.3, the components except JTAGs and PPC405s are available for larger designs (i.e., more memory and components can be added).

200

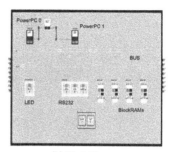

(a) XUP2VP Board   (b) Block Diagram

Figure 6.7: FPGA Implementation

	MUXs	DCMs	Ext.IOBs	JTAG	PPC405s	RAMB16s	SLICES
Used	1	1	26	1	2	128	2159
Available	6	8	556	1	2	136	13696
%	6	12	4	100	100	94	15

Table 6.3: Device Utilisation

6.7.2 Differential Power Analysis (DPA)

The author performed DPA experiments (based on [86] and [127]) on the Single Processor architecture and *MUTE-DES* processor, by executing the DES cryptographic program and analysing each SBOX lookup in each round. Two commonly used selection functions are either based on SBOX output bits, or based on the selection bits to the SBOX. Since the DPA based on the SBOX output bit [86] did not reveal the key in the experiments, results of DPA based on the selection bits to the SBOX [127] is presented. This DPA follows the method proposed by Messerges et al. [156], which predicts the secret key by inspecting all possible SBOX lookups in each round.

The X axis of the displayed DPA plots give all possible key values from 0 to 255 (the first eight bits of a DES encryption key), which is plotted against the DPA values (*Watts*) in the Y axis for each key guess. The attacking point is the store instruction just after the SBOX lookup, where the SBOX output is XORed with the inverted data and stored (as explained in Section 6.3). Figure 6.8 shows a DPA trace performed on Single Processor.

Predicting the correct key corresponds to the significant peak in the DPA trace. In this example (shown in Figure 6.8) the significant peak happens at a key value of 10; DPA was performed on the third selection bit, for the third sbox lookup, in the last round of encryption

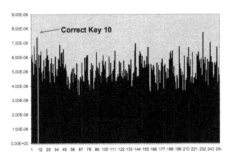

Figure 6.8: DPA on Single Processor

in a Single Processor architecture. Note that another significant peak also appears for the key 233, which is slightly lower than the peak at 10. Reasons for such ghost peaks are given in [46].

Masking of information in the proposed architecture can be achieved when both data and key are inverted. Figure 6.9 is produced when the balancing processor uses the inverted secret key and the inverted data of the first processor (DPA on the third selection bit, for the third sbox lookup, in the last round of encryption). As shown in Figure 6.9, DPA cannot reveal the secret key in the *MUTE-DES* architecture, where the correct key (value of 10) does not produce a significant peak. The DPA values are much less for *MUTE-DES* as shown in Figure 6.9, compared to the Single Processor DPA values shown in Figure 6.8. This is due to the balancing of the information in processing '1's and '0's.

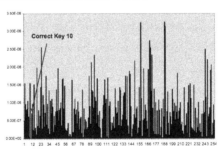

Figure 6.9: DPA on MUTE-DES with inverted Key and inverted Data

To demonstrate the security of *MUTE-DES*, the author compares executions of the encryption algorithm with two different inputs (these were randomly chosen) and subtract the two "clock cycle accurate" power traces. The only information available to the attacker comes

202

from the differences between the power traces for different data inputs chosen. Thus, for an attacker to be able to extract any usable information about the key from the power traces, the power traces for different inputs must be distinguishable.

The author used Fast Fourier Transform (FFT) analysis to examine the spectrum available. The experiments show that the difference when masking is used (shown in Figure 6.10(b)), is an order of magnitude lower than the difference for a single processor (shown in Figure 6.10(a)), and that the frequency spectrum of the difference has far less information (shown in Figure 6.10(d)), unlike the spectrum of the difference for a single processor (shown in Figure 6.10(c)) which exhibits many well defined peaks.

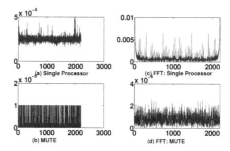

Figure 6.10: Difference between power samples: FFT

To get a better appreciation for the masking ability of the method, an experiment without a perfect balancing is performed, by complementing only the key, but not the data. The DPA graph is presented on Figure 6.11(a), and it clearly shows that the peak that corresponds to the right guess is much lower on *MUTE-DES*. However, when the author finds the differences of the power traces for two different keys as shown in Figure 6.11(b)[1], and examine its spectrum (shown in Figure 6.11(b)[2]), you can still see several well defined peaks, leaving the possibility that there might be some usable information. This shows that both the key and the data must be inverted to preclude the presence of any attacker usable information in the power trace.

Figure 6.12 shows a general picture of the variation of DPA plots for a Single Processor and for a processing system based on the *MUTE-DES* architecture upon the selection bits, for the third sbox lookup in the last round of DES encryption (which was shown to be vulnerable previously). The six plots in each category (each row) is based on the six selection bits (left to

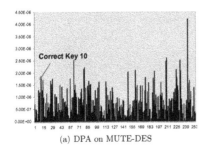
(a) DPA on MUTE-DES

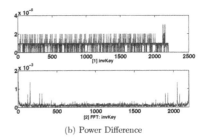
(b) Power Difference

Figure 6.11: Inverted Key and Original Data

right plots start from the most significant bit to least significant bit). First row of Figure 6.12 displays the DPA variation in a Single Processor, while the second row depicts the DPA variation when using the inverted key and inverted data (invKeyinvData) in *MUTE-DES*.

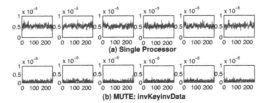

Figure 6.12: DPA plots & Selection Bits

From the variations shown in Figure 6.12(a), the DPA on a single processor produces higher values when compared to *MUTE-DES*. *MUTE-DES* displays a fairly flattened variation (values close to zero) shown in Figure 6.12(b), because of the balanced bit-flips.

6.7.3 Performance Overhead

The performance overhead caused when the second processor is switched for balancing is tabulated in Table 6.4. The normal DES program costs 76,350 clock cycles including memory accesses.

As shown in Table 6.4, every time balancing is performed, there is a delay of 728 clock cycles, which includes saving and restoring necessary registers, setting and clearing the flag for switching, and memory accesses. This delay comprises only 0.94% percent of the runtime. Note that this overhead does not include any delay in software interrupts, which might occur while the system is encrypting. While the masking is performed, the second processor will not

	Clock Cycles
Basic DES	76,350
Delay	
Save Registerfile	320
Save Registers,PC	40
Flush Pipelines	6
Interrupt to switch	1
Exit the interrupt	1
Restore registerfile	320
Restore Registers,PC	40
Total Delay	728
Performance Overhead	0.94%

Table 6.4: Performance Overhead

be doing its usual tasks. Hence, the whole system will have a further delay of 76,350 cycles in the worst case scenario.

6.8   Discussion

In *MUTE-DES*, the primary processor executes the cryptographic program (the second one runs the complementary version), which is enhanced with additional flag registers. But in practice, the operating system can decide upon the processor scheduling. The operating system can force an application to run on a particular processor [14], thus always scheduling the cryptographic program to the primary processor. If the OS is allowed to schedule the cryptographic program to either processor, then additional flag registers have to be attached to all the processors, to enable such a universal execution.

Similar algorithmic level balancing can be performed using a VLIW processor, where a normal instruction and a complementary instruction can be included in a word [71]. But in such cases a VLIW processor will not be able to execute any other program when encryption is not performed.

Since balancing is done by a specific processor all the time, a powerful magnetic probe can be placed on top of the chip to observe the electromagnetic (EM) dissipation of only one of the processors, which is executing the correct program. There is a high probability that the correct key can be exposed from these measurements. To prevent this scenario, the place and route of both processors can be done together with both processors overlaid on top of each other, without a clear partition between the two.

Such on overlaid place and route also prevents one of the processors having a greater power footprint (due to physical variations in the wafer) than the other. If one of the processors did have a greater power footprint, then the encryption key can be deciphered. However, with an overlaid place and route, individual bits in registers can exhibit greater power profile, but such things will be random amongst the two processors and will not remove the masking ability of the MUTE-DES architecture.

Another consideration is if one processor encrypts while the other performs normal computation, then there might be sufficient masking from the noise of the second processor. Masking the actual behaviour in the power profile by the second processor is difficult. Millions of samples taken will statistically average out the noise, which once subtracted will then reveal the encryption key. Hence, MUTE-DES guarantees masking all of the time and does not allow any leakage of secure information to an adversary.

6.9   Summary

This paper presents a multiprocessor balancing technique (*MUTE-DES*) to prevent side channel attacks for the DES algorithm. A second processor is used to mask the effects caused by the secret key from the first processor, by running the same program in parallel to the first processor, using the inverted secret key and inverted data. The hardware architecture of *MUTE-DES* is illustrated, with attacks implemented, to justify its immunity against power analysis. *MUTE-DES* starts balancing when the encryption is scheduled in one of the cores, where the encryption is identified using special instructions, tagged in the program.

The balancing is only performed when necessary, improving the performance of the whole system. The same methodology can be applied with minimal changes to any encryption program which operate in a "bit-wise" manner, by either permuting or flipping bits independently (such as AES, TripleDES, etc.). Similar methods can also be developed to non-bit-wise methods such as RSA, but are harder to implement and, while significantly safer than non-balanced single processor methods, do not result in perfect masking.

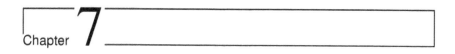

Chapter 7

MUTE-AES: Multiprocessor Balancing for AES *

This chapter presents a multiprocessor balancing architecture for AES (called *MUTE-AES*), similar to *MUTE-DES* discussed in Chapter 6. The complementary version of the algorithm and the architecture are described. *MUTE-AES* utilises the signature detection to capture the encryption routine and synchronises the second processor only during then. Both DPA and FFT analysis are performed to justify the immunity of *MUTE-AES* against power analysis attacks.

7.1 Overview

During an encryption program execution, the bitflips (or the Hamming weights [46]) caused by the secret key are significantly visible in the power trace, causing enough variations to reveal its value. Balancing such bitflips during encryption is one of the most appropriate solutions for power analysis attacks. Chapter 6 explains that balancing can be performed using multiprocessors by executing the algorithm using instructions with proper data in one processor, while executing the inverted data in parallel in the second processor.

This Chapter presents a multiprocessor balancing technique for AES using two processors (called *MUTE-AES*), similar to the one presented in Chapter 6 for DES, where a second processor is utilised to execute instructions of the AES program in parallel with the first processor but with inverted intermediate data. The balancing is performed only when necessary, by combining the second processor during the time when the encryption program is executed

---

*This work is presented in the International Conference on Computer-Aided Design (ICCAD'08) held at San Jose, USA.

in the first processor.

An encryption program starts by accessing the key and the input data from the data memory. In this work, the balancing is triggered when the key or the input data is accessed from the data memory and the balancing is stopped when the signature[1] of the AES encryption expires. Both processors will execute independently and the second processor will start balancing when the first processor identifies an encryption routine (by accessing the input data or key which are in specific locations). The second processor is allowed to continue its original execution after the balancing is ceased.

MUTE-AES has the same contributions and limitations as *MUTE-DES*. The key differences between *MUTE-DES* and *MUTE-AES* are that they target different benchmarks and, use different switching techniques for balancing. *MUTE-DES* uses special instructions to start and end switching (as explained in Chapter 6) whereas *MUTE-AES* uses memory locations and signatures to control switching.

7.2   AES Algorithm

Advanced Encryption Standard (AES) is a symmetric-key block cipher encryption algorithm [167] and is used in a wide range of embedded applications [143]. The 128-bit AES is experimented (AES with 192 bits and 256 bits are also currently used). Figure 7.1 depicts the AES algorithm, specifying only the necessary parts to analyse the attack. A detailed explanation of AES can be found in [72, 214]. The 128-bit AES is considered for the experiments; others (192-bit and 256-bit) can be also treated in a similar way.

As shown in Figure 7.1 the 128-bit input data (which is shown as separate 8-bit blocks — thus input is divided into blocks numbered from 0 to 15) is xor'ed (denoted as $\oplus$) with the 128-bit round key (this initial round key is the actual secret key, and the remaining round keys are generated using a key scheduling algorithm [143]). The result of the xor between the input and key (which are Y0, Y1, Y2 and Y3) will be used as indices for the SBOX (FT0, FT1, FT2 and FT3) lookups. Different lines are used to show which bytes are combined together for different table lookups. For example, the lines are fed into blocks FT0 from Y1[0], FT1 from

---

[1]Signatures can be used to detect the encryption routines in a program based on certain unique patterns of instruction executions. For example, in AES, there are closely clustered XOR instructions, signifying that encryption is taking place. The author uses such a signature in AES encryption, computed based on concomitance analysis [24] as explained in Chapter 5.3

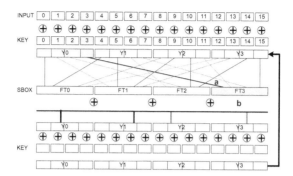

Figure 7.1: AES Algorithm

Y2[1], FT2 from Y3[2] and FT3 from Y0[3] at once. The output from the SBOXes are xor'ed together. Separate xor'ed values are then fed into Y0, Y1, Y2 and Y3. The 128-bit result is then xor'ed with the next round key. This process will continue for several iterations/rounds.

The main part for power analysis is the SBOX lookups. All key bytes have their one and only distinctive place, which they contribute to one of the SBOX lookups. For example, Key byte KEY[3] is only contributing to the FT3 lookup in a round as shown in Figure 7.1. Therefore if an adversary wants to predict KEY[3], the only place for analysis would be the FT3 lookup. a is the input for the FT3 lookup and b is the output.

7.3 Algorithmic Balancing

This section explains the algorithmic balancing as applied to AES to protect AES from power analysis. As shown in Figure 7.2(a), the AES encryption has several main functions: a key scheduling process which will generate subkeys $(K_1, K_2, ...)$ for each round from the original *Key*, the *AddRoundKey* function to XOR the *INPUT* with the *Key*, the *SubBytes* function for the SBOX lookups, *ShiftRows* and *MixColumns* to scramble the intermediate bytes. There are four SBOXes used in the *SubBytes* function.

Figure 7.2(b) and Figure 7.2(c) depict two different inversion approaches (partial and complete) in AES algorithm. The partial inversion approach is presented here only to emphasise the significance of the complete inversion. Both inversion approaches have the same key scheduling function as shown in Figure 7.2. The inverted key $\overline{Key}$ of the original AES is divided into subkeys and the inversion is performed when and where necessary to create

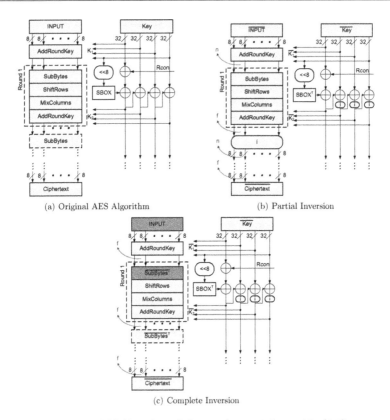

(a) Original AES Algorithm   (b) Partial Inversion

(c) Complete Inversion

Figure 7.2: AES Algorithmic Balancing (images influenced by [210])

inverted subkeys (denoted as i in a round box in Figure 7.2 on the right side segment of both figures). The $SBOX^T$ used in key scheduling is a transposed version (i.e., indices swapped) of the original SBOX, so called due to the inverse value used for the index. As the partial inversion in Figure 7.2(b) reveals, the inverted input $\overline{INPUT}$ is bitwise XORed (the encryption in 128-bit AES is performed in a 4×4 byte matrix) with the inverted first subkey $\overline{K_1}$. Since this will produce the normal output as the original AES (normal output denoted as n) the normal SBOX accesses will be performed. This will be followed by the normal *ShiftRows* and *MixColumn* operations. The final function in the first round (*Round 1*) is the *AddRoundKey* function which will XOR the intermediate data with the second inverted subkey $\overline{K_2}$. Hence, an inverted output will be produced (denoted as f) after *Round 1*. This inverted output is again inverted (the inversion is denoted as a round box labelled i in Figure 7.2(b)) and the normal value of the original AES is sent to the next round. Similar process continues till the end of the AES encryption.

The complete inversion as shown in Figure 7.2(c) has the same key scheduling process of the partial inversion, but has two main different components in the encryption process (the changed components are shaded). Instead of the inverted input $\overline{INPUT}$, the original input $INPUT$ is used. And all the SBOXes (four SBOXes) in $\overline{SubBytes}^T$ are inverted and transposed of the original. The $AddRoundKey$ operation for the original input $INPUT$ and the inverted subkey $\overline{K_1}$ will produce the inverted output of the original (denoted as f to specify *flipped*). Since $\overline{SubBytes}^T$ is inverted and transposed the inverted indices coming into the SBOXes will produce the inverted outputs compared to the SBOX outputs in the original AES. There will be four inverted outputs (each from an SBOX) and the $AddRoundKey$ operation with the inverted subkey $\overline{K_2}$ will produce the inverted outputs of the original. This will continue till the end of the program. These modifications have produced a complete inversion in terms of data bits throughout the encryption.

The partial inversion in Figure 7.2(b) does not process the inverted data at the SBOX operations, but generates inverted outputs after the $AddRoundkey$ operation of each round. This has a considerable effect in balancing (even though it is not completely balanced) especially when you look at the implementation of the AES encryption for each round, which does the XOR with the subkey first and then the SBOX accesses. For example, the first 32 bits intermediate result Y_0 in an encryption round is produced (in the C code) as $Y_0 = \overline{K_1}\,{}^{\wedge}FT0\,{}^{\wedge}FT1\,{}^{\wedge}FT2\,{}^{\wedge}FT3$; where $FT0$, $FT1$, $FT2$ and $FT3$ are the four SBOX lookups. According to this implementation it is visible that there is balancing in the process, since the inverted subkey produces inverted intermediate data after each XOR. However, the SBOXes (which are the main attack points) are receiving the normal input as the original and producing normal output. Since there is pipelining in the processor, there exists a chance that the balancing in the pipelines obfuscates the unbalanced SBOX access pipeline stages.

Since the inverted approaches shown in Figure 7.2 use certain extra flipping operations (denoted as i in round blocks), the original AES program should also have similar operations with the same set of instructions to synchronise both programs (i.e., original and inverted). Note that balancing is performed by executing same instructions in parallel but with comple-

211

mented data values, which shows that the synchronisation between processors is important. Hence, the author created variables for such flipping operations, assigning all 0's in the original program and all 1's in the inverted program. XORing at both instances with that variable will perform the required task.

The attack point (the place where DPA is performed) in AES is the SBOX access, where an 8-bit intermediate data is loaded and stored into the memory as shown in Figure 7.1. The following analysis proves that complete algorithmic balancing will provide an effective countermeasure against power analysis side channel attack for AES. To do this the author considers a power model based on Hamming distance [45], as shown in the following Equation

$$P = kH + n, \tag{7.1}$$

where P is the power consumed, H is the Hamming weight function, k is the scalar gain and n is a noise term. H is given by $Y \oplus X$, where X is the previous value in the register and Y is the new value after the operation. As in the paper by Brier et al. [45] the author assumes that the initial value $X = 0$ (such an assumption is valid for any pre-charged logic [227]).

The 8-bit intermediate data in the Original AES (shown in Figure 7.2) is referred as x and the 8-bit intermediate data in the complete inversion (shown in Figure 7.2(c)) is referred as $\overline{x}$. For example, the intermediate data a and b during FT3 lookup as shown in Figure 7.1 will be complementary for the complete inversion algorithm (i.e., the transpose and inverted values in FT3 will make b complementary). The values of x and $\overline{x}$ are complementary, and as such the Hamming weights between x and $\overline{x}$ will be the number of bits in x. Since the Hamming weights for $x \oplus \overline{x}$ is always 8, the attack point is no longer vulnerable; k and n are constants, and since H is constant, P is a constant value. If the attack also considers the power consumption caused by the bitflips in the bus during load and store, the power model is added with an additional component rH_b as explained in [22]. The modified power model is presented in Equation 7.2, where r is the scalar gain and H_b is the Hamming weight in the bus during load or store.

$$P = kH + rH_b + n \tag{7.2}$$

Since the complete balancing uses complementary index and retrieving complementary outputs from the SBOX (as shown in Figure 7.2), the resulting Hamming weight H_b is also constant. Hence, the power consumption P is still maintained at a constant value.

7.4 System Architecture

In this section, the *MUTE-AES* architecture is presented, which includes an in-built module (called *FUNIT*) for signature detection to stop balancing by identifying the encryption routine in AES. *It is assumed that the key and input data are stored and retrieved from well known fixed memory locations, thus the start time is well understood.* The CONTROLLER for handling the interrupts (as explained in Chapter 6.4.3) is also built into the *FUNIT*.

7.4.1 Signature Detection

The instruction(s) sequences in an execution trace can be monitored and analysed to accurately identify the encryption routines in a processor as explained in Chapter 5.3. Concomitance analysis [112] is used in this Chapter to capture the encryption routine in AES, by looking at instruction executions to realise the patterns of temporal correlation. According to this analysis the signature for the encryption routine of the AES is identified as the consecutive XOR instructions occurring within a 15 instruction window as shown in Figure 7.3.

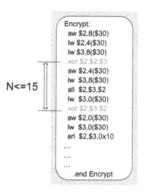

Figure 7.3: Signature to Capture AES encryption

A comprehensive analysis of signature detection within encryption programs, and non-cryptographic programs are reported in Chapter 5, where it is shown that there is almost no signature hits which occur in non-cryptographic programs (with very few false positives). The signature detection unit, *FUNIT*, is shown in Figure 7.4 which exploits two flag registers: (1), *xorreg*, to indicate an XOR instruction execution (i.e., turns on when an XOR instruction is executed); and (2), *sel*, to indicate whether two consecutive XORs are seen within an instruction window of 15 (i.e., turns on when only two consecutive XORs are seen). A counter is used to count each instruction execution for the window computation. When an XOR instruction is executed while the counter is under 15 and above 0, the *sel* flag is either turned on or left on, the *xorreg* is turned off, and the counter is reset. If the counter is above 15, the *sel* is turned off and the *xorreg* is turned off, and the counter is reset.

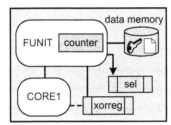

Figure 7.4: Signature Detection Circuit

AES encryption uses key scheduling to create subkeys before encryption. Such an operation also requires balancing where the subkeys need to be created on-the-fly using the inverted secret key. However the signature detection captures only the encryption routine but not the key scheduling part. Therefore in this approach the author proposes to set the *sel* flag when the secret key or input data is initially accessed from the data memory, by using the fixed addresses the key and data are stored. Since the encryption continues after the last access of the memory location where the encryption key or input data is stored, it is not possible to stop the balancing based on memory locations. Note that the only way to stop the second processor from balancing is when the signature expires. Thus, the signature detection unit is a necessity to stop balancing. *i.e., the start of the balancing is triggered by first the access to the memory location of the encryption key or the input data, and the balancing is ended when the signature is no longer detected.*

If there is only a fixed encryption program, then it is possible to use the start and the end of the instruction memory addresses to start and stop balancing. However, the system allows for relocatable AES code to be implemented, by only having to know the data memory locations (which are usually fixed). The operating system can be also used to indicate the encryption program for balancing instead of a signature detection for the encryption routine in AES.

7.4.2 Processor Design

The multiprocessor balancing architecture, *MUTE-AES*, is presented in Figure 7.5, which uses the same base processor as denoted in Chapter 6.4.1. Here the author presents the setup for only the complete balancing, which provides balancing throughout the algorithm as shown in Figure 7.2. Two processors, CORE1 and CORE2, are designed to execute the same program executing in parallel (CORE1 and CORE2 executing the programs designed in Figure 7.2(a), Figure 7.2(c) respectively), and perform independently when no encryption is performed. Separate instruction memories (1 and 2) and data memories (1 and 2) are used for CORE1 and CORE2 as shown in Figure 7.5. The Data Memory 1 of CORE1 is initialised with the proper key (K), input data (D) and proper SBOXes, whereas Data Memory 2 of CORE2 is initialised with the inverted key (K'), input data (D) and modified SBOXes (the key scheduling SBOX is transposed and the SubBytes SBOXes are inverted and transposed as explained in Section 7.3).

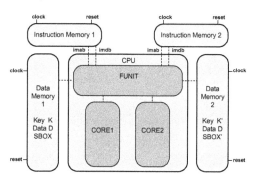

Figure 7.5: Processor Architecture

The interrupt unit (i.e., CONTROLLER) as explained in Chapter 6.4.3 is added into the *FUNIT* to combine the cores for balancing when *sel* flag is set and also when an external interrupt is forced on one of the cores during balancing. The interrupt servicing is explained in Chapter 6.4.3. Note that the caches are disabled during balancing.

215

7.5 Experimental Results

In this section the experimental results are presented, starting with the differential power analysis plots and then with hardware and runtime analysis. The same design flow and experimental setup of *MUTE-DES* are used for *MUTE-AES*, as explained in Chapter 6.5 and Chapter 6.6 respectively.

7.5.1 Differential Power Analysis (DPA)

A DPA on AES is performed to predict the correct 8 bits of the secret key based on the definitions from [86, 127], where the first output bit from the forth SBOX in first round is used for partitioning. The attack point for power measurement is the load instruction from the SBOX. All the DPA plots here are drawn for the DPA bias values (Y axis in *watts*) versus the possible 256 key values (i.e., 0 to 255 for 8 bits). A single processor (without any countermeasure) is attacked to determine the scenario of the attack and also as a base case. Figure 7.6 depicts the DPA plots for a single processor, where the top plot is attacked at the load (LW) instruction, the bottom left at the XOR instruction and the bottom right plot using the average of the power consumption during the SBOX access (i.e., average of the power magnitudes starting from load till the store after the SBOX lookup). In all three cases shown in Figure 7.6 the correct key (value of 14) is clearly identified by a significant peak, thus successfully passing the attack hypothesis.

To justify the necessity of the complete inversion algorithm for the countermeasure, the partial inversion explained in Section 7.3 is attacked using DPA. As Figure 7.7 depicts, the correct key is still predicted using the load (LW) instruction and the XOR instruction, both of which reveal a significant peak. This experiment shows that the balancing effect caused by operations other than the SBOX accesses cannot mask the key. Hence, the SBOX accesses play an important role in revealing the key, and has to be balanced completely.

Figure 7.8 presents the DPA plots for the completely balanced processor architecture which is explained in Section 7.3. As the plots reveal, the DPA signals at the correct key guess (value 14) failed to produce significant peaks for all the three cases (i.e., load instruction, XOR instruction and average during SBOX access). The DPA bias values are much smaller and have a smaller variation when compared to the values observed for the single processor, especially at the load (LW) instruction (which is the main attack point exploited by previous

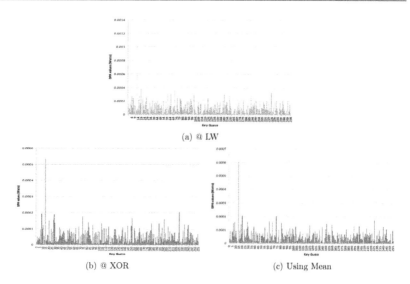

Figure 7.6: DPA plots on a single processor: No Balancing

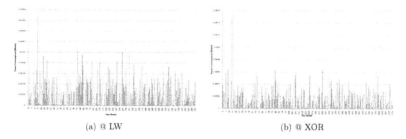

Figure 7.7: DPA plots for Partial Balancing

researchers [86]).

To demonstrate the security of the method the author compares runs of the encryption algorithm with two different inputs (these are randomly chosen) and subtract the two "clock cycle accurate" power traces. The only information available to the attacker comes from the differences between the power traces for different data inputs chosen. Thus, for an attacker to be able to extract any usable information about the key from the power traces, the power traces for different inputs must be distinguishable.

The author used Fast Fourier Transform (FFT) analysis to examine the spectrum available. The experiments show that the difference when balancing is used (shown in Figure 7.9(c)),

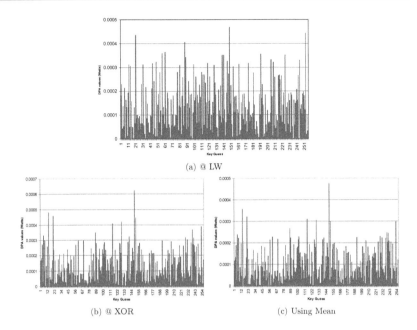

(a) @ LW

(b) @ XOR

(c) Using Mean

Figure 7.8: DPA plots for Complete Balancing

is much lower with more zeroes than the difference for a single processor (shown in Figure 7.9(a)), and that the frequency spectrum of the difference looks much like white noise (shown in Figure 7.9(d)), unlike the spectrum of the difference for a single processor (shown in Figure 7.9(b)) that exhibits many well defined peaks.

This further proves that the balancing technique (*MUTE-AES*) prevents the system from SPA, producing very little variation (or none at all) in the power magnitudes for different data values. Since *MUTE-AES* balances the intermediate data throughout the AES algorithm (i.e., Hamming weight of the processed data is always balanced) there won't be any correlation between Hamming weight and power magnitude.

7.5.2 Hardware Summary

Table 7.1 shows the hardware details of the balanced processor (*MUTE-AES*) architecture, generated by Synopsys Design Compiler. The first column of Table 7.1 categorises the main hardware properties (which are area, clock, dynamic power and leakage power). The second column presents the property values for Single Processor. The properties for the *MUTE-AES*

218

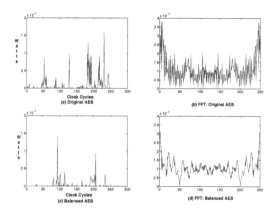

Figure 7.9: FFT Analysis

architecture without the signature detection unit is presented in the third column, and column four details the properties for *MUTE-AES* with the signature detection unit implemented.

	Single	No Sig.	With Sig.
Area (*cell*)	110921.67	213457.61	213855.72
Clock (*ns*)	41.63	49.61	50.50
Power: Dyn. (*mW*)	38.44	76.78	80.19
Leak. (*μW*)	1.49	2.87	2.85

Table 7.1: Hardware Summary

When compared to the single processor the area, dynamic power (Dyn.), leakage power (Leak.) are doubled for the *MUTE-AES* architecture, as shown in Table 7.1, since *MUTE-AES* uses two processors. The clock period slightly increased for *MUTE-AES* compared to the single processor, due to signature detection. The hardware is increased approximately by 0.1% when the signature detection unit is added to *MUTE-AES*.

7.5.3 Performance Overhead

The performance overhead caused, when the second processor is switched for balancing, is tabulated in Table 7.2. Normal AES program costs 175,600 clock cycles including memory accesses. There will not be any delays in finishing the currently executing pipelines before switching, since the signature is detected at the memory stage.

As shown in Table 7.2, every time balancing is performed, there is a delay of 728 clock

	Clock Cycles
Basic AES	175600
Delay	
Save Registerfile	320
Save Registers,PC	40
Flush Pipelines	6
Set start flag	1
Clear start flag	1
Restore registerfile	320
Restore Registers,PC	40
Total Delay	728
Performance Overhead	0.42 %

Table 7.2: Performance Overhead

cycles, which includes saving and restoring necessary registers, setting and clearing the flag for switching and memory accesses. This delay costs only 0.42% percentage in runtime. Note that this overhead does not include any delay in software interrupts which might occur while the system is encrypting.

7.6 Summary

This chapter presents a multiprocessor balancing technique to prevent power analysis attacks in the AES cryptographic program. A dual processor chip is used where the second processor is affixed for balancing only when the encryption program in AES is detected using a signature by the first processor. Two processors execute the same AES encryption (i.e., same instruction sequence) in parallel but with complemented intermediate data.

Since balancing is performed only when necessary, the performance of *MUTE-AES* system is significantly improved in comparison to other balancing methods. *MUTE-AES* successfully prevents power analysis attacks and with careful place and route prevents electro magnetic analysis attacks. The performance penalty is only 0.42% each time balancing is performed with around 2X in hardware cost. Note that there is only 0.1% hardware cost when no balancing is performed.

Chapter 8

Future Extensions for Multiprocessor Balancing Architecture

This chapter introduces the future extensions to be investigated on the multiprocessor balancing architecture. Three different extensions are proposed: (1), *MUTE-C*, a slightly corrupted balancing; (2), *MUTE-SWAP*, swapping consecutive rounds between processors while balancing; and (3), *MUTE-RSWAP*, randomly swap rounds between processors.

8.1   Overview

Multiprocessor balancing architectures (*MUTE-DES* and *MUTE-AES*) proposed in the previous chapters use the second processor to execute the complementary algorithm in parallel with the inverted key. This balances the information in the power profile. However, a slight imbalance between the processors may cause sufficient vulnerability for the adversary to attack the key. Such a scenario can be avoided by confusing the adversary than complete balancing. A popular method to confuse the adversary is to inject a random signal into the vulnerable property (such as dissipated power). When a random signal is added such that it slightly varies with the actual profile, it is very hard for the adversary to differentiate the random component from the original. Adding a random signal when balancing the bitflips (i.e., not balancing completely, but leaving few bits unbalanced at random, for each run) will further reduce the vulnerability. The author proposes an extension (called *MUTE-C*) on the balancing architecture where the second processor uses an inverted data and an inverted key which

221

is slightly randomly corrupted.

As discussed in Chapter 6.8, scheduling the original and complementary programs in fixed cores for balancing might result in a successful attack, when a powerful Electro Magnetic (EM) probe is used to extract only the power footprint of the original program. The author proposes to execute the encryption rounds of both programs (original and complementary) swapped between both processors. This would reduce the vulnerability of extracting the power profile of the original program for the attack. Figure 8.1 presents an overview of two such techniques. The first technique (called *MUTE-SWAP*), shown in Figure 8.1(a), schedules the consecutive DES encryption rounds of both programs (original and inverted) into different cores. For example, the Round 1 of the original program is executed by Core 1 and the Round 1 of the inverted program is executed by Core 2. On the other hand, Round 2 of the original program is executed by Core 2, while Round 2 of the inverted program is executed by Core 1.

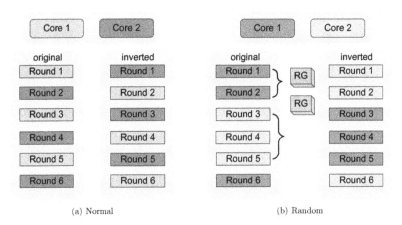

(a) Normal   (b) Random

Figure 8.1: Multiprocessor Balancing with Round Swapping

Figure 8.1(b) depicts the second technique (called *MUTE-RSWAP*) where two additional random number generators (RGs) are used to randomly decide when to swap and how many rounds to continue in that swap. For example, Round 1 and Round 2 of the original program are scheduled to Core 1 and both rounds of the inverted program are scheduled to Core 2 (the first RG created a value of zero to say not to swap and the second RG created a value of two, specifying two rounds to keep without swap). However, Round 3 to Round 5 are swapped to the next cores. At this point, the first RG created a value of one to say do swap and, the other created a value of three to execute three rounds in that manner.

8.2 The Extended Architectures

This section presents the three extended multiprocessor balancing architectures introduced above.

8.2.1 MUTE-C

As shown in Figure 8.2, *MUTE-C* has the same fetching and switching procedures as explained for *MUTE-DES* in Chapter 6. The functional unit (*FUNIT*) in *MUTE-C* framework uses a Random Generator (*R/G*) component to slightly corrupt the inverted key (K'), when K' is retrieved by CORE2.

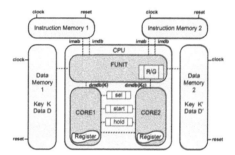

Figure 8.2: MUTE-C Architecture

The *R/G* component, shown in Figure 8.2, is implemented using Linear Feedback Shift Register (LFSR). For the experimentation, the author generated unique seeds for *R/G* using the *date* command in Linux. But in real implementations, several environmental properties like temperature, clock or noise can be sensed to find a unique seed for the random generator at each run. When *FUNIT* retrieves the inverted key (K'), it corrupts two bits in K', in bit positions based on the random values generated by the *R/G*. The corrupted key (Kc) is sent to CORE2, while CORE1 uses the correct key (K).

MUTE-C architecture is expected to confuse the adversary by producing random peaks in the DPA. This is because of the slight random corruption in the key bits which will randomise the behaviour of the selection bit in the DPA plot.

223

8.2.2 MUTE-Swap

Figure 8.3 depicts the *MUTE-SWAP* architecture, where *regSig* and *regSwitch* are flag registers used for signature detection and swapping respectively. Whenever an encryption program is executed the signature detection unit in *FUNIT* sets *regSig* as explained in Chapter 7. The balancing starts when *regSig* is set. Since DES encryption round is implemented as a function, the execution of a *jump* instruction is used to set and clear *regSwitch*. The *jump* execution sets the *regSwitch* if it is cleared already and vice-versa.

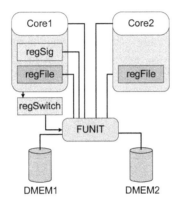

Figure 8.3: MUTE-SWAP Architecture

As shown in Figure 8.3, the *MUTE-SWAP* architecture switches between the original program and the complementary program which are initialised in DMEM1 and DMEM2 respectively. Since the registerfiles (*regFiles*) within the cores are for the original program (in Core1) and the complementary program (in Core2), *FUNIT* switches the control of each *regFile* to the other core when *regSwitch* is set. Such switching is also performed for DMEM1 and DMEM2. The pipelines are flushed (to update the *regFiles* with proper values) before swapping the cores by holding the program counters (PCs) of each core for six clock cycles (note that the cores use six stage pipelines).

Two random number generators are created for *MUTE-RSWAP*, which are embedded into *FUNIT* to randomly swap the encryption rounds, random number of times.

8.3 Experimental Results

This section presents the results for *MUTE-C*, *MUTE-SWAP* and *MUTE-RSWAP*. Experiments were performed for *MUTE-C* to realise the protection it provides against DPA. *MUTE-SWAP* and *MUTE-RSWAP* are not experimented for DPA, but implemented in hardware.

8.3.1 Hardware Summary

Table 8.1 illustrates the hardware details of the *MUTE-DES* processor extensions introduced in this Chapter. The Normal Single Processor is used for reference. *MUTE-C* costs 0.1% in additional hardware compared to *MUTE-DES* without the signature detection. The signature detection unit consumes an additional 0.5% of hardware.

Processor		Area (cell)
Normal Single Processor		110, 921
MUTE-DES	without signature	213, 457
	with signature	213, 855
MUTE-C	without signature	213, 855
	with signature	215, 031
MUTE-SWAP	MUTE-DES	220, 854
	MUTE-C	221, 285
MUTE-RSWAP	MUTE-DES	221, 225
	MUTE-C	221, 656

Table 8.1: Hardware Summary for MUTE-DES extensions

MUTE-SWAP and *MUTE-RSWAP* frameworks are designed in both *MUTE-DES* and *MUTE-C* without signature detection (i.e., *MUTE-DES* refers perfect balancing and *MUTE-C* refers a slightly corrupted balancing). For example, *MUTE-SWAP* in *MUTE-DES* will perform swapping of consecutive rounds for a perfectly balanced technique. *MUTE-SWAP* with *MUTE-DES* costs an additional 3.46% in area compared to the standard *MUTE-DES*, while *MUTE-SWAP* with *MUTE-C* consumes 3.66%. Similarly, *MUTE-RSWAP* costs an additional area of 3.64% and 3.84% with *MUTE-DES* and *MUTE-C* respectively, compared to the standard ones.

8.3.2 DPA on MUTE-C

MUTE-C does not reveal the correct secret key during DPA analysis as shown in Figure 8.4. The DPA value of the correct key (value of 10) does not have significant peaks.

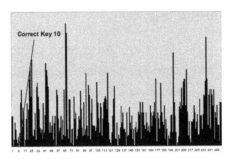

Figure 8.4: DPA on MUTE-C

Figure 8.5 shows a general picture on the variation of DPA plots of Single Processor, *MUTE-DES* and *MUTE-C* on the selection bits, for the third sbox lookup in the last round of DES encryption (which is proved as vulnerable in Chapter 6). The six plots on each category (each column) is based on the six selection bits (top to bottom plots referring least significant to most significant bits).

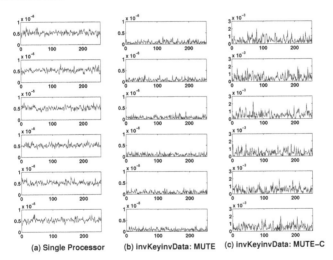

Figure 8.5: DPA using selection bits in DES for MUTE-C

As from the variations shown in Figure 8.5, the DPA on a Single Processor produces higher values compared to *MUTE-DES* and *MUTE-C*. *MUTE-DES* displays a fairly flattened variation, because of the balanced secret key. Even though *MUTE-C* generates lower DPA values, it displays contrasting DPA variations because of the corrupted key balancing. This will further confuse the adversary when deciding upon the significant peaks, where more ghost peaks [46] appear.

8.4 Summary

This chapter explains the initial investigations performed on the extensions of the multiprocessor balancing techniques. *MUTE-C* utilises a slightly corrupted key when balancing, compared to the perfect complementary key in *MUTE-DES*. Such corruption creates random peaks in the DPA plots confusing the adversary. *MUTE-SWAP* swaps consecutive rounds between processors while balancing and *MUTE-RSWAP* randomly swaps rounds between processors. Both *MUTE-SWAP* and *MUTE-RSWAP* protect the system from using highly powerful probes to capture only a single core's power/electromagnetic consumption in a MultiProcessor System-on-Chip (MPSoC). However, *MUTE-SWAP* and *MUTE-RSWAP* have less significance where designs can be carefully routed and placed to make sure EM probes cannot be used to identify separate EM dissipation from the cores and, the latest FPGA chips have built-in EM reduction plates to protect against EM attacks (according to the security experts). DPA will be performed on both these extensions to prove the immunity against power analysis. The extensions will be further tested for AES program.

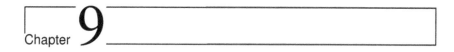

Chapter 9

Conclusions and Future Directions

Power analysis based side channel attacks are getting more and more popular because of the ubiquity of embedded systems. The adversary observes the power consumption/dissipation from the chip, while it is performing an encryption/decryption using the secret key. Power analysis techniques are applied on this recorded power profile to predict the secret key. The most common attacks are Simple Power Analysis (SPA) and Differential Power Analysis (DPA). SPA involves in predicting the Hamming weight [46] of the processed data at an instruction execution, based on the power magnitude. Such prediction will reduce the number of tries, compared to bruteforcing, to attack the system. SPA techniques need only a single power trace, nevertheless not powerful. DPA, a more powerful technique than SPA, uses statistical analysis, based on the principle that there is a significant power variation between manipulating 0's and 1's [127]. Other power analysis techniques discussed in this book are Correlation Power Analysis (CPA), Big Mac attack, template attack, Davies-Murphy power attack and power analysis on FPGA.

Researchers have published various countermeasures at different levels to prevent power analysis. Major solutions are masking, algorithm modification, and balancing. Masking techniques use random values inside the actual computation to obfuscate the real data being processed. Even though masking techniques are considered safe against SPA, they are proved vulnerable against DPAs (especially, multi-order DPAs). Algorithm modification techniques add a substantial amount of extra footprint in the code, costing performance. Balancing techniques are considered the better solutions to prevent power analysis. However, such techniques cost unnecessary hardware overhead. Other countermeasures, discussed in this book, include dummy instruction insertion, signal suppression, current flattening, non-deterministic processors, handling clock and special instructions.

This book presents various countermeasures at system level to prevent power analysis, considering the drawbacks from the previously proposed countermeasures. These techniques mainly focus on compromising area and performance while preventing both SPA and DPA. The following are the key conclusions derived from this book;

1. *RIJID* is a hardware software randomised instruction method, which injects random instructions, random number of times, at random places during the encryption. This prevents the adversary from extracting any useful information by observing the power wave leakage from the processor. A pattern matching methodology (*RIJID* index) is used to measure the degree of randomization to identify suitable injection values. The *RIJID* processor consumes an area overhead of 1.98%, an average runtime overhead of 29.8% and an average energy overhead of 27.1%. *RIJID* prevents both the SPA and DPA, and also the electromagnetic analysis attacks. The randomisation injected into the pipelines creates random nature in the power magnitudes, preventing SPA. Multi-order DPA also fails because of the random number of instruction injections at random places, where the adversary can not pick all the random injections from the power profile.

2. *A-RIJID*, an extension of *RIJID*, utilises dynamic signature detection to prevent side channel attacks. Two different signatures are defined to identify critical blocks (such as encryption blocks) in a cryptographic program. Random number of instructions at random places are injected during the runtime of the processor, based on the detected signatures, to scramble the power wave so that adversaries cannot extract any useful information by observing the power wave leakage from the processor. The *A-RIJID* processor consumes an area overhead of 1.2%, an average runtime overhead of 25% and an average energy overhead of 28.5%. It also prevents both SPA and DPA. The downside of this approach is the small overhead, non-cryptographic programs can occasionally encounter.

3. *MUTE-DES* utilises a dual-core processor, where the second core is synchronised to execute the complementary version of the DES encryption program when the first core starts executing the proper encryption. Both the original and complementary DES

programs have the same instruction sequence, but process complementary data values to produce complementary outputs. Such an execution balances the information in the power profile. The encryption is captured by instrumenting special instructions at the start and at the end of the encryption routine. Interrupts are implemented for servicing higher priority requests during balancing. *MUTE-DES* costs 0.94% in runtime whenever balancing has to be performed. The hardware cost in *MUTE-DES* is just 0.1% compared to the standard dual-core processor. *MUTE-DES* prevents SPA and DPA by balancing the information throughout the DES algorithm.

4. *MUTE-AES* is a similar balancing technique to *MUTE-DES*, where the algorithmic balancing is performed to safeguard AES encryption from power analysis based side channel attacks. Two processors execute the same AES encryption (i.e., same instruction sequence) in parallel but with complemented intermediate data. The balancing is triggered when the key or the input data is accessed from the data memory and the balancing is stopped when the signature (used in *A-RIJID*) of the AES encryption expires. *MUTE-AES* successfully prevents power analysis attacks and with careful place and route prevents electro magnetic analysis attacks. The performance penalty is only 0.42% each time balancing is performed with around 2X in hardware cost. Note that there is only 0.1% hardware cost when no balancing is performed.

5. *MUTE-C*, *MUTE-SWAP* and *MUTE-RSWAP* are the *MUTE-DES* extensions proposed for balancing DES encryption. *MUTE-C* confuses the adversary by creating random peaks in the DPA plot, because of the slight corruption in the complemented key. *MUTE-SWAP* swaps consecutive rounds between processors while balancing, which prevents the attacker from using powerful electro magnetic probes to isolate the individual waves of respective cores. *MUTE-RSWAP*, a slightly different version of *MUTE-SWAP*, randomly swaps the encryption rounds between processors. *MUTE-C* costs 0.1% in additional hardware compared to *MUTE-DES*. *MUTE-SWAP* with *MUTE-DES* costs an additional 3.46% in area compared to the standard *MUTE-DES*, while *MUTE-SWAP* with *MUTE-C* consumes 3.66%. Similarly, *MUTE-RSWAP* costs an additional area of 3.64% and 3.84% with *MUTE-DES* and *MUTE-C* respectively, compared to the standard ones.

Future Directions

Following are the main directions which the author would consider to work in the future;

1. The architectural extensions (i.e., *MUTE-C*, *MUTE-SWAP* and *MUTE-RSWAP*) will be tested for DPA. Implementation of these extensions for AES program will be performed to generalise the idea.

2. Currently, the *RIJID* design injects instructions which are only used for masking, but not for any normal processing. However, such instructions can be used for normal processing by considering the interdependencies. If an instruction can be executed earlier in the program (because of its interdependency with the other earlier instructions), that instruction can be scheduled in the pool to be injected as an instruction for masking. This way of non-deterministic execution will cause less number of instructions to be wasted, improving the performance of the application. A table mechanism can be introduced to preprocess the code and populate interdependent instructions with their possible places of execution. Whenever a normal instruction is not available for masking, a fake instruction can be used as already been implemented in *RIJID*.

3. The author realises that the randomness created in the power profile from *RIJID* could still be isolated using humongous amount of samples. One interesting way to approach this would be to perform averaging on the power samples at each clock cycle to recreate the original power profile. Phase shifting techniques would be also needed, since the instructions are injected at random places.

4. Power analysis attacks on a multiprocessor environment would be another interesting concept to investigate. The author assumes in his book that *MUTE-DES* and *MUTE-AES* guarantee the security of the system, where the adversary can implement a successful power analysis attack on a general multiprocessor environment (i.e., without balancing). An investigation on what is possible using power analysis in a general multiprocessor environment would be very useful for the future multiprocessor systems.

5. *MUTE-DES* and *MUTE-AES* utilised two processors, where these techniques can be adapted for VLIW architectures, multipipeline systems, multithreading, etc. Investigations on such systems for balancing will be interesting, which will allow us to broaden

the solutions to different types of applications.

6. The author attempted FPGA implementations for the solutions (as briefed in the Appendices), but did not perform a complete power analysis attack on those systems. Investigations on such FPGA implementations would be useful to justify the practicality of the countermeasures. This will also open more research problems (such as, how a power analysis free system can be implemented in an FPGA, what are the design factors to be considered in an FPGA implementation to prevent power analysis, etc.).

Anatomy of Differential Power Analysis for AES*

This Appendix presents a detailed study of attacking AES cryptographic algorithm using DPA.

Overview

Advanced Encryption Standard (AES) [214] is one of the mostly used encryption programs in embedded systems [143]. Latest secure embedded devices, such as RFID (Radio-frequency identification), are using AES for authentication and encryption [80], which shows its effectiveness and preference in industry over other encryption algorithms. Hence, a detailed explanation of how an AES can be attacked using power analysis will be beneficial for the researchers who endeavour to find effective countermeasures to such attacks.

AES Analysis

AES, a symmetric block cipher, is one of the widely used encryption programs in embedded systems [101, 143]. It is important for an adversary to understand and master the algorithm and its implementation before performing power analysis. It is even more important for the designer of countermeasures. In this section The author presents a detailed description of the

---

*This work is presented in the international workshop on Real Time and Embedded Systems (RTES'08) held at Timisoara, Romania.

algorithmic and implementation parts of AES, which are important for power analysis.

AES Encryption Algorithm

Figure A.1 depicts the AES algorithm, specifying only the necessary parts to analyse the attack. A detailed explanation of AES can be found in [72, 214]. The 128-bit AES is considered for the experiments; others (192-bit and 256-bit) can be also treated in a similar way.

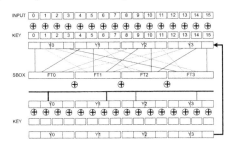

Figure A.1: AES Algorithm

As shown in Figure A.1 the 128 bits input data (which is shown as separate 8 bits blocks — thus input is divided into blocks numbered from 0 to 15) is xor'ed (denoted as $\oplus$) with the 128 bits round key (this initial round key is the actual secret key, and the remaining round keys are generated using a key scheduling algorithm [143]). The result of the xor between the input and key (which are Y0, Y1, Y2 and Y3) will be used as indices for the SBOX (FT0, FT1, FT2 and FT3) lookups. Different lines are used to show which bytes are combined together for different table lookups. For example, the lines are fed into blocks FT0 from Y1[0], FT1 from Y2[1], FT2 from Y3[2] and FT3 from Y0[3] at once. The output from the SBOXes are xor'ed together. Separate xor'ed values are then fed into Y0, Y1, Y2 and Y3. The 128 bits result is then xor'ed with the next round key. This process will continue for several iterations/rounds.

The main part of concern for the attack demonstration is the first round and the blocks which are shaded in Figure A.1. The author chooses the first round as the best place to attack because that is the only round which is affected by the original key (all the other rounds are contributed by round keys). The forth byte of input (INPUT[3]) is xor'ed with the forth byte of key (KEY[3]) and the result (Y0[3]) is sent as index for the lookup in FT3. Key byte KEY[3] is only contributing to the FT3 lookup in a round as shown in Figure A.1. Likewise, all the other bytes of the key have their one and only distinctive place, which they contribute to one of the SBOX lookups. Therefore if an adversary wants to predict KEY[3], the only place for analysis would be the FT3 lookup. Once the algorithm is understood, it is necessary to look at the code to understand the implementation of the algorithm, in particular to understand how and where the SBOX lookups are implemented.

Code Analysis

Figure A.2(a) depicts the AES round implementation in C. The FT3 lookup in the first round (which is the execution of concern to predict KEY[3] as explained in the previous section) using the index of Y0 (the least significant byte of Y0) is highlighted. Each statement receives values from SBOXes based on a byte index and xor'ed together with the round key. The values (Y0, Y1, Y2 and Y3) are fed to the next round as explained.

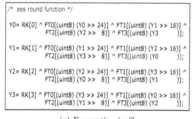

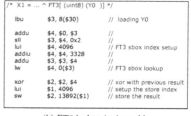

(a) Encryption in C   (b) FT3 lookup in Assembly

Figure A.2: Code Analysis

As shown in Figure A.2(a) the least significant byte of Y0 is only used for the FT3 SBOX lookup in statement two, within a round, which has to be investigated for power analysis to predict KEY[3]. The attacker still needs to find the instructions involved in executing the FT3 lookup using Y0, since the attack is based on specific instructions executed. Note that the exploited property in power analysis is the bitflips or the Hamming weights during instruction executions.

Figure A.2(b) shows the assembly instruction sequence of the FT3 lookup segment in statement two of Figure A.2(a). This assembly is produced using the GNU/GCC cross compiler for the PISA instruction set (SimpleScalar Tool Set [51]). The adversary should also realise (if the architecture of the processor is not known) that a different compiler might produce slightly different instruction sequence, but will include all necessary instructions like load, xor and store (lw, xor and sw in Figure A.2(b)). As per the instruction sequence, the least significant byte of Y0 is loaded (using *lbu*) and the index for the SBOX lookup is calculated using several instructions. FT3 lookup is performed using a load instruction (*lw*) and the output is xor'ed with the previous result. The xor'ed result is then stored (*sw*) into memory.

As shown in Figure A.2(b), the key instructions for the adversary will be the instructions involved in the SBOX lookup, namely the load (*lw*), *xor* and store (*sw*) instructions. The attacker should look for the places where these instructions are executed in the power profile.

Differential Power Analysis (DPA)

In this section the author details the DPA, starting with the definition of DPA and then discuss related research. The author explains and demonstrates only the traditional DPA [86, 127] (also called as single-bit DPA [247]), which is most commonly used. Other types of DPA, such as Multi-bit DPA [44, 154], DPA based on hamming weights [101, 185], higher order DPA [180, 188] and Correlation Power Analysis (CPA) [46] can be also experimented in a similar fashion.

Definition

The secret key, which is embedded inside the processor, is the one which the adversary has to successfully predict. Input values to a chip (i.e., data to be encrypted) are given from an external source, which can be controlled by the adversary. Multiple input values are fed into the chip and the adversary observes and records the power profile during encryption for each of the inputs. The adversary seeks to predict the correct key based on the input values fed into the system, and the power values which are dissipated for those inputs.

As shown in Figure A.3, a byte data and a byte key are xor'ed together and the result is used for the SBOX lookup. If the data is 8 bits, the range of values the adversary can feed into the chip is $0 <= i <= 255$. The dissipated power during the SBOX load process (where the index Y is calculated, and FT is looked up) when data value i is input, is P_i (power profile will contain the dissipated power signature of all instructions, and the adversary has to identify only the section of the power profile of interest, for use in the attack). The power dissipation (P_i) at the load process, can be identified in different ways (i.e, the average power over the whole index calculation and lookup can be used, or only the load instruction (*lw*) power where the SBOX data is looked up, or the XOR instruction power when Y is calculated). Note that

238

in a single attack, only one of these ways will be employed.

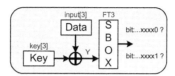

Figure A.3: Differential Power Analysis

Input: Power Values P

Output: DPA bias

$S_0 = 0; S_1 = 0; CNT_0 = 0; CNT_1 = 0;$

for *Key j=0 to 255* **do**

> **for** *Input i=0 to 255* **do**
>
> > Simulate the AES to get SBOX output bit bit_i;
> >
> > Determine Corresponding Power P_i;
> >
> > **if** $bit_i = 0$ **then**
> > > $S_0 = P_i + S_0$;
> > >
> > > $CNT_0 = CNT_0++$;
> > >
> > **end**
> >
> > **if** $bit_i = 1$ **then**
> > > $S_1 = P_i + S_1$;
> > >
> > > $CNT_1 = CNT_1++$;
> > >
> > **end**
>
> **end**
>
> DPA bias$_j = |(S_0/CNT_0) - (S_1/CNT_1)|$;

end

Algorithm 1: DPA algorithm for AES

Algorithm 1 illustrates the DPA approach in AES, where the power values P measured for all possible Inputs are given as inputs and output is the DPA bias value for each Key assumption. The algorithm performs a loop with key j varying from 0 to 255. For each key j the Input values i, are varied from 0 to 255. At each Input i the SBOX output value is extracted and the least significant bit of the output as shown in Figure A.3 is examined. If bit_i is 0, the power value P_i corresponding to Input i will be added to S_0. If bit_i is 1, the power value P_i corresponding to Input i will be added to S_1. Likewise, all the power values corresponding to all possible Inputs will be added to either S_1 or S_0. The DPA bias for a

239

Key guess j (DPA bias$_j$) is computed as the difference between the averages of S_0 and S_1 as shown in Algorithm 1 (CNT_0 and CNT_1 are used to divide the S_0 and S_1 respectively). A set of DPA bias values will be computed using all possible Key values (from 0 to 255). The key which gives the highest DPA bias value is predicted as the correct key, because that is where the highest correlation is observed between prediction and the actual processing [127].

For the attack, key[3] and input[3] are xor'ed together for the FT3 lookup (indicated in Figure A.3). The task is to correctly predict the value of key[3]. The input[3] is only used with key[3] as shown in Figure A.1. Hence, the author assign values from 0 to 255 to input[3] for power measurements and all the other input values (e.g., input[0], input[2]) to a fixed value so that the noise from the other inputs will cancel out.

Power Profile Analysis

One of the hardest tasks for the adversary in power analysis is to analyse the whole power profile and capture power values from specific places (such as load operation at SBOX). Several researchers [87, 106, 180] have showed in practical power measurements that the encryption parts in a program are significantly visible for the adversary. Mangard [143] states that finding specific power values is manageable for someone who knows the assembly code that runs in the device. Biham and Shamir [37] highlight several possible methods to find necessary sections from the whole power profile: (1), execute the program large number of times in different contexts and align the power measurements; (2), repeat (1) with different devices of the similar model which execute with different keys, to eliminate the standard operations (data independent regions). In this section the author presents an example of how an adversary will analyse a power trace for patterns to capture only the necessary power values. The analysis is based on the fact that similar patterns in the power profile will be produced for same sequence of instruction executions, and distinguishable power patterns will be produced for different sequence of instruction executions.

Figure A.4(a) shows the whole power trace of an AES encryption executed using a key and an input. The encryption part is circled, where the key expansion is also quite visible with a distinguishable pattern. Most of the time the encryption is executed at the end of the program. The adversary first examines the last distinguishable part (a segment with similar patterns for the ten rounds, but different from the other segments in the power profile) as the possible power profile for the encryption rounds

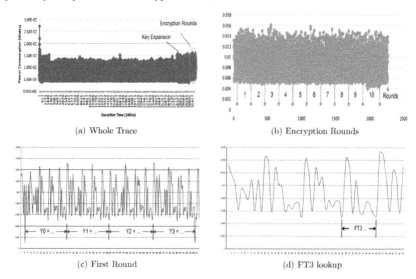

(a) Whole Trace

(b) Encryption Rounds

(c) First Round

(d) FT3 lookup

Figure A.4: Power Traces

The encryption rounds part is extracted and plotted in Figure A.4(b). Since the AES program has ten rounds, there should be ten similar patterns representing each round. If such a pattern does not exist, the adversary will try the next segment prior to the last one, as encryption in the whole trace (shown in Figure A.4(a)). As shown in Figure A.4(b) the predicted encryption rounds segment has ten similar patterns, which are numbered. The main concern in the experiments for the attack is the first round as explained above.

The power trace segment for the first round is expanded in Figure A.4(c). As shown in Figure A.2, there are four sets of similar instruction segments executed in the first round. This can be clearly seen in Figure A.4(c) where four similar patterns (labelled) are visible in the power profile. The second pattern (which represents Y1, as shown in Figure A.2(a)) is the part in which the attack is implemented. With experience it is fairly easy to see the similarities in patterns quickly.

Figure A.4(d) shows the extracted power profile of the second segment (Y1) from the first round (Figure A.4(c)). The access for **FT3 SBOX** is highlighted, which is the attack point in this approach. This is the place the adversary has to concentrate on the assembly implementation of the code as shown in Figure A.2(b). The power value(s) at necessary

241

instruction executions or the average of certain executions can be extracted from the separated power profile of the SBOX access which is shown in Figure A.4(d). The example shown in Figure A.4 is based on a single sample taken in one try. There might be time shifts in power profile for different samples due to various noise effects. Advanced techniques like phase correction [91] can be applied to synchronise the power profiles before power analysis. In the experiments each instruction takes six clock cycles (six stage pipeline). However, in a different processor like Xtensa LX [13], some instructions (such as load and store) take different number of clock cycles. The adversary also has to consider this when extracting power values. Consideration of caches makes this identification of power values more complex, since memory instructions will vary in the number of clock cycles depending upon whether there has been a cache miss or a hit.

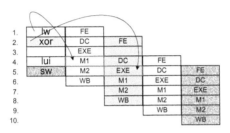

Figure A.5: Instructions and Pipeline Stages

As shown in Figure A.5, the six stages in the pipeline are fetch (*FE*), decode (*DC*), execution (*EXE*), memory one (*MEM1*), memory two (*MEM2*) and write back (*WB*). When the adversary extracts the power value for the *lw* instruction, the *M1* stage of the *lw* is the place for measurement (i.e., the clock 3114610 is the place for power measurement as stated in Table A.1). Likewise, for *xor* as shown in Figure A.5, *EXE* stage is the place where the power should be measured (i.e., clock 3114710 in Table A.1). Hence, after the adversary extracts the power profile segment of the SBOX lookup as shown in Figure A.4(d), it is important to consider pipeline stages before extracting power values for necessary instructions.

Table A.1 depicts the FT3 SBOX lookup segment of the execution trace. The free space without an instruction execution (at clock 3114510) denotes the holds to prevent data hazards.

As tabulated in Table A.1, the load instruction (*lw*) to lookup FT3 is the attack point (i.e., that is where the power value should be extracted). Since the processor has a six stage

Exe. (ns)	Address	Instruction		Comments
3114310	0x401FA0	lw	$4.0($3)	**Attack pt.**
3114410	0x401FA8	xor	$2,$2,$4	
3114510				
3114610	0x401FB0	lui	$1,4096	lw power
3114710	0x401FB8	sw	$2,13892($1)	xor power

Table A.1: Execution Trace

pipeline, the memory stage of *lw* instruction (*M1* as shown in Figure A.5) is executed after four clock cycles from the fetch (*FE* as shown in Figure A.5). The actual load from the memory happens only at the *M1* stage. Likewise, the actual execution of the *xor* instruction takes place at the execution stage (*EXE* as shown in Figure A.5).

The Attack Process

This section presents a complete summary of the DPA process. As shown in Figure A.6, the adversary tries to understand the code of the AES and attempts to select the part of the key for prediction. After identifying which inputs are related to the segment of the key for prediction, all possible input values are fed into the chip and the power traces are captured.

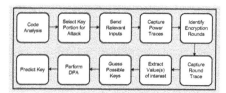

Figure A.6: Process of DPA

The captured power traces for all the inputs are analysed to identify the encryption rounds. The rounds traces are captured as shown in Figure A.6 and the power value(s) of interest are extracted. After the power values are extracted, possible key values (0 to 255 in experiments) are guessed and the DPA analysis is performed (Algorithm 1). There will be 256 values in the DPA plot, since 256 keys are guessed. The key which has the highest DPA value is predicted as the correct secret key stored inside the chip.

In the experiment the author demonstrates and predicts only an 8-bit key of the AES program. All the other key bits can be predicted in similar fashion. Hence, the number of samples needed to predict the 128-bit key using DPA is $16 * 2^8$.

243

Results

This section presents the DPA plots which were plotted based on an attack of AES where the forth byte (key[3]) of the secret key is predicted. The x axis of the DPA plots represent the key guesses (0 to 255), and the y axis displays the DPA values in $Watts$. Figure A.7 shows that the DPA successfully predicts the correct key (which is 14), when lw instruction is exploited, which is the FT3 SBOX lookup. Note that the power values are extracted at the memory stage, considering the pipelining. A clear significant peak is observed at the correct key guess as shown in Figure A.7.

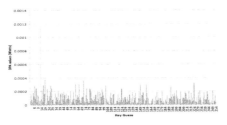

Figure A.7: DPA at LW (Load)

A DPA analysis on the xor instruction, as shown in Figure A.8(a) also produced a significant peak at the correct key (value is 14), where the power values are taken at the execution stage. The author also tested a DPA analysis on the average power value of the FT3 lookup (extracting the average value of the power profile which belongs to FT3 lookup, as shown in Figure A.4(d)).

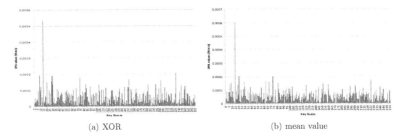

(a) XOR   (b) mean value

Figure A.8: DPA plots

As shown in Figure A.8(b) the correct key can be successfully predicted even with the average power value of the FT3 lookup power profile. This clearly shows that the adversary does not necessarily have to predict power values at specific instructions to successfully attack the AES. Predicting an approximity place for the SBOX lookup and finding the average will be enough to find the key, even though identifying power values for certain instructions would make the attack more successful. However, the attack at the store instruction (SW) does not produce a significant peak at the correct key guess as shown in Figure A.9. This shows that the adversary could not be able to attack the key using the power signature of the store instruction.

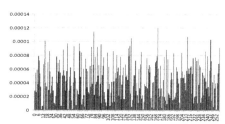

Figure A.9: DPA at SW (Store)

Note that depending upon the processor architecture, different instructions (in this case LW and XOR) would be vulnerable for DPA, producing significant data dependent signatures in the power profile.

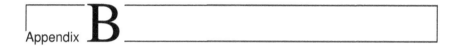

Development of the RINDEX tool in Matlab

This Appendix provides a brief explanation on the development of RINDEX tool using Matlab. RINDEX tool computes the RIJID index (see Chapter 4.5) of a given sequence.

GUIDE in Matlab

GUIDE [4] is a Graphical User Interface (GUI) development tool in matlab which has very flexible drag and drop features. Figure B.1 depicts the GUIDE interface during the RINDEX tool development, where necessary widgets are chosen from the set. GUIDE also allows positioning of the components.

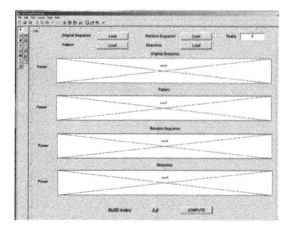

Figure B.1: GUIDE for GUI development in Matlab

247

After the required components are added, integration between the components has to be done by modifying the *m* file created by the GUIDE. Each button as shown in Figure B.1 should be attached to one of the axis areas. Pressing a button should open a file and plot it in the attached axis. The following piece of code in matlab shows such a task, where the press of *pattern* button captures the axes area.

```
function patternbutton_Callback(hObject, eventdata, handles)
  axes(handles.axes)
    file = uigetfile('*.txt');
        if ~isequal(file, 0)
            global pattern;
            pattern = load(file);
        end
    plot(pattern);
```

A file is allowed to be browsed (using *uigetfile*) and the loaded file is plot in the axes. Similar piece of code is added to all the necessary buttons so that the sequences (i.e., original, pattern, random and current sequences) will be plot to different axes components. The sequences are stored in arrays before they are plot. The RIJID index calculation (explained in Chapter 4.5) is added into the *compute* button press function.

RINDEX tool

Figure B.2 depicts a screen shot of the RINDEX tool where the original sequence, the pattern from the original sequence, the complete random sequence and the sequence to measure the RIJID index are loaded from files and plot in respective axes areas. The user can also specify the number of peaks which would appear in the correlation of original sequence and the chosen pattern (i.e., denotes the number of occurrences of the pattern in the original sequence).

Pressing the COMPUTE button will calculate and display the RIJID index. The RINDEX tool is then generated as a stand-alone application using the *mcc* compiler, with the following command;

mcc -B sgl rindex.m

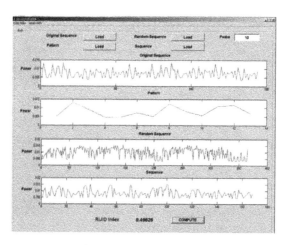

Figure B.2: RINDEX tool outlook

MUTE in XUPV2P using EDK8.2i

This Appendix presents the necessary steps to implement muliprocessor balancing (MUTE) in the XUPV2P FPGA evaluation board.

XUPV2P

XUPV2P is a XUP Virtex-II Pro Development System [2], which includes several key components like JTAG, Ethernet, LED, Serial, Speaker, etc. It contains two PowerPC processors and can be programmed using Embedded Development Kit (EDK). XUPV2P has *xc2vp30* FPGA with the FF896-7 package.

Embedded Development Kit (EDK)

EDK is an integrated software solution, which is efficient in designing embedded processing systems [7]. The EDK provides the IP to configure the PowerPC or to design a MicroBlaze. A base configuration is built by the EDK from the libraries of the specific FPGA. Such a base configuration can be modified by creating necessary buses and connecting necessary ports for different functionalities. The source code in C can be attached with the processor and the EDK does an automatic map of the source into relevant memories (i.e., Data Memory and Program Memory). PowerPC has its on-chip memories (Instruction-side On Chip Memory (ISOCM) and Data-side On Chip Memory (DSOCM) as shown in Figure C.1(a)) and off-chip memories (blockRAMs connected using Data-side Processor Local Bus (DPLB) and Instruction-side Processor Local Bus (IPLB) as shown in Figure C.1(b)), which can be enabled and configured using EDK.

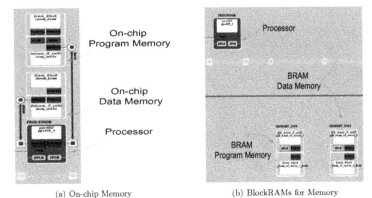

(a) On-chip Memory   (b) BlockRAMs for Memory

Figure C.1: Block Diagrams for Memory Accesses by PowerPC (generated by EDK8.2i)

As shown in Figure C.1, EDK can be configured to use different memory modes by using the library of the target FPGA.

MUTE implementation

MUTE is explained in Chapter 6. The multiprocessor balancing is implemented here in the FPGA. The main task is to use both the built-in PowerPC processors in the XUPV2P FPGA using the library provided. Both processors should execute in parallel, one with the original program and the other with the balanced program. EDK8.2i creates a base setup in the FPGA using the XUPV2P library, which is provided by the FPGA vendor. Figure C.2 shows a block diagram of the base configuration in XUPV2P, where PowerPC0 is neither connected nor configured. PowerPC1 is using the Processor Local Bus (PLB) to connect to the BlockRAM (BRAM) and other components.

Similar to the setup of PowerPC1 in the base configuration, shown in Figure C.2, PowerPC0 has to be also connected with another PLB. A new PLB is created for PowerPC0 and necessary ports are connected. Figure C.3 depicts the final configuration, where 4 BlockRAMs are created one for program memory and another for data memory for each PowerPC processor. Mapping the BlockRAMs to DPLB and IPLB bus in each PowerPC will allow the processor to access the BlockRAMs as Data Memory and Program Memory automatically. LED and

252

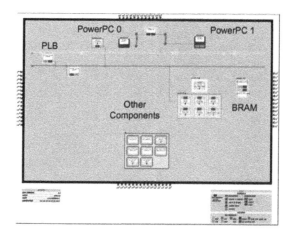

Figure C.2: Base configuration in XUPV2P (generated by EDK8.2i)

Serial are connected to PowerPC1 and PowerPC0 respectively for debugging purposes.

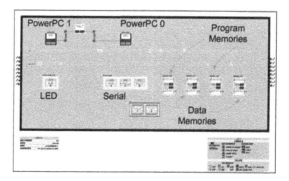

Figure C.3: Final Implementation of MUTE in XUPV2P (generated by EDK8.2i)

After the ports are mapped and the final setup is done (block diagram shown in Figure C.3) EDK8.2i allows designer to attach source codes to both PowerPCs separately. The original version of the program is attached to PowerPC0 and the balanced program is attached with PowerPC1. Note that both programs should have the same instruction sequence, hence will be executed in parallel for balancing. The following piece of code illustrates the steps needed to output values into RS232 (Serial) for debugging,

```
#include ''xuartns550_1.h''      // header
#include ''xparameters.h''       // header
```

```
XUartNs550_SetBaud(XPAR_RS232_UART_1_BASEADDR,XPAR_XUARTNS550_CLOCK_HZ,9600);
XUartNs550_mSetLineControlReg(XPAR_RS232_UART_1_BASEADDR,XUN_LCR_8_DATA_BITS);
xil_printf(''Key'');
```

The following piece of code briefs the steps in using LED for debugging.

```
#include ''xgpio.h''          // header
#include ''xparameters.h''    // header

XGpio GpioOutput;
XStatus Status;
XGpio_Initialize(&GpioOutput,XPAR_LEDS_4BIT_DEVICE_ID);
XGpio_SetDataDirection(&GpioOutput,1,0x0);
XGpio_DiscreteWrite(&GpioOutput,1,0xC);
```

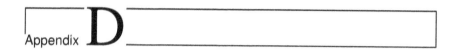

SimpleScalar processor in FPGA using Xilinx8.2i

This Appendix presents the implementation flow of the SimpleScalar processor in an FPGA using Xilinx8.2i.

SimpleScalar

SimpleScalar architecture (PISA instruction set) is a close derivative of the MIPS architecture and a tool set is developed by Burger and Austin [51]. PISA has 65 instructions, which are of 64 bits in length. Both little-endian and big-endian are supported by the SimpleScalar, compiled using **sslittle-na-sstrix-gcc** and **ssbig-na-sstrix-gcc** cross compilers respectively. Several simulators such as **sim-fast, sim-safe, sim-cache, sim-profile**, etc. are provided with the SimpleScalar tool set. **sim-fast** performs a pure functional check, executing instructions in serial.

ASIPMeister

ASIPMeister [10] is an Application Specific Instruction set Processor (ASIP) tool. It allows creation of necessary components (such as adder, shifter, multiplier, etc.), bus interfaces and designing instructions using microinstructions [83]. Thus, the Instruction Set Architecture (ISA) for the target processor is fed into the ASIPMeister. The VHDL description of the processor is provided as the output from the ASIPMeister. The author used the PISA (Portable

Instruction Set Architecture) instruction set (as implemented in SimpleScalar [51] tool set with a six stage pipeline) processor without cache. The source code (to be executed in the processor) is compiled using the SimpleScalar crosscompiler and the memories (i.e., instruction memory and data memory) are setup using the compiled binary.

FPGA Implementation

The author used Xilinx8.2i to implement the SimpleScalar processor in a Virtex2-XC2V3000-FG676 FPGA. Figure D.1 depicts the block diagram of the implementation, highlighting the main components used. The CPU (i.e., processor) is generated using the ASIPMeister tool set in VHDL. All the author needed is to setup the memories (Instruction Memory (IMEM) and Data Memory (DMEM)). Since the author wanted the memory access to be performed in a single clock cycle, DCM (Digital Clock Manager) is used to devide the clock for the CPU to run in half the speed of the memory. BUFG's are used to synchronise the clocks. When the DCM finishes its task, the CPU is given the Reset signal to start the execution. This operation is performed using the SRL16 (16-bit shift register LUT) module. A toplevel file in VHDL is used to connect all the components together with the CPU.

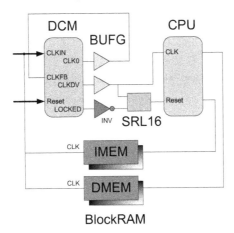

Figure D.1: Implementation in Virtex2

BlockRAM IP cores are used for both IMEM and DMEM. To create a BlockRAM: File → New Source → IP (Coregen & Architecture Wizard) → Memories & Storage Elements

256

→ Block Memory Generator. Figure D.2 shows the BlockRAM creation wizard. Required pins are selected based on the CPU connections. For example, the instruction memory has to be a single port ROM with an Address in and Data out. This is created as illustrated in the figure. The wizard also allows defining the memory address width and also an init file to initialize the memory. Two headers are required in the memory initialisation file: 'memory_initialization_radix=16'; and 'memory_initialization_vector=' followed by the data values in proper sequence (in hexadecimal).

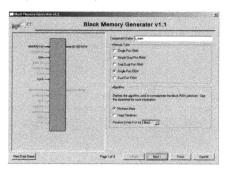

Figure D.2: BlockRAM IP creation wizard

Two BlockRAMs are created, one single port ROM and one double port RAM for IMEM and DMEM respectively. Initialisation files are provided for both memories. The DCM component in Virtex2 is used by creating an instance of the DCM module and the VHDL template is copied from: Edit → Language Templates → VHDL → FPGA → Clock Components → Digital Clock Manager → DCM for VirtexII. Likewise, the VHDL instances for BUFG and SRL16 are copied to the toplevel.

The DCM needs a feedback which is derived from CLK0 as shown in Figure D.1, a zero shift clock output. A four-cycle shift register is used for the reset circuit of the DCM. The reset circuit in VHDL is as follows;

```
flop1: FDS port map (D => '0', C => clkin, Q => out1, S => '0');
flop2: FD port map (D => out1, C => clkin, Q => out2);
flop3: FD port map (D => out2, C => clkin, Q => out3);
flop4: FD port map (D => out3, C => clkin, Q => out4);
Reset => out2 or out3 or out4;   //Reset for DCM
```

The divided clock signal (CLKDV) is given as the clock for CPU. However, DCM output clocks are only valid when LOCKED signal is high. Hence, an SRL16 is used in between for

257

the Reset of CPU, as shown in Figure D.1, by inverting the LOCKED signal and also feeding in the CLKDV signal. The SRL16 configuration in VHDL is as follows,

```
LOCKEDINV <= not LOCKED;         //invert LOCKED signal
A0 <= '1';
A1 <= '0';
A2 <= '0';
A3 <= '0';

    NewReset: SRL16              // SRL16 instance
    generic map (
      INIT => x''0000'';
    port map (
      Q => Reset,                // Reset for the CPU
      A0 => A0,
      A1 => A1,
      A2 => A2,
      A3 => A3,
      CLK => CLKDV,              // CLKDV from the DCM
      D => LOCKEDINV             // inverted LOCKED signal from DCM
    );
```

BUFGs are inserted for synchronisation of the clock as shown in Figure D.1. A testbench is created: Project → New Source → Test Bench WaveForm. The required clock and reset signals are modified in the testbench GUI as shown in Figure D.3. The duration of the simulation is also specified (i.e., the execution time of the program to be executed). ModelSim [5] hardware simulator is separately installed and used as the simulator for Xilinx8.2i. The simulation is verified for correctness and the binary is created.

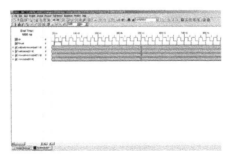

Figure D.3: Testbench Wizard in Xilinx8.2i

Bibliography

[1] cellular-news. Available at: http://www.cellular-news.com/story/27497.php Viewed on: April 2008. (Cited on page 1.)

[2] Digilent, XUPV2P. Available at: http://www.digilentinc.com/xupv2p Viewed on: April 2008. (Cited on page 251.)

[3] Embedded System Applications. Available at: http://www.lynuxworks.com/solutions/index.php3 Viewed on: December 2008. (Cited on page 1.)

[4] The MathWorks. Viewed on: April, 2008 Available at: http://www.mathworks.com/access/helpdesk/help/techdoc . (Cited on page 247.)

[5] ModelSim Technical Resources. Available at: http://www.model.com/resources/mainpage.asp. (Cited on page 258.)

[6] Sourcebank. Available at: http://archive.devx.com/sourcebank. (Cited on page 185.)

[7] XILINX, Platform Studio and the EDK. Available at: http://www.xilinx.com/ise/embedded_design_prod/platform_studio.htm Viewed on: April 2008. (Cited on page 251.)

[8] IEEE P1363/D7. Standard Specifications for Public Key Cryptography. September 11, 1998. (Cited on page 111.)

[9] Building a high-performance, programmable secure coprocessor. *Comput. Netw.*, 31(9):831–860, 1999. (Cited on page 152.)

[10] The PEAS Team. ASIP Meister, 2002. Available at: http://www.asip-solutions.com/english/. (Cited on pages 162, 166, 184, 198, 199, and 255.)

[11] The Evolution and Regulation of the Payments System (Australia). 2006. Available at: http://www.ladlass.com/ice/archives/cat_payments.html Viewed on: April 2008. (Cited on page 2.)

[12] Chip Multi Processor Watch, 2007. Available at: http://view.eecs.berkeley.edu/wiki/Chip_Multi_Processor_Watch. (Cited on page 192.)

[13] Xtensa 7 Feature Summary, 2007. Available at: http://www.tensilica.com/products/x7_features.htm. (Cited on page 242.)

[14] howstuffworks: How Operating Systems Work, 2009. Available at: http://computer.howstuffworks.com/operating-system.htm. (Cited on page 205.)

[15] WATCHDATA: Singapore's CEPAS 2.0 Transport Card Case, 2009. Available at: http://www.watchdata.com/page.php?id=20. (Cited on page 194.)

[16] M. A. E. Aabid, S. Guilley, and P. Hoogvorst. Template attacks with a power model. Cryptology ePrint Archive, Report 2007/443, 2007. (Cited on pages 4, 24, 67, 91, and 92.)

[17] O. Aciiçmez, Çetin Kaya Koç, and J.-P. Seifert. On the power of simple branch prediction analysis. In *ASIACCS '07: Proceedings of the 2nd ACM symposium on Information, computer and communications security*, pages 312–320, New York, NY, USA, 2007. ACM. (Cited on pages 16, 17, and 132.)

[18] O. Aciicmez, J.-P. Seifert, and C. K. Koc. Predicting secret keys via branch prediction. Cryptology ePrint Archive, Report 2006/288, 2006. (Cited on page 32.)

[19] D. Agrawal, J. R. Rao, and P. Rohatgi. Multi-channel Attacks. In *CHES*, pages 2–16, 2003. (Cited on page 92.)

[20] D. Agrawal, J. R. Rao, P. Rohatgi, and K. Schramm. Templates as Master Keys. In *CHES*, pages 15–29, 2005. (Cited on page 92.)

[21] M. Aigner and E. Oswald. Power analysis tutorial. Technical report, University of Technology Graz. (Cited on pages 22, 51, and 81.)

[22] M.-L. Akkar, R. Bevan, P. Dischamp, and D. Moyart. Power analysis, what is now possible... In *ASIACRYPT '00: Proceedings of the 6th International Conference on the Theory and Application of Cryptology and Information Security*, pages 489–502, London, UK, 2000. Springer-Verlag. (Cited on pages 12, 19, 25, 26, 101, and 212.)

[23] M.-L. Akkar and C. Giraud. An Implementation of DES and AES, Secure against Some Attacks. In *CHES '01: Proceedings of the Third International Workshop on Cryptographic Hardware and Embedded Systems*, pages 309–318, London, UK, 2001. Springer-Verlag. (Cited on pages 100, 101, 102, 103, 106, 125, and 126.)

[24] J. A. Ambrose, R. G. Ragel, and S. Parameswaran. A Smart Random Code Injection to Mask Power Analysis Based Side Channel Attacks. In *CODES+ISSS '07: Proceedings of the 5th international conference on Hardware/software codesign and system synthesis*, pages 51–56, New York, NY, USA, 2007. ACM Press. (Cited on page 208.)

[25] R. Anderson, E. Biham, and L. Knudsen. Serpent: A Proposal for the Advanced Encryption Standard. (Cited on page 103.)

[26] K. Aoki, T. Ichikawa, M. Kanda, M. Matsui, S. Moriai, J. Nakajima, and T. Tokita. Camellia: A 128-bit block cipher suitable for multiple platforms - design and analysis. In *Selected Areas in Cryptography*, pages 39–56, 2000. (Cited on page 29.)

[27] C. Archambeau, E. Peeters, F.-X. Standaert, and J.-J. Quisquater. Template Attacks in Principal Subspaces. In *CHES*, pages 1–14, 2006. (Cited on page 92.)

[28] L. R. Avery, J. S. Crabbe, S. A. Sofi, H. Ahmed, J. R. A. Cleaver, and D. J. Weaver. Reverse Engineering Complex Application-Specific Integrated Circuits (ASICs). In *DMSMS*, page 4, 2002. (Cited on page 2.)

[29] H. Bar-El, H. Choukri, D. Naccache, M. Tunstall, and C. Whelan. The sorcerer's apprentice guide to fault attacks. *Proceedings of the IEEE*, 94(2):370–382, 2006. (Cited on page 41.)

[30] M. Barbosa and D. Page. On the Automatic Construction of Indistinguishable Operations. In *Cryptography And Coding*, pages 233–247. Springer-Verlag LNCS 3796, November 2005. (Cited on pages 18, 32, 132, 135, 136, 158, and 174.)

[31] E. G. Barrantes, D. H. Ackley, T. S. Palmer, D. Stefanovic, and D. D. Zovi. Randomized instruction set emulation to disrupt binary code injection attacks. In *CCS '03: Proceedings of the 10th ACM conference on Computer and communications security*, pages 281–289, New York, NY, USA, 2003. ACM Press. (Cited on page 134.)

[32] L. Batina, N. Mentens, B. Preneel, and I. Verbauwhede. Balanced point operations for side-channel protection of elliptic curve cryptography. *Information Security, IEE Proceedings*, 152(1):57–65, 2005. (Cited on page 132.)

[33] L. Benini, A. Macii, F. Macii, E. Omerbegovic, F. Pro, and M. Poncino. Energy-aware design techniques for differential power analysis protection. In *DAC '03: Proceedings of the 40th conference on Design automation*, pages 36–41, New York, NY, USA, 2003. ACM. (Cited on page 152.)

[34] L. Benini, G. D. Micheli, E. Macii, M. Poncino, and R. Scarsi. Symbolic synthesis of clock-gating logic for power optimization of synchronous controllers. *ACM Transactions on Design Automation of Electronic Systems.*, 4(4):351–375, 1999. (Cited on page 152.)

[35] E. Biham and A. Biryukov. An improvement of Davies' attack on DES. *Journal of Cryptology: the journal of the International Association for Cryptologic Research*, 10(3):195–205, Summer 1997. (Cited on page 93.)

[36] E. Biham, A. Biryukov, and A. Shamir. Cryptanalysis of skipjack reduced to 31 rounds using impossible differentials. *J. Cryptol.*, 18(4):291–311, 2005. (Cited on page 101.)

[37] E. Biham and A. Shamir. Power Analysis of the Key Scheduling of the AES Candidates. In *In Second Advanced Encryption Standard (AES) Candidate Conference*, pages 343–347, 2003. (Cited on pages 1, 9, 26, 101, and 240.)

[38] I. Blake, G. Seroussi, N. Smart, and J. W. S. Cassels. *Advances in Elliptic Curve Cryptography (London Mathematical Society Lecture Note Series)*. Cambridge University Press, New York, NY, USA, 2005. (Cited on page 10.)

[39] I. Blake, G. Seroussi, N. Smart, and J. W. S. Cassels. *Advances in Elliptic Curve Cryptography (London Mathematical Society Lecture Note Series)*. Cambridge University Press, New York, NY, USA, 2005. (Cited on page 156.)

[40] I. F. Blake, G. Seroussi, and N. P. Smart. *Elliptic Curves in Cryptography*. Cambridge University Press, July 1999. (Cited on pages 114 and 115.)

[41] J. Blomer, J. Guajardo, and V. Krummel. Provably Secure Masking of AES. In *SAC 2004: Selected Areas in Cryptography, 11th International Workshop*, pages 69–83. Springer, 2004. (Cited on page 106.)

[42] B. D. Boer, K. Lemke, and G. Wicke. A DPA Attack against the Modular Reduction within a CRT Implementation of RSA. In *CHES '02: Revised Papers from the 4th International Workshop on Cryptographic Hardware and Embedded Systems*, pages 228–243, London, UK, 2003. Springer-Verlag. (Cited on pages 48, 49, 50, and 51.)

[43] D. Boneh. Twenty years of attacks on the RSA cryptosystem. *Notices of the American Mathematical Society (AMS)*, 46(2):203–213, 1999. (Cited on page 108.)

[44] G. Boracchi and L. Breveglieri. A Study on the Efficiency of Differential Power Analysis on aes S-Box, 2007. (Cited on pages 45, 46, 47, 56, 70, 71, 72, 117, and 238.)

[45] E. Brier, C. Clavier, and F. Olivier. Optimal Statistical Power Analysis, 2003. Cryptology ePrint Archive, Report 2003/152. (Cited on pages 25, 84, 195, and 212.)

[46] E. Brier, C. Clavier, and F. Olivier. Correlation power analysis with a leakage model. In *CHES*, pages 16–29, 2004. (Cited on pages 3, 21, 83, 84, 86, 87, 202, 207, 227, 229, and 238.)

[47] E. Brier and M. Joye. Weierstraβ Elliptic Curves and Side-Channel Attacks. In *PKC '02: Proceedings of the 5th International Workshop on Practice and Theory in Public Key Cryptosystems*, pages 335–345, London, UK, 2002. Springer-Verlag. (Cited on pages 32, 33, 34, 130, 136, and 137.)

[48] E. O. Brigham. *The fast Fourier transform and its applications*. Prentice-Hall, Inc., Upper Saddle River, NJ, USA, 1988. (Cited on page 32.)

[49] D. Brumley and D. Boneh. Remote timing attacks are practical. In *Proceedings of the 12th USENIX Security Symposium*, August 2003. (Cited on page 2.)

[50] M. Bucci, M. Guglielmo, R. Luzzi, and A. Trifiletti. A Power Consumption Randomization Countermeasure for DPA-Resistant Cryptographic Processors. In *PATMOS*, pages 481–490, 2004. (Cited on page 144.)

[51] D. Burger, T. M. Austin, and S. Bennett. Evaluating future microprocessors: The simplescalar tool set. Technical Report CS-TR-1996-1308, 1996. (Cited on pages 237, 255, and 256.)

[52] C. Burwick, D. Coppersmith, E. D'Avignon, R. Gennaro, S. Halevi, C. Jutla, S. Matyas, L. O'Connor, M. Peyravian, D. Safford, and N. Zunic. MARS — A Candidate Cipher for AES, 1998. (Cited on page 103.)

[53] S. Chari, C. Jutla, J. R. Rao, and P. Rohatgi. A cautionary note regarding evaluation of AES candidates on smart-cards. In *Second Advanced Encryption Standard (AES) Candidate Conference*, Rome, Italy, 1999. http://csrc.nist.gov/encryption/aes/round1/conf2/aes2conf.htm. (Cited on pages 11, 12, 101, 130, and 134.)

[54] S. Chari, C. S. Jutla, J. R. Rao, and P. Rohatgi. Towards sound approaches to counteract power-analysis attacks. In *CRYPTO*, pages 398–412, 1999. (Cited on pages 59, 99, 101, 138, 152, 158, and 174.)

[55] S. Chari, J. R. Rao, and P. Rohatgi. Template Attacks. In *CHES '02: Revised Papers from the 4th International Workshop on Cryptographic Hardware and Embedded Systems*, pages 13–28, London, UK, 2003. Springer-Verlag. (Cited on pages 89, 90, 92, and 108.)

[56] D. Chaum. Blind Signatures for Untraceable Payments. In *CRYPTO '82: In Proceedings of Advances in Cryptology*, pages 199–203, 1983. (Cited on page 98.)

[57] D. Chaum. Security without identification: transaction systems to make Big Brother obsolete. *Commun. ACM*, 28(10):1030–1044, 1985. (Cited on page 111.)

[58] S. Chaumette and D. Sauveron. New security problems raised by open multiapplication smart cards. (Cited on page 9.)

[59] B. Chevalier-Mames, M. Ciet, and M. Joye. Low-cost solutions for preventing simple sidechannel analysis: Side-channel atomicity. *IEEE Transactions on Computers*, 53(6):760–768, 2004. (Cited on pages 132, 135, and 136.)

[60] D. V. Chudnovsky and G. V. Chudnovsky. Sequences of numbers generated by addition in formal groups and new primality and factorization tests. *Advances in Applied Mathematics*, 7:385–434, 1986. (Cited on page 136.)

[61] C. Clavier, J.-S. Coron, and N. Dabbous. Differential Power Analysis in the Presence of Hardware Countermeasures. In *CHES '00: Proceedings of the Second International Workshop on Cryptographic Hardware and Embedded Systems*, pages 252–263, London, UK, 2000. Springer-Verlag. (Cited on pages 82, 83, 130, 157, 159, and 174.)

[62] C. Clavier and M. Joye. Universal Exponentiation Algorithm. *Lecture Notes in Computer Science*, 2162:300–310, 2001. (Cited on pages 109, 128, and 137.)

[63] Computer Systems Laboratory (U.S.). *Data Encryption Standard (DES)*, 1994. Category: computer security, subcategory: cryptography. Supersedes FIPS PUB 46-1–1988 January 22. Reaffirmed December 30, 1993. Shipping list no.: 94-0171-P. (Cited on pages 14, 100, 122, and 193.)

[64] T. H. Cormen, C. E. Leiserson, R. L. Rivest, and C. Stein. *Introduction to Algorithms, Second Edition*. The MIT Press, September 2001. (Cited on page 49.)

[65] J. Coron. Resistance against Differential Power Analysis for Elliptic Curve Cryptosystems. In *Cryptographic Hardware and Embedded Systems*, number Generators, pages 292–302, 1999. (Cited on pages 18, 32, 51, 52, 53, 110, 111, 112, 113, 114, 116, 128, 130, 131, 134, and 135.)

[66] J. Coron, P. C. Kocher, and D. Naccache. Statistics and secret leakage. In *FC '00: Proceedings of the 4th International Conference on Financial Cryptography*, pages 157–173, London, UK, 2001. Springer-Verlag. (Cited on page 12.)

[67] J.-S. Coron and A. Tchulkine. A New Algorithm for Switching from Arithmetic to Boolean Masking. In *CHES '03: Proceedings of the Fifth International Workshop on Cryptographic Hardware and Embedded Systems*, pages 89–97, London, UK, 2003. Springer-Verlag. (Cited on page 104.)

[68] J.-S. Coron and L. Goubin. On Boolean and Arithmetic Masking against Differential Power Analysis. In *Ches '00*, pages 231–237, London, UK, 2000. (Cited on pages 40, 41, 56, 99, 101, 104, 130, 158, 174, and 193.)

[69] N. Courtois and L. Goubin. An Algebraic Masking Method to Protect AES Against Power Attacks. In *ICISC*, pages 199–209, 2005. (Cited on page 127.)

[70] J. Daemen, M. Peeters, and G. V. Assche. Bitslice Ciphers and Power Analysis Attacks. In *FSE '00: Proceedings of the 7th International Workshop on Fast Software Encryption*, pages 134–149, London, UK, 2001. Springer-Verlag. (Cited on pages 59 and 120.)

[71] J. Daemen and V. Rijmen. Resistance against implementation attacks: a comparative study of the AES proposals, 1999. URL: http://csrc.nist.gov/CryptoToolkit/aes/round1/pubcmnts.htm. (Cited on pages 19, 35, 42, 43, 45, 130, 138, 144, 151, 155, and 205.)

[72] J. Daemen and V. Rijmen. *The Design of Rijndael: AES - The Advanced Encryption Standard*. Springer-Verlag, 2002. (Cited on pages 103, 208, and 236.)

[73] S. Danil, M. Julian, B. Alexander, and Y. Alex. Design and analysis of dual-rail circuits for security applications. *IEEE Trans. Comput.*, 54(4):449–460, 2005. (Cited on pages 142, 143, 192, and 193.)

[74] B. S. David, C. Lap-Wai, and M. C. William. Cryptographic architecture with random instruction masking to thwart differential power analysis. *U.S. Patent 20050271202*, 2005. (Cited on pages 133, 134, and 174.)

[75] D. Davies and S. Murphy. Pairs and triplets of DES s-boxes. *Journal of Cryptology*, 8(1):1–25, 1995. (Cited on page 93.)

[76] J.-F. Dhem and N. Feyt. Hardware and Software Symbiosis Helps Smart Card Evolution. *IEEE Micro*, 21(6):14–25, 2001. (Cited on page 139.)

[77] M. T. DiBrino. Apparatus and method for managing interrupts in a multiprocessor system. *U.S. Patent 5265215*, 1993. (Cited on page 198.)

[78] Z. Dongyao. Side channel analysis on rsa cryptosystem. Diploma Thesis, Department of Computer Science, Technology University Darmstadt, Darmstadt, 2005. (Cited on page 32.)

[79] P. F. Dunn. *Measurement and Data Analysis for Engineering and Science*. McGraw-Hill, New York, NY, USA, 2005. (Cited on page 61.)

[80] M. Feldhofer, S. Dominikus, and J. Wolkerstorfer. Strong Authentication for RFID Systems using the AES Algorithm. In M. Joye and J.-J. Quisquater, editors, *Workshop on Cryptographic Hardware and Embedded Systems - CHES 2004*, volume 3156 of *Lecture Notes in Computer Science*, pages 357–370, Boston, Massachusetts, USA, August 2004. IACR, Springer-Verlag. (Cited on page 235.)

[81] A. Fiskiran and R. Lee. Evaluating instruction set extensions for fast arithmetic on binary finite fields. *Application-Specific Systems, Architectures and Processors, 2004. Proceedings. 15th IEEE International Conference on*, pages 125–136, 2004. (Cited on page 153.)

[82] S. R. Fluhrer and D. A. McGrew. Statistical analysis of the alleged rc4 keystream generator. In *FSE '00: Proceedings of the 7th International Workshop on Fast Software Encryption*, pages 19–30, London, UK, 2001. Springer-Verlag. (Cited on page 89.)

[83] M. J. Flynn and M. D. McLaren. Microprogramming revisited. In *Proceedings of the 1967 22nd national conference*, pages 457–464, New York, NY, USA, 1967. ACM. (Cited on page 255.)

[84] S. Fruhauf and L. Sourge. Safety device against the unauthorized detection of protected data. *U.S. Patent 4932053*, 1990. (Cited on page 145.)

[85] B. M. Gammel and S. J. Ruping. Smart cards inside. *Solid-State Circuits Conference, 2005. ESSCIRC 2005. Proceedings of the 31st European*, pages 69–74, 2005. (Cited on pages 3 and 10.)

[86] C. Gebotys. A Table Masking Countermeasure for Low-Energy Secure Embedded Systems. *IEEE Transactions on Very Large Scale Integration (VLSI) Systems*, 14(7):740–753, 2006. (Cited on pages 4, 12, 40, 41, 43, 45, 117, 121, 122, 124, 158, 159, 174, 193, 194, 201, 216, 217, and 238.)

[87] C. H. Gebotys. Design of Secure Cryptography Against the Threat of Power-Attacks in DSP-Embedded Processors. *Trans. on Embedded Computing Sys.*, 3(1):92–113, 2004. (Cited on pages 20 and 240.)

[88] C. H. Gebotys and R. J. Gebotys. Secure Elliptic Curve Implementations: An Analysis of Resistance to Power-Attacks in a DSP Processor. In *CHES '02: Revised Papers from the 4th International Workshop on Cryptographic Hardware and Embedded Systems*, pages 114–128, London, UK, 2003. Springer-Verlag. (Cited on pages 4, 32, 131, 132, 134, 158, and 174.)

[89] C. H. Gebotys, S. Ho, and C. C. Tiu. EM Analysis of Rijndael and ECC on a Wireless Java-Based PDA. In *CHES*, pages 250–264, 2005. (Cited on page 96.)

[90] C. H. Gebotys and B. A. White. Methodology for attack on a Java-based PDA. In *CODES+ISSS '06*, pages 94–99, New York, NY, USA, 2006. ACM Press. (Cited on pages 1 and 9.)

[91] C. H. Gebotys and B. A. White. A Phase Substitution Technique for DEMA of Embedded Cryptographic Systems. In *ITNG*, pages 868–869, 2007. (Cited on page 242.)

[92] B. Gierlichs, K. Lemke-Rust, and C. Paar. Templates vs. Stochastic Methods. In *CHES*, pages 15–29, 2006. (Cited on page 92.)

[93] C. Giraud. An RSA Implementation Resistant to Fault Attacks and to Simple Power Analysis. *IEEE Trans. Comput.*, 55(9):1116–1120, 2006. (Cited on pages 32 and 135.)

[94] J. D. Golic and C. Tymen. Multiplicative Masking and Power Analysis of Aes. In *CHES '02: Revised Papers from the 4th International Workshop on Cryptographic Hardware and Embedded Systems*, pages 198–212, London, UK, 2003. Springer-Verlag. DPA on AES. (Cited on pages 43, 102, 103, 117, 125, and 126.)

[95] D. M. Gordon. A survey of fast exponentiation methods. *J. Algorithms*, 27(1):129–146, 1998. (Cited on page 116.)

[96] A. Gordon-Ross and F. Vahid. Frequent loop detection using efficient non-intrusive on-chip hardware. In *CASES '03: Proceedings of the 2003 international conference on Compilers, architecture and synthesis for embedded systems*, pages 117–124, New York, NY, USA, 2003. ACM Press. (Cited on pages 174 and 181.)

[97] L. Goubin and J. Patarin. DES and Differential Power Analysis (The "Duplication" Method). In *CHES '99: Proceedings of the First International Workshop on Cryptographic Hardware and Embedded Systems*, pages 158–172, London, UK, 1999. Springer-Verlag. (Cited on pages 118, 119, 120, 152, 158, and 174.)

[98] J. Großschädl and E. Savas. Instruction set extensions for fast arithmetic in finite fields gf(p) and gf(2^m). In *CHES*, pages 133–147, 2004. (Cited on page 153.)

[99] N. Gura, A. Patel, A. Wander, H. Eberle, and S. C. Shantz. Comparing elliptic curve cryptography and rsa on 8-bit cpus. In *CHES*, pages 119–132, 2004. (Cited on page 17.)

[100] M. R. Guthaus, J. S. Ringenberg, D. Ernst, T. M. Austin, T. Mudge, and R. B. Brown. Mibench: A free, commercially representative embedded benchmark suite. In *WWC '01: Proceedings of the Workload Characterization, 2001. WWC-4. 2001 IEEE International Workshop on*, pages 3–14, Washington, DC, USA, 2001. IEEE Computer Society. (Cited on page 185.)

[101] Y. Han, X. Zou, Z. Liu, and Y. Chen. Improved differential power analysis attacks on aes hardware implementations. In *WiCom '07*, pages 2230–2233, 2007. (Cited on pages 74, 75, 76, 87, 235, and 238.)

[102] M. A. Hasan. Power analysis attacks and algorithmic approaches to their countermeasures for koblitz curve cryptosystems. *IEEE Trans. Comput.*, 50(10):1071–1083, 2001. (Cited on pages 53, 54, 113, 114, and 135.)

[103] C. Herbst, E. Oswald, and S. Mangard. An AES Smart Card Implementation Resistant to Power Analysis Attacks. In J. Zhou, M. Yung, and F. Bao, editors, *Applied Cryptography and Network Security, Second International Conference, ACNS 2006*, volume 3989 of *Lecture Notes in Computer Science*, pages 239–252. Springer, 2006. (Cited on pages 106, 107, 132, and 133.)

[104] G. Hollestelle, W. Burgers, and J. I. den Hartog. Power analysis on smartcard algorithms using simulation. Technical report CSR 04-22, Eindhoven University of Technology, Eindhoven, 2004. (Cited on pages 31 and 32.)

[105] J. Huiping and M. Zhigang. Design of an RSA module Against Power Analysis Attacks. *ASIC, 2003. Proceedings. 5th International Conference on*, 2:1308–1311 Vol.2, 2003. (Cited on pages 16, 31, and 135.)

[106] D. Hwang, K. Tiri, A. Hodjat, B.-C. Lai, S. Yang, P. Schaumont, and I. Verbauwhede. Aes-Based Security Coprocessor IC in 0.18um CMOS With Resistance to Differential Power Analysis Side-Channel Attacks. *IEEE Journal of Solid-State Circuits*, 41(4):781–792, 2006. (Cited on pages 141, 142, 192, 193, and 240.)

[107] D. D. Hwang, P. Schaumont, K. Tiri, and I. Verbauwhede. Securing embedded systems. *IEEE Security and Privacy*, 4(2):40–49, 2006. (Cited on pages 140, 192, and 193.)

[108] J. Irwin, D. Page, and N. P. Smart. Instruction stream mutation for non-deterministic processors. In *ASAP '02: Proceedings of the IEEE International Conference on Application-Specific Systems, Architectures, and Processors*, page 286, Washington, DC, USA, 2002. IEEE Computer Society. (Cited on pages 150, 151, and 158.)

[109] K. Itoh, M. Takenaka, and N. Torii. DPA Countermeasure Based on the "Masking Method". In *ICISC '01: Proceedings of the 4th International Conference Seoul on Information Security and Cryptology*, pages 440–456, London, UK, 2002. Springer-Verlag. (Cited on pages 123 and 124.)

[110] K. Itoh, J. Yajima, M. Takenaka, and N. Torii. DPA Countermeasures by Improving the Window Method. In *CHES '02: Revised Papers from the 4th International Workshop*

on *Cryptographic Hardware and Embedded Systems*, pages 303–317, London, UK, 2003. Springer-Verlag. (Cited on pages 98, 108, 128, 129, and 130.)

[111] T. Itoh and S. Tsujii. A fast algorithm for computing multiplicative inverses in gf(2m) using normal bases. *Information and Computation*, 78(3):171–177, 1988. (Cited on page 127.)

[112] A. Janapsatya, A. Ignjatovic, and S. Parameswaran. Exploiting statistical information for implementation of instruction scratch memory in embedded system. *IEEE Transactions on Very Large Scale Integration (VLSI) Systems*, 14(8):816–829, 2006. (Cited on pages 5, 175, and 213.)

[113] M. Johnson. *Superscalar Microprocessor Design*. Prentice Hall, 1991. (Cited on page 149.)

[114] I. T. Jolliffe. *Principal Component Analysis (2nd ed.)*. Springer, 2002. (Cited on page 91.)

[115] M. Joye, P. Paillier, and B. Schoenmakers. On Second-Order Differential Power Analysis. In *CHES*, pages 293–308, 2005. (Cited on pages 62, 63, 64, 67, 69, and 158.)

[116] M. Joye and J.-J. Quisquater. Hessian Elliptic Curves and Side-Channel Attacks. In *CHES '01: Proceedings of the Third International Workshop on Cryptographic Hardware and Embedded Systems*, pages 402–410, London, UK, 2001. Springer-Verlag. (Cited on pages 113 and 137.)

[117] M. Joye and C. Tymen. Protections against Differential Analysis for Elliptic Curve Cryptography. In *CHES '01: Proceedings of the Third International Workshop on Cryptographic Hardware and Embedded Systems*, pages 377–390, London, UK, 2001. Springer-Verlag. (Cited on pages 113, 114, 115, and 128.)

[118] M. Kaminaga, T. Watanabe, T. Endo, and T. Okochi. Power Analysis and Countermeasure of RSA Cryptosystem. In *The Transactions of the Institute of Electronics, Information and Communication Engineers*, volume 88, pages 606–615. The Institute of Electronics, Information and Communication Engineers, 2006. (Cited on pages 89, 108, 109, and 110.)

[119] C. Karlof and D. Wagner. Hidden Markov model cryptanalysis, 2003. (Cited on page 120.)

[120] J. Kelsey, B. Schneier, D. Wagner, and C. Hall. Side channel cryptanalysis of product ciphers. *J. Comput. Secur.*, 8(2,3):141–158, 2000. (Cited on page 48.)

[121] J. Kessels, T. Kramer, G. den Besten, A. Peeters, and V. Timm. Applying asynchronous circuits in contactless smart cards. *Advanced Research in Asynchronous Circuits and Systems, 2000. (ASYNC 2000) Proceedings. Sixth International Symposium on*, pages 36–44, 2000. (Cited on page 145.)

[122] A. Khatibzadeh and C. H. Gebotys. Enhanced current-balanced logic (ecbl): An area efficient solution to secure smart cards against differential power attack. In *ITNG*, pages 898–899, 2007. (Cited on page 141.)

[123] M. A. Kishinevskiµi and A. V. Yakovlev. *Self-Timed Control of Concurrent Processes: The Design of Aperiodic Logical Circuits in Computers and Discrete Systems*. Kluwer Academic Publishers, Norwell, MA, USA, 1990. (Cited on page 139.)

[124] L. R. Knudsen, W. Meier, B. Preneel, V. Rijmen, and S. Verdoolaege. Analysis methods for (alleged) rc4. In *ASIACRYPT*, pages 327–341, 1998. (Cited on page 89.)

[125] N. Koblitz. CM-Curves with Good Cryptographic Properties. In *CRYPTO '91: Proceedings of the 11th Annual International Cryptology Conference on Advances in Cryptology*, pages 279–287, London, UK, 1992. Springer-Verlag. (Cited on pages 113 and 114.)

[126] P. Kocher, J. Jaffe, and B. Jun. introduction to differential power analysis and related attacks. *Technical Report*, 1998. (Cited on pages 9 and 10.)

[127] P. Kocher, J. Jaffe, and B. Jun. Differential Power Analysis. *Lecture Notes in Computer Science*, 1666:388–397, 1999. (Cited on pages 3, 4, 9, 10, 19, 20, 21, 31, 35, 36, 37, 38, 40, 41, 47, 55, 57, 82, 97, 117, 130, 134, 156, 191, 201, 216, 229, 238, and 240.)

[128] P. Kocher, J. Jaffe, and B. Jun. Using unpredictable information to minimize leakage from smartcards and other cryptosystems. *U.S. Patent 6327661*, 1999. (Cited on page 151.)

[129] P. Kocher, R. Lee, G. McGraw, and A. Raghunathan. Security as a new dimension in embedded system design. In *DAC '04: Proceedings of the 41st annual conference on Design automation*, pages 753–760, New York, NY, USA, 2004. ACM. Moderator-Srivaths Ravi. (Cited on page 2.)

[130] P. C. Kocher. Timing Attacks on Implementations of Diffie-Hellman, RSA, DSS, and Other Systems. In *CRYPTO '96: Proceedings of the 16th Annual International Cryptology Conference on Advances in Cryptology*, pages 104–113, London, UK, 1996. Springer-Verlag. (Cited on pages 98 and 108.)

[131] F. Koeune and J. Quisquater. A timing attack against Rijndael: Tech. Report CG, 1999. (Cited on page 34.)

[132] F. Koeune and F.-X. Standaert. A Tutorial on Physical Security and Side-Channel Attacks. In *Foundations of Security Analysis and Design III : FOSAD 2004/2005*, pages 78–108, 2006. (Cited on pages 9, 40, 41, 56, 84, and 85.)

[133] A. Kondratyev and K. Lwin. Design of Asynchronous Circuits Using Synchronous CAD Tools. *IEEE Des. Test*, 19(4):107–117, 2002. (Cited on page 139.)

[134] K. J. Kulikowski, A. Smirnov, and A. Taubin. Automated Design of Cryptographic Devices Resistant to Multiple Side-Channel Attacks. In *CHES*, pages 399–413, 2006. (Cited on page 140.)

[135] K. J. Kulikowski, M. Su, A. Smirnov, A. Taubin, M. G. Karpovsky, and D. MacDonald. Delay Insensitive Encoding and Power Analysis: A Balancing Act. In *ASYNC '05: Proceedings of the 11th IEEE International Symposium on Asynchronous Circuits and Systems*, pages 116–125, Washington, DC, USA, 2005. IEEE Computer Society. (Cited on page 140.)

[136] S. Kunz-Jacques, F. Muller, and F. Valette. The Davies-Murphy Power Attack. In *ASIACRYPT*, pages 451–467, 2004. (Cited on pages 25, 93, and 94.)

[137] D. Kwon, J. Kim, S. Park, S. H. Sung, Y. Sohn, J. H. Song, Y. Yeom, E.-J. Yoon, S. Lee, J. Lee, S. Chee, D. Han, and J. Hong. New Block Cipher: ARIA. In *ICISC*, pages 432–445, 2003. (Cited on page 72.)

[138] A. K. Lenstra and E. R. Verheul. The XTR Public Key System. In *CRYPTO '00: Proceedings of the 20th Annual International Cryptology Conference on Advances in Cryptology*, pages 1–19, London, UK, 2000. Springer-Verlag. (Cited on page 135.)

[139] P.-Y. Liardet and N. P. Smart. Preventing SPA/DPA in ECC Systems Using the Jacobi Form. In *CHES '01: Proceedings of the Third International Workshop on Cryptographic Hardware and Embedded Systems*, pages 391–401, London, UK, 2001. Springer-Verlag. (Cited on pages 113, 115, and 137.)

[140] R. G. Lyons. *Understanding Digital Signal Processing (2nd Edition)*. Prentice Hall PTR, Upper Saddle River, NJ, USA, 2004. (Cited on page 82.)

[141] P. Lysaght, J. Irvine, and R. W. Hartenstein, editors. *Field-Programmable Logic and Applications, 9th International Workshop, FPL'99, Glasgow, UK, August 30 - September 1, 1999, Proceedings*, volume 1673 of *Lecture Notes in Computer Science*. Springer, 1999. (Cited on page 94.)

[142] D. J. C. MacKay. *Information Theory, Inference and Learning Algorithms*. Cambridge University Press, 2003. (Cited on page 91.)

[143] S. Mangard. A Simple Power-Analysis (SPA) Attack on Implementations of the AES Key Expansion. In P. J. Lee and C. H. Lim, editors, *Information Security and Cryptology - ICISC 2002, 5th International Conference Seoul, Korea, November 28-29, 2002, Revised Papers*, volume 2587 of *Lecture Notes in Computer Science*, pages 343–358. Springer, 2003. (Cited on pages 2, 3, 15, 16, 27, 28, 29, 156, 208, 235, 236, and 240.)

[144] S. Mangard. Hardware Countermeasures against DPA – A Statistical Analysis of Their Effectiveness. In T. Okamoto, editor, *Topics in Cryptology - CT-RSA 2004, The Cryptographers' Track at the RSA Conference 2004, San Francisco, CA, USA, February 23-27, 2004, Proceedings*, volume 2964 of *Lecture Notes in Computer Science*, pages 222–235. Springer, 2004. (Cited on page 130.)

[145] D. May, H. L. Muller, and N. P. Smart. Non-deterministic Processors. In *ACISP '01: Proceedings of the 6th Australasian Conference on Information Security and Privacy*, pages 115–129, London, UK, 2001. Springer-Verlag. (Cited on pages 148, 149, 150, and 158.)

[146] D. May, H. L. Muller, and N. P. Smart. Random register renaming to foil dpa. In *CHES '01: Proceedings of the Third International Workshop on Cryptographic Hardware and Embedded Systems*, pages 28–38, London, UK, 2001. Springer-Verlag. (Cited on pages 150, 158, 161, and 183.)

[147] R. Mayer-Sommer. Smartly Analyzing the Simplicity and the Power of Simple Power Analysis on Smartcards. In *CHES '00: Proceedings of the Second International Workshop on Cryptographic Hardware and Embedded Systems*, pages 78–92, London, UK, 2000. Springer-Verlag. (Cited on pages 21, 22, and 156.)

[148] A. J. Menezes. *Elliptic Curve Public Key Cryptosystems*. Springer, 1993. (Cited on page 111.)

[149] A. J. Menezes, S. A. Vanstone, and P. C. V. Oorschot. *Handbook of Applied Cryptography*. CRC Press, Inc., Boca Raton, FL, USA, 1996. (Cited on pages 35 and 49.)

[150] N. Mentens, K. Sakiyama, L. Batina, B. Preneel, and I. Verbauwhede. A side-channel attack resistant programmable pkc coprocessor for embedded applications. In *ICSAMOS*, pages 194–200, 2007. (Cited on page 110.)

[151] M. C. Merten, A. R. Trick, R. D. Barnes, E. M. Nystrom, C. N. George, J. C. Gyllenhaal, and W. mei W. Hwu. An architectural framework for runtime optimization. *IEEE Transactions on Computers*, 50(6):567–589. (Cited on page 174.)

[152] T. S. Messerges. Using second-order power analysis to attack dpa resistant software. In *CHES '00: Proceedings of the Second International Workshop on Cryptographic Hardware and Embedded Systems*, pages 238–251, London, UK, 2000. Springer-Verlag. (Cited on pages 5, 57, 58, 59, 62, 63, 65, 69, 70, 98, 99, and 101.)

[153] T. S. Messerges. Securing the AES Finalists Against Power Analysis Attacks. In *FSE '00: Proceedings of the 7th International Workshop on Fast Software Encryption*, pages 150–164, London, UK, 2001. Springer-Verlag. (Cited on pages 60, 103, 104, and 123.)

[154] T. S. Messerges, E. A. Dabbish, and R. H. Sloan. Investigations of power analysis attacks on smartcards. In *WOST'99: Proceedings of the USENIX Workshop on Smartcard Technology on USENIX Workshop on Smartcard Technology*, pages 17–17, Berkeley, CA, USA, 1999. USENIX Association. (Cited on pages 10, 11, 21, 23, 24, 69, and 238.)

[155] T. S. Messerges, E. A. Dabbish, and R. H. Sloan. Power analysis attacks of modular exponentiation in smartcards. In *CHES '99: Proceedings of the First International Workshop on Cryptographic Hardware and Embedded Systems*, pages 144–157, London, UK, 1999. Springer-Verlag. (Cited on pages 32, 33, 48, 51, 67, 78, 79, 80, 81, 98, 108, 130, and 156.)

[156] T. S. Messerges, E. A. Dabbish, and R. H. Sloan. Examining smart-card security under the threat of power analysis attacks. *IEEE Trans. Computers*, 51(5):541–552, 2002. (Cited on pages 3, 12, 22, 23, 24, 25, 37, 38, 39, 40, 41, 55, 56, 98, 99, 104, 131, 191, 193, and 201.)

[157] V. S. Miller. Use of elliptic curves in cryptography. In *Lecture notes in computer sciences; 218 on Advances in cryptology—CRYPTO 85*, pages 417–426, New York, NY, USA, 1986. Springer-Verlag New York, Inc. (Cited on pages 18 and 31.)

[158] A. Miyaji, T. Ono, and H. Cohen. Efficient Elliptic Curve Exponentiation. In *Proc. 1st International Information and Communications Security Conference*, pages 282–290, 1997. (Cited on page 136.)

[159] B. Möller. Securing elliptic curve point multiplication against side-channel attacks. In *ISC '01: Proceedings of the 4th International Conference on Information Security*, pages 324–334, London, UK, 2001. Springer-Verlag. (Cited on pages 114, 137, and 138.)

[160] B. Moller. Parallelizable elliptic curve point multiplication method with resistance against side-channel attacks. In *ISC '02: Proceedings of the 5th International Conference on Information Security*, pages 402–413, London, UK, 2002. Springer-Verlag. (Cited on page 137.)

[161] P. L. Montgomery. Modular Multiplication without Trial Division. In *Mathematics of Computation 44 no. 70*, pages 519–521, 1985. (Cited on pages 33, 54, and 112.)

[162] P. L. Montgomery. Speeding the Pollard and Elliptic Curve Methods of Factorizations. *Mathematics of Computation*, 48(177):243–264, 1987. (Cited on page 54.)

[163] S. Moore, R. Anderson, and M. Kuhn. Improving Smart card Security Using Self-Timed Circuit Technology. In *ACiD-WG '00: Forth ACiD-WG Workshop*, Grenoble, 2000. (Cited on page 139.)

[164] S. Moore, R. Anderson, R. Mullins, G. Taylor, and J. Fournier. Balanced Self-Checking Asynchronous Logic for Smart Card Applications, 2003. (Cited on page 139.)

[165] R. Muresan and C. H. Gebotys. Current flattening in software and hardware for security applications. In *CODES+ISSS*, pages 218–223, 2004. (Cited on pages 146, 147, 148, 159, 174, and 193.)

[166] R. Muresan, H. Vahedi, Y. Zhanrong, and S. Gregori. Power-smart system-on-chip architecture for embedded cryptosystems. In *CODES+ISSS '05: Proceedings of the 3rd IEEE/ACM/IFIP international conference on Hardware/software codesign and system synthesis*, pages 184–189, New York, NY, USA, 2005. ACM. (Cited on pages 145 and 146.)

[167] National Institute of Standards and Technology. *Advanced Encryption Standard (AES)*, 2001. Supersedes FIPS PUB 197–2001 November. (Cited on pages 15, 16, 42, 101, 123, 124, and 208.)

[168] N. Nedjah, L. de Macedo Mourelle, and R. M. da Silva. Efficient Hardware for Modular Exponentiation Using the Sliding-Window Method. In *ITNG '07: Proceedings of the International Conference on Information Technology*, pages 17–24, Washington, DC, USA, 2007. IEEE Computer Society. (Cited on pages 128 and 130.)

[169] W. Ng. Countermeasure for Differential Power Analysis using Boolean and Arithmetic masking. Technical report, School of Electrical Engineering and Computer Science, Oregon State University, 2004. (Cited on page 104.)

[170] M. Nikitovic and M. Brorsson. An adaptive chip-multiprocessor architecture for future mobile terminals. In *CASES '02: Proceedings of the 2002 international conference on Compilers, architecture, and synthesis for embedded systems*, pages 43–49, New York, NY, USA, 2002. ACM Press. (Cited on page 192.)

[171] C. NIST. The digital signature standard. *Commun. ACM*, 35(7):36–40, 1992. (Cited on page 34.)

[172] R. Novak. SPA-Based Adaptive Chosen-Ciphertext Attack on RSA Implementation. In *PKC '02: Proceedings of the 5th International Workshop on Practice and Theory in Public Key Cryptosystems*, pages 252–262, London, UK, 2002. Springer-Verlag. (Cited on pages 20, 32, and 156.)

[173] K. Okeya, H. Kurumatani, and K. Sakurai. Elliptic Curves with the Montgomery-Form and Their Cryptographic Applications. In *PKC '00: Proceedings of the Third International Workshop on Practice and Theory in Public Key Cryptography*, pages 238–257, London, UK, 2000. Springer-Verlag. (Cited on pages 54 and 112.)

[174] K. Okeya, K. Miyazaki, and K. Sakurai. A Fast Scalar Multiplication Method with Randomized Projective Coordinates on a Montgomery-Form Elliptic Curve Secure against Side Channel Attacks. In *ICISC '01: Proceedings of the 4th International Conference Seoul on Information Security and Cryptology*, pages 428–439, London, UK, 2002. Springer-Verlag. (Cited on pages 113 and 128.)

[175] K. Okeya and K. Sakurai. Power Analysis Breaks Elliptic Curve Cryptosystems even Secure against the Timing Attack. In *INDOCRYPT '00: Proceedings of the First International Conference on Progress in Cryptology*, pages 178–190, London, UK, 2000. Springer-Verlag. (Cited on pages 54, 111, 112, and 113.)

[176] A. One. Smashing The Stack For Fun And Profit. *Phrack*, 49, 1996. (Cited on page 134.)

[177] S. B. Ors, F. Gurkaynak, E. Oswald, and B. Preneel. Power-analysis attack on an asic aes implementation. *itcc*, 02:546, 2004. (Cited on pages 3, 43, 44, 47, 86, 87, and 191.)

[178] E. Oswald and M. Aigner. Randomized Addition-Subtraction Chains as a Countermeasure against Power Attacks. In *CHES '01: Proceedings of the Third International Workshop on Cryptographic Hardware and Embedded Systems*, pages 39–50, London, UK, 2001. Springer-Verlag. (Cited on pages 5, 32, 54, 81, 115, 116, and 135.)

[179] E. Oswald and S. Mangard. Template Attacks on Masking—Resistance is Futile. In M. Abe, editor, *Topics in Cryptology - CT-RSA 2007, The Cryptographers' Track at the RSA Conference 2007, San Francisco, CA, USA, February 5-9, 2007, Proceedings*, volume 4377 of *Lecture Notes in Computer Science*, pages 243–256. Springer, February 2007. ISBN 978-3-540-69327-7. (Cited on pages 92 and 93.)

[180] E. Oswald, S. Mangard, C. Herbst, and S. Tillich. Practical Second-Order DPA Attacks for Masked Smart Card Implementations of Block Ciphers. In D. Pointcheval, editor, *Topics in Cryptology - CT-RSA 2006, The Cryptographers' Track at the RSA Conference 2006, San Jose, CA, USA, February 13-17, 2006, Proceedings*, volume 3860 of *Lecture Notes in Computer Science*, pages 192–207. Springer, 2006. (Cited on pages 5, 19, 20, 65, 66, 67, 99, 107, 156, 158, 159, 191, 238, and 240.)

[181] E. Oswald, S. Mangard, and N. Pramstaller. Secure and Efficient Masking of AES - A Mission Impossible? Cryptology ePrint Archive, Report 2004/134, 2004. (Cited on page 126.)

[182] E. Oswald, S. Mangard, N. Pramstaller, and V. Rijmen. A Side-Channel Analysis Resistant Description of the AES S-box. In H. Gilbert and H. Handschuh, editors, *Fast Software Encryption, 12th International Workshop, FSE 2005, Paris, France, February 21-23, 2005, Proceedings*, volume 3557 of *Lecture Notes in Computer Science*, pages 413–423. Springer, 2005. (Cited on page 127.)

[183] E. Oswald and K. Schramm. An Efficient Masking Scheme for AES Software Implementations. In J. Song, T. Kwon, and M. Yung, editors, *Information Security Applications: 6th International Workshop, WISA 2005, Jeju Island, Korea, August 22-24, 2005, Revised Selected Papers*, volume 3786 of *Lecture Notes in Computer Science*, pages 292–305. Springer, 2006. (Cited on page 127.)

[184] D. Page and M. Stam. On XTR and Side-Channel Analysis. In *Selected Areas in Cryptography (SAC 2004)*, pages 54–68. Springer Verlag LNCS 3357, January 2005. (Cited on page 135.)

[185] J. Park, H. Lee, J. Ha, Y. Choi, H. Kim, and S. Moon. A differential power analysis attack of block cipher based on the hamming weight of internal operation unit. In *CIS '06*, pages 417–426, 2007. (Cited on pages 21, 22, 23, 71, 72, 73, 74, 81, and 238.)

[186] Paul Bourke. Cross Correlation: AutoCorrelation – 2D Pattern Identification. Available at http://astronomy.swin.edu.au/ pbourke/other/correlate/ index.html, 1996. (Cited on page 163.)

[187] J. Peddersen, S. L. Shee, A. Janapsatya, and S. Parameswaran. Rapid embedded hardware/software system generation. In *VLSID '05*, pages 111–116, 2005. (Cited on page 199.)

[188] E. Peeters, F.-X. Standaert, N. Donckers, and J.-J. Quisquater. Improved Higher-Order Side-Channel Attacks with FPGA Experiments. In *CHES*, pages 309–323, 2005. (Cited on pages 64, 65, 68, 69, 92, 120, 121, 191, and 238.)

[189] L. A. Plana, P. Riocreux, W. Bardsley, J. Garside, and S. Temple. SPA – A Synthesisable Amulet Core for Smartcard Applications. In *ASYNC '02: Proceedings of the 8th International Symposium on Asynchronus Circuits and Systems*, pages 201 – 210, Washington, DC, USA, 2002. IEEE Computer Society. (Cited on page 139.)

[190] T. Popp, M. Kirschbaum, T. Zefferer, and S. Mangard. Evaluation of the Masked Logic Style MDPL on a Prototype Chip. In P. Paillier and I. Verbauwhede, editors, *Cryptographic Hardware and Embedded Systems – CHES 2007, 9th International Workshop, Vienna, Austria, September 10-13, 2007, Proceedings*, volume 4727 of *Lecture Notes in Computer Science*, pages 81–94. Springer, September 2007. (Cited on page 144.)

[191] T. Popp and S. Mangard. Masked Dual-Rail Pre-Charge Logic: DPA-Resistance without Routing Constraints. In J. R. Rao and B. Sunar, editors, *Cryptographic Hardware and Embedded Systems – CHES 2005, 7th International Workshop, Edinburgh, Scotland, August 29 - September 1, 2005, Proceedings*, volume 3659 of *Lecture Notes in Computer Science*, pages 172–186. Springer, 2005. (Cited on pages 143, 192, and 193.)

[192] J. Quisquater and D. Samyde. ElectroMagnetic Analysis (EMA): Measures and Counter-Measures for Smart Cards. In *E-smart*, pages 200–210, 2001. (Cited on page 2.)

[193] J.-J. Quisquater and D. Samyde. Automatic Code Recognition for smart cards using a Kohonen neural network. In *CARDIS'02: Proceedings of the 5th conference on Smart Card Research and Advanced Application Conference*, pages 6–6, Berkeley, CA, USA, 2002. USENIX Association. (Cited on page 19.)

[194] R. G. Ragel and S. Parameswaran. Impres: integrated monitoring for processor reliability and security. In *DAC '06: Proceedings of the 43rd annual conference on Design automation*, pages 502–505, 2006. (Cited on page 2.)

[195] P. Rakers, L. Connell, T. Collins, and D. Russell. Secure Contactless Smartcard ASIC with DPA Protection. *IEEE Journal of Solid-State Circuits*, pages 559–565, 2001. (Cited on page 145.)

[196] G. B. Ratanpal, R. D. Williams, and T. N. Blalock. An On-Chip Signal Suppression Countermeasure to Power Analysis Attacks. *IEEE Transactions on Dependable and Secure Computing*, 01(3):179–189, 2004. (Cited on pages 145 and 158.)

[197] S. Ravi, A. Raghunathan, and S. Chakradhar. Tamper Resistance Mechanisms for Secure, Embedded Systems. *vlsid*, 00:605, 2004. (Cited on page 156.)

[198] C. Rechberger and E. Oswald. Practical Template Attacks. In C. H. Lim and M. Yung, editors, *Information Security Applications, 5th International Workshop, WISA 2004, Jeju Island, Korea, August 23 – 25, 2004, Revised Papers*, volume 3325 of *Lecture Notes in Computer Science*, pages 443–457. Springer, 2004. (Cited on pages 90 and 91.)

[199] R. L. Rivest, M. J. B. Robshaw, R. Sidney, and Y. L. Yin. The RC6 Block Cipher. RSA Laboratories, v1.1, August 20, 1998. (Cited on pages 62 and 103.)

[200] A. Rostovtsev and O. Shemyakina. AES side channel attack protection using random isomorphisms. Cryptology ePrint Archive, Report 2005/087, 2005. http://eprint.iacr.org/. (Cited on page 107.)

[201] K. Rothbart, U. Neffe, C. Steger, R. Weiss, E. Rieger, and A. Mühlberger. High level fault injection for attack simulation in smart cards. In *Asian Test Symposium*, pages 118–121, 2004. (Cited on page 2.)

[202] Y. Sakai and K. Sakurai. Simple Power Analysis on Fast Modular Reduction with Generalized Mersenne Prime for Elliptic Curve Cryptosystems. *IEICE Trans. Fundam. Electron. Commun. Comput. Sci.*, E89-A(1):231–237, 2006. (Cited on pages 34 and 138.)

[203] T. Samuelsson, M. Akerholm, P. Nygren, J. Stärner, and L. Lindh. A comparison of multiprocessor real-time operating systems implemented in hardware and software. In *International Workshop on Advanced Real-Time Operating System Services (ARTOSS)*, 2003. (Cited on page 198.)

[204] H. Saputra, N. Vijaykrishnan, M. Kandemir, M. J. Irwin, R. Brooks, S. Kim, and W. Zhang. Masking the energy behavior of des encryption. *date*, 01:10084, 2003. (Cited on pages 139, 152, 158, 192, and 193.)

[205] A. Satoh, S. Morioka, K. Takano, and S. Munetoh. A Compact Rijndael Hardware Architecture with S-Box Optimization. In *ASIACRYPT '01: Proceedings of the 7th International Conference on the Theory and Application of Cryptology and Information Security*, pages 239–254, London, UK, 2001. Springer-Verlag. (Cited on page 127.)

[206] B. Schneier. *Applied cryptography (2nd ed.): protocols, algorithms, and source code in C.* John Wiley & Sons, Inc., New York, NY, USA, 1995. (Cited on pages 16, 31, and 108.)

[207] B. Schneier, J. Kelsey, D. Whiting, D. Wagner, C. Hall, and N. Ferguson. *The Twofish encryption algorithm: a 128-bit block cipher*. John Wiley & Sons, Inc., New York, NY, USA, 1999. (Cited on pages 57 and 103.)

[208] R. Schoof. Elliptic curves over finite fields and the computation of square roots *mod p*. *Math. Comp.*, 44:483–494, 1985. (Cited on page 136.)

[209] Z. J. Shi and F. Zhang. New Attacks on Randomized ECC Algorithms. In *Proceedings of EITC*, pages 22–25, 2006. (Cited on page 116.)

[210] S. Shimizu, H. Ishikawa, A. Satoh, and T. Aihara. On-demand design service innovations. *IBM J. Res. Dev.*, 48(5/6):751–765, 2004. (Cited on pages 15 and 210.)

[211] K. G. Shin. On Securing Networked Real-Time Embedded Systems. In *EUC*, page 1, 2006. (Cited on page 2.)

[212] J. Sparsø and S. Furber. *Principles of Asynchronous Circuit Design - A Systems Perspective*. Kluwer Academic Publishers, dec 2001. (Cited on page 139.)

[213] E. Sprunk. Clock frequency modulation for secure microprocessors. *U.S. Patent WO 99/63696*, 1999. (Cited on pages 151 and 152.)

[214] W. Stallings. The advanced encryption standard. *Cryptologia*, XXVI(3):165–188, 2002. (Cited on pages 208, 235, and 236.)

[215] F.-X. Standaert, S. B. Ors, and B. Preneel. Power Analysis of an FPGA Implementation of Rijndael: Is Pipelining a DPA Countermeasure? In *CHES 2004*, pages 30–44. Springer-Verlag, 2004. (Cited on page 95.)

[216] F.-X. Standaert, S. B. Ors, J.-J. Quisquater, and B. Preneel. Power Analysis Attacks against FPGA Implementations of the DES. In *FPL 2004*, pages 84–94. Springer-Verlag, 2004. (Cited on page 95.)

[217] F.-X. Standaert, E. Peeters, and J.-J. Quisquater. On the Masking Countermeasure and Higher-Order Power Analysis Attacks. In *ITCC 2005*, pages 562–567. IEEE Computer Society, 2005. (Cited on pages 158, 159, and 174.)

[218] F.-X. Standaert, L. van Oldeneel tot Oldenzeel, D. Samyde, and J.-J. Quisquater. Differential Power Analysis of FPGAs : How Practical is the Attack? In *FPL 2003*, pages 701–709. Springer-Verlag, 2003. (Cited on pages 94 and 95.)

[219] S. Tillich and J. Großschädl. Instruction Set Extensions for Efficient AES Implementation on 32-bit Processors. In *CHES*, pages 270–284, 2006. (Cited on page 153.)

[220] S. Tillich and J. Großschädl. Power-Analysis Resistant AES Implementation with Instruction Set Extensions. In P. Paillier and I. Verbauwhede, editors, *Cryptographic Hardware and Embedded Systems – CHES 2007, 9th International Workshop, Vienna, Austria, September 10-13, 2007, Proceedings*, volume 4727 of *Lecture Notes in Computer Science*, pages 303–319. Springer, September 2007. (Cited on page 153.)

[221] K. Tiri, M. Akmal, and I. Verbauwhede. A Dynamic and Differential CMOS Logic with Signal Independent Power Consumption to Withstand Differential Power Analysis on Smart Cards. In *ESSCIRC 2002: 29 European Solid-State Circuits Conference*, 2002. (Cited on pages 140, 141, and 143.)

[222] K. Tiri, D. Hwang, A. Hodjat, B. Lai, S. Yang, P. Schaumont, and I. Verbauwhede. A side-channel leakage free coprocessor ic in 0.18um cmos for embedded aes-based cryptographic and biometric processing. In *DAC '05: Proceedings of the 42nd annual conference on Design automation*, pages 222–227, New York, NY, USA, 2005. ACM Press. (Cited on pages 13, 43, 68, 69, 86, 87, 141, 158, 169, 174, and 187.)

[223] K. Tiri, D. Hwang, A. Hodjat, B.-C. Lai, S. Yang, P. Schaumont, and I. Verbauwhede. AES-based cryptographic and biometric security coprocessor IC in 0.18-/spl mu/m CMOS resistant to side-channel power analysis attacks. *VLSI Circuits, 2005. Digest of Technical Papers. 2005 Symposium on*, pages 216–219, 2005. (Cited on page 141.)

[224] K. Tiri and I. Verbauwhede. Securing Encryption Algorithms against DPA at the Logic Level: Next Generation Smart Card Technology. In *CHES*, pages 125–136, 2003. (Cited on page 140.)

[225] K. Tiri and I. Verbauwhede. A Logic Level Design Methodology for a Secure DPA Resistant ASIC or FPGA Implementation. In *DATE '04: Proceedings of the conference on Design, automation and test in Europe*, page 10246, Washington, DC, USA, 2004. IEEE Computer Society. (Cited on pages 141, 142, 143, 192, and 193.)

[226] K. Tiri and I. Verbauwhede. A vlsi design flow for secure side-channel attack resistant ics. In *DATE '05: Proceedings of the conference on Design, Automation and Test in Europe*, pages 58–63, 2005. (Cited on page 141.)

[227] K. Tiri and I. Verbauwhede. A Digital Design Flow for Secure Integrated Circuits. *IEEE Trans. on CAD of Integrated Circuits and Systems*, 25(7):1197–1208, 2006. (Cited on pages 141, 192, 193, and 212.)

[228] N. Torii and K. Yokoyama. Elliptic curve cryptosystem. In *Journal of FUJITSU Sci. Tech.*, pages 140–146, 2000. (Cited on pages 18 and 136.)

[229] E. Trichina. Combinational logic design for aes subbyte transformation on masked data. eprint archive: Report 2003/236, IACR, november 11, 2003. (Cited on pages 104, 105, and 123.)

[230] E. Trichina and A. Bellezza. Implementation of Elliptic Curve Cryptography with Built-In Counter Measures against Side Channel Attacks. In *CHES '02: Revised Papers from the 4th International Workshop on Cryptographic Hardware and Embedded Systems*, pages 98–113, London, UK, 2003. Springer-Verlag. (Cited on page 132.)

[231] E. Trichina, T. Korkishko, and K.-H. Lee. Small Size, Low Power, Side Channel-Immune AES Coprocessor: Design and Synthesis Results. In *AES Conference*, pages 113–127, 2004. (Cited on page 105.)

[232] E. Trichina, D. D. Seta, and L. Germani. Simplified Adaptive Multiplicative Masking for AES. In *CHES '02: Revised Papers from the 4th International Workshop on Cryptographic Hardware and Embedded Systems*, pages 187–197, London, UK, 2003. Springer-Verlag. (Cited on pages 103, 123, 126, and 127.)

[233] TUG. *SMEPP: D5.1.1 Specification of Secure Instruction Sets for EP2P Devices*, 2007. http://www.smepp.org/. (Cited on page 153.)

[234] F. Vater, S. Peter, and P. Langendörfer. Combinatorial logic circuitry as means to protect low cost devices against side channel attacks. In *WISTP*, pages 244–253, 2007. (Cited on page 152.)

[235] J. Waddle and D. Wagner. Towards efficient second-order power analysis. In *CHES*, pages 1–15, 2004. (Cited on pages 59, 60, 61, 62, and 158.)

[236] J. Waddle and D. Wagner. Fault Attacks on Dual-Rail Encoded Systems. In *ACSAC '05: Proceedings of the 21st Annual Computer Security Applications Conference*, pages 483–494, Washington, DC, USA, 2005. IEEE Computer Society. (Cited on page 139.)

[237] D. Wagner and B. Schneier. Analysis of the SSL 3.0 protocol. In *WOEC'96: Proceedings of the 2nd conference on Proceedings of the Second USENIX Workshop on Electronic Commerce*, pages 4–4, Berkeley, CA, USA, 1996. USENIX Association. (Cited on page 90.)

[238] C. D. Walter. Sliding Windows Succumbs to Big Mac Attack. In *CHES '01: Proceedings of the Third International Workshop on Cryptographic Hardware and Embedded Systems*, pages 286–299, London, UK, 2001. Springer-Verlag. (Cited on pages 32 and 88.)

[239] C. D. Walter. Simple Power Analysis of Unified Code for ECC Double and Add. In *CHES*, pages 191–204, 2004. (Cited on pages 33, 34, 116, and 137.)

[240] C. D. Walter and S. Thompson. Distinguishing Exponent Digits by Observing Modular Subtractions. In *CT-RSA 2001: Proceedings of the 2001 Conference on Topics in Cryptology*, pages 192–207, London, UK, 2001. Springer-Verlag. (Cited on pages 33, 108, and 110.)

[241] P. Wayner. Code Breaker Cracks Smart Cards' Digital Safe. In *New York Times*, page C1, 1998. (Cited on page 99.)

[242] W. Wolf. Multimedia applications of multiprocessor systems-on-chips. In *DATE '05: Proceedings of the conference on Design, Automation and Test in Europe*, pages 86–89, Washington, DC, USA, 2005. IEEE Computer Society. (Cited on pages 1, 9, and 192.)

[243] J. Wolkerstorfer, E. Oswald, and M. Lamberger. An ASIC Implementation of the AES SBoxes. In *CT-RSA '02: Proceedings of the The Cryptographer's Track at the RSA Conference on Topics in Cryptology*, pages 67–78, London, UK, 2002. Springer-Verlag. (Cited on page 126.)

[244] L. Xiao and H. M. Heys. A simple power analysis attack against the key schedule of the Camellia block cipher. *Inf. Process. Lett.*, 95(3):409–412, 2005. (Cited on pages 29, 30, and 31.)

[245] L. Yang and J. S. Yuan. Enhanced techniques for current balanced logic in mixed-signal ics. In *ISVLSI '03: Proceedings of the IEEE Computer Society Annual Symposium on VLSI (ISVLSI'03)*, page 278, Washington, DC, USA, 2003. IEEE Computer Society. (Cited on pages 140 and 141.)

[246] S. Yang, J. Park, and Y. You. The Smallest ARIA Module with 16-Bit Architecture. In *ICISC*, pages 107–117, 2006. (Cited on page 72.)

[247] S.-M. Yen. Amplified Differential Power Cryptanalysis on Rijndael Implementations with Exponentially Fewer Power Traces. In *ACISP*, pages 106–117, 2003. (Cited on pages 34, 35, 55, 76, 77, 78, and 238.)

[248] S.-M. Yen, S. Kim, S. Lim, and S.-J. Moon. RSA Speedup with Chinese Remainder Theorem Immune against Hardware Fault Cryptanalysis. *IEEE Trans. Comput.*, 52(4):461–472, 2003. (Cited on page 49.)

[249] D. F. YongBin Zhou. Side-Channel Attacks: Ten Years After Its Publication and the Impacts on Cryptographic Module Security Testing. 2005. (Cited on pages 2, 3, and 9.)

[250] P. Yu and P. Schaumont. Secure FPGA Circuits Using Controlled Placement and Routing. In *CODES+ISSS '07: Proceedings of the 5th international conference on Hardware/software codesign and system synthesis*, pages 45–50, New York, NY, USA, 2007. ACM Press. (Cited on page 142.)

[251] F. Zhang and Z. J. Shi. Power analysis attacks on ecc randomized automata. In *ITNG '07: Proceedings of the International Conference on Information Technology*, pages 900–901, Washington, DC, USA, 2007. IEEE Computer Society. (Cited on page 116.)

VDM publishing house ltd.

Scientific Publishing House

offers

free of charge publication

of current academic research papers, Bachelor´s Theses, Master's Theses, Dissertations or Scientific Monographs

If you have written a thesis which satisfies high content as well as formal demands, and you are interested in a remunerated publication of your work, please send an e-mail with some initial information about yourself and your work to *info@vdm-publishing-house.com*.

Our editorial office will get in touch with you shortly.

VDM Publishing House Ltd.
Meldrum Court 17.
Beau Bassin
Mauritius
www.vdm-publishing-house.com

www.ingramcontent.com/pod-product-compliance
Lightning Source LLC
LaVergne TN
LVHW042331060326
832902LV00006B/109